'ENGLAND'S MICHELANGELO'

BY THE SAME AUTHOR

The Art of Botanical Illustration
Pietro's Pilgrimage
A Persian Spring
Of Flowers and a Village
Cockerell
Isfahan
The Dream King
The Compleat Naturalist
John Christie of Glyndebourne
The Golden Road to Samarkand
On Wings of Song

WILFRID BLUNT

'ENGLAND'S MICHELANGELO'

a biography of

GEORGE FREDERIC WATTS, O.M., R.A.

HAMISH HAMILTON
LONDON

HOUSTON PUBLIC LIBRARY

First published in Great Britain 1975
by Hamish Hamilton Ltd
90 Great Russell Street London WC1

Copyright © 1975 by Wilfrid Blunt

SBN 241 89174 4

Printed in Great Britain
by W & J Mackay Limited, Chatham

To RICHARD JEFFERIES

CONTENTS

ILLUSTRATIONS

Photos, black and white
Jeremy Marks, 4b, 5, 6, 9b, 10, 12b, 12c, 13b, 18c, 19a, 20, and re-photographs of 22, 23a and b, 24b; John Donat, 1, 11; Courtauld Institute, 2a, 7; Tate Gallery, 2c, 8, 18a, 21b; Todd-White, 3; Alinari, 4a; Messrs Colnaghi, 9a; Fine Art Society, 13b; Royal Photographic Society, 16; National Portrait Gallery, 13c, 17; Wilfrid Blunt, 18b; Leighton House, 21a; Hollyer, 2b.

ENDPAPER ILLUSTRATION

Watts's bookplate, containing his motto *The Utmost for the Highest*, of which he wrote that he was 'more proud' than of any of his pictures.

FOREWORD

THE ONLY relatively recent biography of George Frederic Watts is Ronald Chapman's *The Laurel and the Thorn* (Faber & Faber, 1945). Unfortunately this has long been out of print, and the publishers have twice rejected my appeal to them to bring out a fresh edition. But with the revival of interest in Victorian art there is now a considerable demand for an up-to-date life of one of the most important English painters of the nineteenth century. I therefore approached Mr Chapman, the son of Watts's adopted daughter the late Mrs Michael Chapman, and asked him whether, if I undertook to write one, he would give it his blessing and allow me to make use of material of which he now owns the copyright. He replied very kindly: 'Of course I should not think you poaching on my territory if you do the Watts book! As a matter of fact I do not think *The Laurel and the Thorn* should be reprinted without considerable alteration. . . . Watts certainly needs another biographer and no-one other than yourself should do it. . . . As to quotations of course you have my permission in every way'. Thus reassured, I set to work.

I have received help and encouragement from many people. My assistant Mr Richard Jefferies, to whom I gratefully dedicate this book, readily put his specialised knowledge of Watts and his wide knowledge of the Victorian age at my disposal. The Hon. Mrs Hervey-Bathurst and Sir Andrew Duff Gordon, Bt., kindly invited me to stay, thus enabling me to study at leisure and in comfort their fine collections of Watts's paintings and drawings. Mr Richard Ormond was good enough to read my typescript and to make a number of helpful suggestions. Miss Susan Radcliffe, an expert genealogist, added useful branches to the rather bare family trees I xiv *Foreword*

had sketched of the Pattles and other clans who play a part in my story. The photographs of about one-third of the pictures were taken for me by Mr Jeremy Marks, whose skill and patience never ceased to amaze me. Last but not least I acknowledge with gratitude the permission of the Trustees of the Watts Gallery to make free use of material at Compton.

I am also indebted to the following for help of one kind or another: Mrs Quentin Bell, Sir Weldon Dalrymple-Champneys, Bt., Mr Marcus Edwards, Mr John Gage, Mr Hubert Hartley, Mr J. S. Hogg, Mrs Judith Jeffreys, Mrs Sadie Kilpatrick, Mr David Loshak, Lady Mander, Miss Betty C. Monkman, the Rev. Andrew Morrison, Mrs Marion Rawson, Mrs Jenny Stein, Mrs Virginia Surtees, Mr Christopher Sykes, the Rev. Gordon Taylor, Mr L. S. Thompson, Mr D. S. Emrys Williams, Mr Christopher Wood, and my efficient typist Miss Charmian Young. Mrs Ellen Crampton kindly prepared the index. Several local inhabitants who knew Mary Watts gave me interesting information but enjoined anonymity. And as always I have never turned in vain for help to my brother Anthony.

For the illustrations I acknowledge with gratitude the gracious permission of H.M. the Queen to reproduce the portrait of Lady Holland in the Royal Collection. I am also grateful to the following for permission to reproduce paintings, drawings, sculpture and photographs: Mr Brinsley Ford, Mrs B. Granger-Taylor, Mr Robert Bailey, the Trustees of the Tate Gallery and the National Portrait Gallery, the Witt Library (Courtauld Institute), the National Trust (Wightwick Manor), Leighton House, the executors of the late Mr Kerrison Preston, the Fine Art Society, Messrs Alinari; Messrs John Donat, and Messrs Colnaghi. I am particularly glad that it has been made possible for me to include eight sides of colour illustrations, for colour meant so much to Watts that to have left him 'penny plain' would have been a tragedy. The choice here has not been easy, but I have tried to represent all stages of his development, and have preferred small paintings, or details of larger ones, so as to give some idea of his method of handling paint. It also seemed to me only fair that one side should be allotted to Mary Watts and her Mortuary Chapel.

I further acknowledge permissions for quotations in the text: Messrs John Murray (*Lady Charlotte Schreiber, Journal*, ed. the Earl of Bessborough; *The Chronicles of Holland House*, by the Earl of Ilchester, and *Letters, 1852–1862*, by the Hon. Mrs Edward Twistleton); Messrs Faber & Faber (*The Laurel and the Thorn*, by Ronald Chapman); Messrs Duckworth (*G. F. Watts*, by G. K. Chesterton); Messrs Heinemann (*Memories and Reflections*, by Laura, Lady Troubridge); Messrs Allen & Unwin (*The Story of my Life*, by Augustus Hare; *G. F. Watts, Reminiscences*, by Mrs Russell Barrington, and *The Winnington Letters*, ed. by Van Akin Bond), and Messrs Macmillan (*George Frederic Watts; the Annals of an Artist's Life* by Mary Watts). For any sins of omission I ask forgiveness.

INTRODUCTION

THIS IS not a reverent biography: it is not intended to be. It is Watts, 'warts and all'; nor have the warts of Mary, his adoring second wife, been overlooked. Her three-volume *Annals of an Artist's Life*, fortunately published without the originally intended sub-title, 'The Life Story of a Noble Soul seeking Beauty, Truth and Goodness', has already provided us with a surfeit of adulation.

Yet *'England's Michelangelo'* has been written with both admiration and affection. For Watts had so many splendid qualities. He was a completely dedicated and very gifted artist. He was enormously industrious, even in oldest age rising (health permitting) at dawn so as not to squander a single God-given minute. He was enormously generous and public-spirited. He charmed all who came into contact with him. But the gods who gave much also withheld much; and in particular his health, though he lived to see his eighty-seventh birthday, was always precarious. Had he been blessed with a robust constitution and a sense of humour; had he married the right wife at the right time; had he been born in Italy at the end of the fifteenth century instead of in England at the beginning of the nineteenth—he might well have become one of the greatest of all artists. As it was, and unequal though his works are, he showed himself to be in many ways more original, interesting and adventurous than Millais, Rossetti or Burne-Jones—all of whom have now overtaken him, temporarily at any rate, in the popularity stakes.

Mrs Watts—by which of course we mean Mary Fraser-Tytler, whom he married when he was nearly seventy—became at once his companion, his nurse, his slave; his 'guide, philosopher and friend'; his watchdog, and finally, by her biography of him, his advocate and publicity agent. She worshipped him blindly. She gave him a new lease of life, and the best years of her own to establishing him as a national monument; yet she sadly lived on to hear a fickle world declare that after all he was just a prosy old bore. Her own very considerable artistic gifts, which she willingly sacrificed, can at least be gauged from the remarkable mortuary chapel that she designed and built at Compton.

Now, with the general revival of interest in everything Victorian, Watts is at last beginning to find his true level; and if, as we have said, he has lagged a little behind some of his no more gifted contemporaries it is in part because his allegories (by which he set such store) are still unpalatable to many, in part because his output was so enormous that the inflated prices which result from rarity rather than from merit do not come his way. His name is still little known to the younger generation, and more than one visitor to the Gallery at Compton, confusing him with James Watt, has gone away disappointed at finding no steam engines. For many of the middle-aged and what we are now urged to call 'senior citizens' he is simply the painter of 'Hope'—the best-known version of which was, in fact, mostly carried out by a pupil. Some are aware that he married Ellen Terry, though one loquacious know-all informed our amazed Custodian that he married Nell Gwynne 'and then painted her sitting on the top of the world'.

It is extremely important for the reader of this book to bear in mind that almost all the information for the first twenty-five years of Watts's life, and not a little for his later years, comes to us from what the artist thought fit to tell Mary Watts in his old age. This material was no doubt further sifted, for she aimed at excluding from her *Annals* anything that showed him in an unfavourable light. (For example, the unfortunate Ellen Terry episode, which being common knowledge could not be completely omitted, is dismissed in a few lines in which poor Nell is not even mentioned by name.) The fifteen volumes of correspondence that Mrs Watts assembled contain letters with passages blacked out, and no doubt other letters were destroyed. She was, on occasions, not above a deliberate distortion of the truth.

Watts never learnt even the rudiments of writing English, and his punctuation would be counted a disgrace in a child of ten. This one would never guess from the quotations from his letters in Mrs Watts's book, for (though she nowhere admits it) she has freely 'edited' them. I hereby confess that I too, for the sake of the reader, have taken some small liberties; one passage has, however, purposely been left exactly as he wrote it.[1]

Did Mrs Watts also destroy some of her husband's pictures? One frankly erotic study, with the typically Wattsian title of 'Satan and Sin' (see Plate 18c), has come down to us; did he paint no others, or is this the only one that slipped through the net? We shall never know, for Mrs Watts has covered her tracks only too well. William Etty, who painted nudes as voluptuous as those of Rubens, was 'a shy, pious bachelor [who] found in his painting a sensuous outlet';[2] perhaps the veiled eroticism of many of Watts's female nudes was also a kind of sublimation.

So the task of the biographer of Watts is not an easy one. He does not want to go looking for scandal, and yet he cannot but feel that Mrs Watts's stained-glass-window saint of a husband is too good to be true. Twentieth-century research, not always untinged with malice, has revealed that so many of the Great Victorians had their little human weaknesses, their feet of clay; what were Watts's feet really made of? I think we may probably rest assured that they were of flesh and bone, not of Compton pottery, and that what Mary suppressed were for the most part peccadilloes or trivialities that made her god look mortal or merely silly. For example, it is not from her that we learn that Watts was called 'Betty' by the sailors on board H.M.S. *Gorgon*: 'Betty' is no name even for a goddess, still less for a god. Yet as we shall see, her devoted recording of her husband's more vacuous table-talk and casual scribblings produces on the reader exactly the effect she sought so hard to avoid.

Finally, though a serious study of Watts's art, together with a *catalogue raisonné* of his works, is badly needed, this book, like my life of Mendelssohn (*On Wings of Song*), is simply a biography—or rather, what once used to be called a 'life and times' of its subject. It is intended to interest the reader in Watts the man and in his wide circle of friends, thereby arousing a curiosity about Watts the artist that some art historian must surely soon satisfy. It is with this in mind that '*England's Michelangelo*' should be judged.

W.J.W.B.

[1] See p. 67.
[2] T. S. R. Boase, *English Painting, 1800–1870*, O.U.P. 1959.

1

A CLEVER BOY

GEORGE FREDERIC[1] WATTS, the son of a Hereford piano manufacturer who had transferred his business to London, was born in Queen Street,[2] Bryanston Square, on 23 February 1817. He was, wrote one of his more gushing biographers, 'indeed a child of the spring, having the fresh vernal influences of nature in his blood from the beginning, fitting him to give a new impulse to the artistic and philosophic life of his day . . .'[3]

Watts liked to believe that he had Celtic blood in his veins, but, writing nearly sixty years later to a friend who had inquired about the origin of his name, he confessed, 'I really know nothing about it. Being a lover of the beautiful its want of music is distasteful to me, and when I was younger I often had serious thoughts of changing it—and would have done so if taking what did not belong to me had not seemed to be a very unsatisfactory alternative.' He envied Tennyson, who could derive inspiration from the mere mechanical repetition of his name, whereas the reiteration of 'Watts' produced no comparable vibrations; and when he chanced to hear a name that pleased him—'Wynn', for example, 'which has a fragrance about it for me'—he would sadly say, 'Ah, if only I had had one like that I should have done my work better!' Though he was twice to refuse a

[1] So spelt on his grave, by Mary Watts in her biography of her husband, and in the *Dictionary of National Biography*; but the certificate of baptism and other official documents give Frederick.
[2] Now Harrowby Street, leading out of Cato Street where the notorious conspiracy was hatched in 1820.
[3] *The Life-work of George Frederick Watts, R.A.* by Hugh Macmillan, Dent, 1903—one of a number of laudatory little biographies of Watts which appeared in the opening decade of the present century.

1

baronetcy, might he not have accepted a barony if (like Leighton) he had been offered one? 'Lord Limnerslease, of Compton in the county of Surrey'? That would have sounded very well.

Equally he regretted, though he was never ashamed of, his humble birth, and would sometimes daydream that he was the scion of a distinguished family that had come down in the world. In the letter already quoted, he adds, 'I confess I should like to have a fine name and a great ancestry; it would have been delightful to me to feel as though a long line of worthies were looking down upon me and urging me to sustain their dignity.' Later a rumour (quite without foundation) circulated in London that Watts's father was a son of the third Lord Holland, who had at all events one other bastard. If it ever came to the artist's ears he would certainly have been more shocked than uplifted by the thought that his 'long line of worthies' might be urging him onwards from the wrong side of the blanket.

The biographer of Watts cannot but be grateful that he is not obliged (as is so often a biographer's lot) to hold up his story by much tedious genealogy. A Watts may have fought at the side of Gruffudd ab Llywelyn or Owen Glendower, but if he did we know nothing of it. In fact, the recorded family tree is no more than a few inches high. It comprises the artist's grandfather, another George, who in 1774 married a certain Elizabeth Bradford, both of Hereford, and whose son, yet another George, was born there a year later. They were craftsmen in a family business which began as cabinet-makers and later became piano manufacturers.

Mr Watts (if, to avoid confusion, we may so call the artist's father) had by his first wife a son and two daughters—Thomas, Maria and Harriet. Then in 1815 Mrs Watts died, and a year later the widower married a widow, Harriet, daughter of Frederic Smith. By this second marriage there were four sons in quick succession. One died in infancy, and George Frederic, the eldest, alone (and only just) survived a sharp attack of measles that soon carried off his brothers.

Young George's childhood was no bed of roses. He was sickly, and already suffered constantly from those migraines, vertigos and vomitings that were to be the bane of his whole life. He was lonely, for his mother was often ill, his father often busy, and with his two half-sisters he had little in common. Some of his hours of strangest happiness were those he spent lying in his darkened bedroom in a kind of ecstasy that always followed the cessation of his attacks.

With him would be the perfect companion, a sparrow that he had tamed and taught to perch on his head and share with him the food on his plate—till the awful day when, as he was shutting it up in its cage for the night, 'he accidentally caught in the door the little head which, unnoticed by him, popped out for another last word'. The death of his pet, the result of his carelessness, was, he alleged, the greatest grief he ever experienced.

Mrs Watts was a good but dull and puritanically pious woman, and the boy was never to forget the gloom of Sundays when his beloved translation of the *Iliad* and the novels of Sir Walter Scott were locked away and his reading restricted to the Bible, the Prayer Book and *Pilgrim's Progress*. Misguidedly she stuffed him with edifying tales which sadly miscarried, and even in old age he would recall with revulsion that of a man who, having neglected to read his Bible during the week, was struck dead by God on the following Sunday when in the act of penitently taking it down from the shelf. He was regularly dragged to a hideous church where 'a preacher in a black gown spoke of wrath to come', and where his reason and his aesthetic instincts were so shocked that at the time he firmly believed all religious teachers to be humbugs. 'While I felt,' he said, 'for the subject of religion so great a reverence that it was difficult for me to speak about it, I reasoned and rebelled against the unreality of ordinary religious teaching.'

The cause of Mrs Watts's ill-health was at last diagnosed: she was consumptive; soon she was wholly bedridden, and in 1826 she died. Thus Mr Watts, once more a widower, found himself in the care and at the mercy of his two daughters: girls just out of their teens, both (according to George) ill-tempered, and one of them 'dotty'. The elder son, Thomas, of whom we hear no more, was twenty-five. For the nine-year-old George, the death of his mother brought little respite from the tyranny of a Puritan Sunday, for his father was also a strict sabbatarian.

According to George, Mr Watts was 'a good man and a very thoughtful man, but weak—weak in health and in purpose'. By this time he was also disappointed and disillusioned. Having a taste for invention, he had put much time, skill and good money into the development of a musical instrument[1] (a kind of Aeolian harp?)

[1] The craze for building strange musical instruments seems to have started in the 1780s with the publication of a book on the setting of music for barrel

which was to combine wind and string and so make him rich and famous; but it never materialised, and soon, for lack of capital, he was obliged to exchange the making of pianos for the humbler and less lucrative occupation of tuning them, and to move from his drab house in Queen Street to a yet drabber and even cheaper one in Marylebone. We can see him as he appeared a few years later, in two portraits painted of him by his son in about the year 1835. The features are distinguished—indeed almost aristocratic—and the greying hair (for he was then sixty) is brushed back to reveal an intellectual forehead; but the dark brown eyes betray infinite sadness. He had failed, and his sense of failure now weighs heavily on him. But George, his beloved George, shall succeed; and to this end is henceforth to be directed all his paternal love and solicitude.

Prevented by ill health from regularly attending school or playing games, George had learned to read at home and turned instinctively to drawing for recreation.[1] He could not remember a time when he did not draw, and many of his early sketches have survived. Among these are figure studies from life and from the antique (including the Elgin marbles), illustrations to Homer and the novels of Sir Walter Scott, domestic scenes, and copies of engravings from one or two books in his father's humble library. They show considerable talent and still greater industry, but give no more than a hint of what was to come.

At the age of ten the boy was sent, when well enough, to draw and make himself generally useful in the studio of William Behnes—one of the three sons of a Hanoverian piano manufacturer, a friend of Mr Watts, who had married an English wife and set up in business in London. William was a very able, but very unstable, man in his late thirties, then making a considerable name for himself as a sculptor. But success was turning his head, and (according to Ernest Radford)[2] as commissions multiplied he fell into 'unsatisfactory habits' apparently too dreadful to specify, neglecting his pupils, doing scant justice to his sitters, and forcing his respectable brother Henry to

---

organs. From about 1780 to 1830 many strange instruments were devised, some of which proved successful while others led to the bankruptcy of their inventors.

[1] Sketching had been a hobby of his father, and a drawing by him of Hereford Cathedral was auctioned at Limnerslease in March 1939; it cannot now be traced.
[2] *Dictionary of National Biography.*

change his surname. In 1861, after much 'tossing about in a sea of trouble', William was declared bankrupt, and three years later he was picked up in a London gutter and taken to the Middlesex Hospital to die.

William, besides being a sculptor, was also an exceptional draughtsman, and however idle he may have been as a teacher—'I never studied under him in the ordinary acceptation of the term,' George said later—it is probable that George picked up from him much that was to be of great value later. But hardly less important to the lonely, almost uneducated boy was the friendship he now formed with William's youngest brother, Charles,—deformed, a cripple, and some twenty years his senior, but (unlike William) well-read, cultured, and a man of great integrity. George spent many long evenings with him in William's studio in Osnaburgh Street, discussing Shakespeare, Virgil and Ossian and widening his outlook by contact with a maturer mind. Charles was the only steadying influence on his depraved brother, with whom he lived, and it was after the former's death in the middle forties that William finally went to pieces.

It was no doubt William Behnes who, probably in the very early thirties (for the exact dating of the events of George's boyhood is difficult), arranged for Mr Watts to get an opinion on his son's work from the President of the Royal Academy, Sir Martin Archer Shee—poet as well as painter, of whom Byron had written:

And here let Shee and genius find a place,
Whose pen and pencil yield an equal grace . . .

Shee thumbed through the portfolio of competent but immature drawings and said with icy frankness, 'I can see *no* reason why your son should take up the profession of art.'

One cannot wholly blame him for not seeing where these boyish sketches might one day lead. Or did he perhaps feel that real genius and dedication could never be deterred by even the coldest of douches? If so, he was right. Mr Watts was undaunted; and as for George—blessed with that strange mixture of humility and absolute self-assurance that was to be so typical of the Victorians, he *knew* that he would be an artist, and not a dozen Shees would have deflected him from his chosen path.

By 1833 the sixteen-year-old boy was making a useful contribution to his keep by drawing portraits in pencil or chalk at five shillings a time, and within a year he was able proudly to boast that he was no longer costing his father anything. And then, suddenly, he painted a head-and-shoulder self-portrait—no more than a sketch, yet something that even Shee could hardly have dismissed as just the work of a rather clever boy. It shows a serious, romantic-looking youth—eager, sensitive, poetical—with dark, lustrous eyes which (wrote Chesterton) 'seemed to have been at this time the largest and hungriest part of him'. The face is pale, and almost framed in a tangle—though a modest one by today's standards—of crisp brown hair that suggests no calculated attempt to appear bohemian but is long merely 'because he has forgotten to have it cut'; it is Shelley as one might perhaps imagine him, rather than as he actually was. A happy chance has preserved this brilliant and charming study from destruction, whereas a second self-portrait, made about the same time and showing the artist shading his face with his left hand (in emulation, perhaps, of Reynolds's youthful self-portrait), has vanished without trace.

Other scraps of information about his life in the early thirties were recalled by George some sixty years later and recorded for posterity by his indefatigable and adoring second wife. A friend of Charles Behnes, a miniature painter, gave the boy his first lesson in the use of oils and lent him a little Lely to copy; this copy, like the self-portrait, is now at Compton. George also 'faked' a Vandyke, gave it an antique appearance by treating it with soot, and then submitted it to William Behnes for his opinion. The sculptor studied it carefully. 'I wouldn't like to say it *is* a Vandyke,' he said guardedly, but it's certainly by no mean hand.' When George confessed, Behnes cried out angrily, 'Then why the devil don't you always paint like that?'

George remembered being stopped in the street one day by a man who, noticing the sketchbook in his hand, said amiably, 'May a fellow-student look at your work?' The 'student' proved to be Benjamin Haydon, the famous historical painter, exponent of High Art and champion of the Elgin marbles, who praised what he saw and invited the youth to visit his studio. It may have been shyness which prevented him from following up this friendly suggestion; or was the earnest, upright youth perhaps shocked by stories he had heard of Haydon's rather stormy life? As for Haydon—could anyone have told him that, before very long, he was to be routed in open competition by this fledgling, he would never have believed him.

Mary Watts also informs us that George, in order to make use of every moment of daylight, disciplined himself to rise at dawn. This state of grace he achieved by 'not going to bed at all. I didn't undress, but rolled myself in a thick dressing-gown and lay on the floor of my studio, or on two chairs, until I had taught myself to wake and rise with the sun.' The habit, once acquired, was never lost, and, even in his eighty-eighth year, except when he was ill he would get up at dawn and go straight to his easel.

We now come to a firm date. On 30 April 1835, George, just turned eighteen, was admitted to the Royal Academy Schools, still at that time at Somerset House, to study initially in that part of it which was devoted to drawing from the antique.[1] Though his name remained on the books for two years, he gained (he said) little or nothing from his very irregular attendance there beyond what he taught himself by drawing from the casts and later from the live model. 'There was no teaching at all; no tests and no examinations. I learned in one school only: that of Pheidias.' Medals were, however, awarded from time to time, and on two occasions both the Keeper (William Hilton) and the students in general felt certain that George would win one. When, on the first occasion, he did not, he bravely maintained that Hilton's whispered 'Never mind, you *ought* to have had it,' meant more to him than any medal. Hilton, a man much loved by the students, seems to have been among the first to recognise George's exceptional gifts, and held up his work as an example to the rest of the class. Was the boy being, perhaps, rather unfair in alleging that there was *no* teaching at all at the School?

By this time George had a small studio in Clipstone Street, not far from where Broadcasting House now stands. There in the winter of 1836–37 he painted three pictures which were accepted for the 1837 Summer Exhibition of the Royal Academy, which was held that year for the first time in one wing of the newly-built National Gallery in Trafalgar Square; it may be noted that Hilton was one of the five members of the Hanging Committee. Two of these pictures

[1] Another youth of exactly George's age, Patrick Branwell Brontë, came to London in 1835 to apply for admission to the R.A. Schools, but it is doubtful whether he ever attended them.

were portraits, one of which has disappeared. The other, now known as 'Little Miss Hopkins', is a technically very accomplished, if not very original, portrait of a child; it might almost be described as a large miniature,[1] so highly finished is its enamelled surface. Watts had long since forgotten the identity of the sitter when, one day some sixty years later, a 'pretty, silver-haired old lady' came to his studio and introduced herself as Mrs Mallorie, the original of the portrait.

The third painting, listed in the Academy catalogue as 'A Wounded Heron', is far more remarkable; indeed it might almost be claimed that this youth, barely twenty and largely self-taught, was never to paint anything more technically perfect. Watts was all his life interested in falconry,[2] and this picture was preceded by a small study entitled 'Hawking' (1836, and now at Compton) in which the artist portrays himself holding his horse while the same heron (but reversed) lies at his feet. No doubt Watts was also familiar with Landseer's 'Hawking in the Olden Time' (1832, now at Kenwood).

The 'wounded' heron was in fact already dead when Watts acquired it; the bird had caught his eye in a poulterer's shop, where he had instantly fallen in love with the soft silver-grey of its plumage and bought it.[3] Then out of this still-life material he created, by the introduction of a falconer on horseback and a landscape setting, a little drama with (thought Mary Watts) a symbolic meaning: 'It is impossible not to see in the pathos of the outstretched wing something more than a prophecy of the pathos of the wing of Love defending the door of Life of forty years later—young Love impotent against the inevitable—much also of the same mind [kind?], taking note of the mysteries in the drama of life suggested by the falcon[4] high in the blue over the dying heron—one beautiful child of nature joyfully pursuing another to the death, and the mounted falconer also following gaily, and possessed with the joy of the chase.'

[1] The size is $10'' \times 8''$. The picture is now at Compton.
[2] The equestrian statue of Hugh Lupus (see p. 192) shows the rider about to release his hawk.
[3] The heron was not then, if indeed ever, a luxury for the rich, and at an earlier date had been so abundant that some London apprentices had once gone on strike 'as a protest against being called upon to eat the bird's dark and fishy flesh more than three times a week'. (*Searchlight on Animals* by E. G. Boulanger, Robert Hale, 1936.)
[4] Now barely visible.

Chesterton, too, found a moral in it. 'The Wounded Heron', he wrote, was 'painted clearly with a humanitarian object: it depicts the suffering of a stricken creature; it depicts the helplessness of life under the cruelty of inanimate violence; it depicts the pathos of dying and the greater pathos of living. Since then, no doubt, Watts has improved his machinery of presentation and found larger and more awful things to tell his tale with than a bleeding bird. The wings of the heron have widened till they embrace the world with the terrible wings of Time or Death . . .' Certainly Watts, who had wept over his pet sparrow accidentally killed, all his life felt deeply about birds, and in his 'A Dedication' (1898–99) attacked the 'barbarous and abominable practice of destroying myriads of exquisite birds' for the base purpose of adorning women's hats. 'The Wounded Heron' may therefore perhaps be considered at least an anticipation of those allegories with which Watts's name was later to become so closely associated.

The picture was sold from the walls of the exhibition, and Watts lost all track of it. Then in 1888 (wrote Mary Watts) 'one Sunday, talking to Mrs Henry Holiday of his early work, he spoke of it as his first picture at the Royal Academy, and regretted that it was lost . . . By a strange coincidence a letter from the possessor, a dealer in Newcastle, was already in the post offering the picture to us for a small sum [five pounds].' On seeing it again, Watts was embarrassed by the realisation that in certain respects he had scarcely made any advance over a period of half a century, and when, the following year, he sent it with five other pictures to an exhibition at the New Gallery, it 'put him to the greatest confusion' that it was singled out by the critics for special acclaim. 'The "Heron" they are now all praising,' he complained, 'had no notice taken of it when it was first painted.' He also denied that he had been in any way indebted to the paintings of Hondecoeter,[1] an artist of whom he had at that time never even heard; 'it is strange,' he told a friend, that one can never do anything in the way of painting without being supposed to be prompted by some old master.'

Who, then, were the artists who influenced the young Watts— for influenced, of course, he was? He was early familiar with the

[1] Melchior d'Hondecoeter (1636–95), famous Dutch painter of birds, especially poultry. He is said to have trained a cockerel to pose for him. Watts's painting can stand comparison with Oudry's famous 'White Goose'.

work of Reynolds, Fuseli, Flaxman and probably Morland—partly, perhaps, through engravings. Then came Lawrence and Etty, who guided his hand as a portrait-painter and may also have been behind the sure brushwork of 'The Wounded Heron'. The first impact of the Elgin Marbles had been overwhelming, though it was not until rather later that they were to affect his own work. Soon, too, we see Watts warming himself before the glowing fires of the Venetians, especially Titian. In the late thirties Turner was at his greatest, but Watts wrote later, 'I can see in nature what Turner saw, and can appreciate the excellence of his imitation, but my natural tendency is to see nature with such eyes as Giorgione and Titian had.'[1] Constable, who had died in 1837, left no mark on Watts, even when in the forties he turned for a while to landscape; nor did Wilkie, the most popular artist of the day, except by his unhappy advocacy of bitumen.

About this time there came into Watts's life two men who were to have a considerable influence, the one on his intellectual develop-ment and the other on his career as a portrait-painter in search of commissions: Nicholas Wanostrocht and Constantine Ionides.

Wanostrocht, an Englishman of Belgian origin, had inherited a flourishing family coaching establishment, the Alfred House Academy, which had recently moved from Camberwell to Black-heath. Instruction there, always unorthodox, was at this time also unbalanced; for Wanostrocht was a fanatical cricketer under whose régime academic subjects (except singing—his other hobby) suffered some neglect. He was a brilliant left-handed bat, his 'cut to the off from the shoulder' being memorable, and as a bowler his slow lobs were described as 'very fatal'. He first played, though on this occasion to little effect, for the Gentlemen against the Players at Lord's in 1831 (bowled Pilch for 0, bowled Lillywhite for 1), and thereafter fairly regularly for the next twenty years, using, so as not to embarrass his family, the pseudonym 'M. Felix'.

In 1845 Wanostrocht published a slim quarto entitled *Felix on the Bat; being a scientific Enquiry into the use of the Cricket Bat, together with the History and Use of the Catapulta*; further editions were called for in 1850 and 1855. It was illustrated with lithographs made by Watts, his original drawings for them being now in the pavilion

[1] 'Loch Ness' (1899) is clearly Turneresque.

at Lord's, and the title-page shows Felix flying on a bat's back high above the green English countryside. The text, at times facetious, is however strictly practical, and describes in detail what a cricketer should wear—for example: 'I strongly recommend a cap made of chequered woollen: it is light and cool to the head, absorbs perspiration and (which is not an insignificant fact) is not likely to be blown off and hit the wicket.'

The catapulta was an ingenious mechanical bowler of Felix's invention, which could project a cricket ball at a batsman at any desired velocity—'so fast, that it would split your bat in two; or so slow, that the ball would scarcely reach the wicket'. At eleven guineas it failed to sell. More successful financially were Felix's patent tubular indiarubber batting-gloves and other contrivances for the protection of the batsman against 'the uncertainty and irregularity of the present system of throwing bowling'.

We do not know how the paths of Watts and Felix chanced to cross. Undoubtedly the young man was very conscious of his neglected education—'I only knew one thing,' he said, 'which was that I knew nothing'—and possibly one of the flowery prospectuses of Alfred House caught his eye and stirred him to action. At all events, under Felix and his staff he now acquired a smattering of French, Italian and Greek. One day, half a century later, Mary Watts came upon his copy of *Il Pastor Fido*, sadly inscribed in a boyish scribble, *'Qui ne le sait lire, qu'il est malheureux!'* Watts probably suffered all his life from an inferiority complex induced by his defective education. His thinking was, and remained, confused; his endless high-minded reflections, so devotedly garnered by Mary Watts from his *obiter dicta* and barely legible jottings on the backs of a thousand envelopes, are for the most part pathetically trite.

At Alfred House Watts trained his voice and throughout his life was a happy songster of the 'Tom Bowling' brand, singing as he worked or for relaxation. No doubt he also played a good deal of cricket, for even in old age the sound of ball on bat would bring him running (or his nearest equivalent) from his studio to see the sport; and perhaps it was also now that he learned to ride. In short, the hours he spent at Felix's Academy were to be often recalled as 'happy old times . . . I think they were to many of us happier than any of our later years.'

*   *   *

In the spring of 1837 a Greek named Alexander Constantine Ionides, the head of a Merchant House in London with branches in Athens and Constantinople, was looking for an artist to make a copy of a portrait[1] of his father for the firm's office in Constantinople. A friend recommended Watts, who agreed to do the work for £10. The copy was duly brought to Ionides, who to everyone's astonishment announced that he much preferred it to the original (which had cost him £63) and that he therefore proposed sending the latter to Constantinople instead of the copy. It so happened that an art connoisseur arrived at that moment in the office, and he was asked to say which was the original. 'I can't tell you that,' he answered, but (pointing to the Watts), 'I can tell you which is by far the better painting of the two.' Thus began Watts's long and mutually profitable association with the Ionides family, five generations of whom he was to paint over a period of nearly sixty years.

Frank Brangwyn once said[2] that no artist need ever starve in Paris; he had only to paint another picture of the Pont Neuf for the tourist trade. So for Watts there was always another Ionides, waiting in the queue to be painted as soon as a financial crisis obliged him to take time off from unprofitable 'High Art' and stoop to vulgar but lucrative portraiture. The very names of these compatriots of Pheidias were music to him: Euterpe, Aglaia, Euphrosyne, Agathonike, Anthea Chariclea, Demetrius, Eustratius, Zoë—some of them through marriage members of other Greek families such as the Coronio, Cassavetti, Lascarides, Zambaco, Fenerli or Craies. Constantine Alexander Ionides, a son of Alexander Constantine, became famous as an art collector, and through his generosity his fine collection, which contained a number of pictures by Watts, passed on his death in 1900 to the Victoria and Albert Museum, London.

From this time on, Watts was able to keep himself in modest comfort by portrait painting, with something left over for his impecunious father and half-sisters; he was now the breadwinner of the family, and long after his father's death he continued conscientiously to contribute towards the support of those two unattractive and unloved women 'of fibre different from his own' (as he charitably put it) with whom he severed all other connection. Among paintings made during the next four or five years are several

[1] By the deaf-and-dumb artist, Samuel Lane.
[2] To the author, in 1920, when he was considering taking a studio in Paris.

Ionides family groups. These appear to be the artist's first attempts to work on six-foot canvases—to 'think big'; very soon he was to be thinking enormous. There were also smaller portraits of various Ionides, a Captain and Mrs Hamilton and their little son (the infant 'thrown in' because Watts considered he had been overpaid for the other two!), the Rev. Alfred Wellsted, Miss Brunton, the Radical parliamentarian John Roebuck, and the three children of Lord Gainsborough. From Roebuck Watts also received the curious commission for a portrait of Jeremy Bentham (who had died in 1832), to be made from the wax effigy which covers the philosopher's skeleton and is dressed in his clothes; this macabre object is, I believe, still preserved in University College, London. It was generally agreed that the most successful of his early subject pictures was his 'Aurora' —a work which foreshadows the large classical compositions of his later years.

2

ELEVEN DAVIDS AND ONE GOLIATH

THE HIGH PRIEST and missionary of 'High Art' in England in the early part of the nineteenth century was one of the strangest figures in the whole long story of painting: Benjamin Robert Haydon—'historical painter' (as he liked to sign himself). His brief encounter with Watts has already been mentioned.

First, let us hear him pray—for when he was not painting or borrowing money he was mostly on his knees:

O God Almighty! who so mercifully assisted me during my last picture; who enabled me to combat and conquer so many difficulties, and gave me strength of mind superior to all, desert me not now O Lord . . . My difficulties are again accumulating, and will yet accumulate. Grant me that I may be able to proceed unchecked by sickness with my present great picture, and conclude it as it ought to be concluded. Let not the progress of this picture be disgraced by the vice which disgraced the last. Let me be pure, holy, and virtuous—industrious, indefatigable, and firm. Enable me to conceive all the characters with the utmost possible acuteness and dignity, and execute them with the utmost possible greatness and power. O God, in pecuniary emergencies Thou hast never deserted me; still in such moments stretch forth Thy protecting hand. Amen. Amen.

The prayer tells us, by implication, much about the man. It tells us that he was deeply and morbidly religious. It tells us also that he believed in his divine mission: that the Almighty had sent him to rescue English art from triviality and direct it along a nobler path. 'His impassioned prayers [wrote George Paston[1]] read as though

[1] *B. R. Haydon and his Friends*, by George Paston, James Nisbet, London, 1905.

14

they were offered up to some omnipotent President of a celestial Academy, who demanded oblations in the shape of historical pictures. Haydon daily implored his Creator to grant him success in his calling, promising in return to raise the standard of national taste, and to produce works which should redound to the glory of his God and the honour of his country.' And lastly, it hints that Haydon was incessantly in financial crises from which God was expected repeatedly to rescue his chosen instrument. 'I have been imprisoned four times for persevering to improve the people,' he wrote in his fascinating Journals,[1] in the London Library copy of which a reader, in defiance of the Library's regulations, has deleted the last five words of this sentence and substituted for them, 'living beyond my income'.

The dreadful story of Haydon's agonizing decline from fame and glory into neglect, chronic debt, despair, and eventual suicide in 1846 at the age of sixty, all meticulously and self-pityingly recorded by him in twenty-six 'bulky parchment-bound ledger-like folios', cannot be related here. The part he played in championing and establishing the reputation of the Elgin Marbles, an act which earned for him the immortality of several sonnets by Keats, may again be briefly mentioned because of the importance of these sculptures in the artistic development of the young Watts. But it was Haydon's lifelong crusade to get the walls of England's public buildings made available for decoration by British artists that is principally relevant, in that it led to Watts achieving his first great public success.

In October 1834 the Houses of Parliament had been destroyed by fire, but it was not until nearly six years later, in April 1840, that the first stone was laid of the new buildings, designed by (Sir) Charles Barry. Here at last was the great opportunity for Haydon to achieve his ambition, and in his Journal for 10 July 1840 he notes that he has seen Barry, who has promised him 'sections and plans of the Houses of Lords and Commons. We talked of it. He said whether anything were done or no, he would leave the Hall and House of Lords so that they would be in a mess if painting was not introduced . . . I said, "I hope you won't forget me, Mr Barry." "It

[1] *Life of Benjamin Robert Haydon, Historical Painter, from his Autobiography and Journals*, edited and compiled by Tom Taylor, Longmans, London, 1853, 3 volumes.

will be a great shame if they do, Mr Haydon." "I hope *you* won't forget me, Mr Barry." He blushed!'

A Fine Arts Committee was set up under the presidency of the Prince Consort, and a number of witnesses, including Shee, Dyce and Eastlake, were examined; but Haydon was not called. He was bitterly disappointed, and already began to fear that there might be further disappointments in store for him. Then in April 1842 came the announcement of an open competition. Cartoons were to be submitted, illustrating scenes from British history or the works of Spenser, Shakespeare or Milton. They were to be carried out in chalk or charcoal, without colour, in size not less than ten and not more than fifteen feet in their longest dimension, with figures not less than life-size. The closing date for entries was fixed for the beginning of May 1843, but subsequently the time was extended by a month.

The prizes were tempting: three of £300, three of £200 and five of £100—and everywhere in England artists set feverishly to work. Haydon was at first delighted by the news. The 'glorious' Report made his heart 'leap with gratitude and joy to the good and great Creator, who has blessed me through every variety of fortune to this first great accomplishment of my ardent hopes. O God! Bless me with life, and health, and intellect, and eyes to realise the wishes of the Commissioners.' Then, on reflection, he felt slighted in that he had not been directly invited to undertake the work. Perhaps God wished to mortify his pride and ambition. 'I bow,' he wrote; 'but I am pained.' But supposing—was it possible?—that he did not win a prize. To his old pupil (Sir) Charles Eastlake, Secretary to the Commission, he wrote to beg that, *'employed* or *not employed'*, he would, as a reward for all his labours over the years in the cause of High Art, be allowed 'to take the *first* brush, and dip into the *first* colour, and put the *first* touch on the *first* intonaco.[1] If that is not granted, I'll haunt every noble Lord and you, till you join my disturbed spirit on the banks of the Styx.'

In July, Haydon, though handicapped through being obliged to pawn his spectacles and lay figure, began one of the two cartoons he intended to submit—'the Curse of Adam and Eve':

Huzza—huzza—huzza; and one cheer more!

[1] Wet plaster.

My cartoon is up, and makes my heart beat, as all large bare spaces do, and ever have done. Difficulties to conquer. Victories to win. Enemies to beat. The Nation to please. The honour of England to be kept up.

Huzza—huzza—huzza; and one cheer more!

Then came the second cartoon, 'The Entry of Edward the Black Prince and King John into London'. 'The moment I touch a great canvas,' he wrote, 'I think I see my Creator smiling on all my efforts . . .' But the Creator omitted to sustain him when he was 'fixing' his cartoon (by the then clumsy practice of steaming it), and he was laid up for several weeks with a burnt foot. His feet seem to have been accident prone; only a year before he had run a bayonet through one of them while painting 'The Maid of Saragossa'. His financial troubles were more acute than ever, but he had found an ingenious method of extracting further loans from his long-suffering creditors while still behaving like a gentleman: 'February 3rd [1843] . . . In one hour and a half I had £10 to pay upon my honour, and only £2 15s. in my pocket. I drove away to Newton, paid hims £2 15s., and borrowed £10. I then drove away to my friend, paid him the £10, and borrowed £5 more, but felt relieved I had not broke my honour.'

On 1 June he wrote:

O God, I thank Thee that this day I have safely placed my cartoons in Westminster Hall. Prosper them! . . . Spare my life, O Lord, until I have shown Thy strength unto this generation, and Thy power unto that which is to come . . .

I found Eastlake, my pupil, walking about. He was most happy to see me . . . 'Do you remember,' said he, 'coming with me into Westminster Hall, and drawing a gigantic limb on the wall with the end of the umbrella, saying "This is the place for art"? I did not. He said I actually did so, thirty years ago; and he remembered my jumping up to reach high. Now here we were, master and pupil, marching about, and the first act of this great drama of art just beginning . . .

Meanwhile young Watts, though he had never before attempted to work on so large a scale, had also decided to try his luck. He took for his subject Caractacus, the captive British chieftain, being led in chains through the streets of Rome; and the defiant look that he needed in his hero, which long eluded him, he finally achieved by studying a lion at the Zoo. It was a strange subject to choose, and Watts was later to be castigated by the art critic of the *Athenaeum* for selecting for his theme a moment of British humiliation—'A British captive led in triumph to "make a Roman holiday"!' Could anyone, the critic added, imagine a Delaroche or a Delacroix adorning the *Palais de Justice* with Napoleon dying under the eyes of English sentinels? One is reminded of the naive question put by the Algerian patriot, Abd el-Kader, after he had been shown the great series of battle pictures in the *Galerie des Batailles* at Versailles: 'And where are the pictures of the French defeats?'

Watts, too, ran into trouble when he came to fix his cartoon. True, he did not damage his foot; what was almost worse, he damaged the drawing. He was in fact so disheartened that he turned it face to the wall and took up other work. Then, a morning or two before sending-in day, he looked at it again with a fresh eye, decided that the damage might not after all be irreparable, set to work feverishly, and at the eleventh hour took it to Westminster Hall where the competing cartoons—a hundred and forty in all—were to be exhibited.

Before long, rumours about the probable prize-winners began to circulate, and young Horsley (Mendelssohn's great friend, who was also a competitor) reported to Watts that his (Watts's) entry[1] was considered likely to receive one of the three top prizes. Watts could not credit it. He was disappointed with his drawing and had come very near to destroying it; and in any case he was competing against artists of established reputation such as Haydon. But to poor Haydon now came ill tidings that were more than a rumour: on 27 June, a week before the exhibition was due to open, Eastlake called to tell him that he had not succeeded in winning even one of the third prizes.

It took Haydon several days to summon up courage to break the bitter news to his wife, Mary. On 1 July he wrote in his Journal:

A day of great misery. I said to my dear love, 'I am not included.' Her expression was a study. She said, 'We shall be ruined.' I

[1] Actually the cartoons had been entered anonymously.

looked up my lectures, papers and journals, and sent them to my dear Æsculus Barrett,[1] with two jars of oil twenty-seven years old. I burnt loads of private letters, and prepared for executions . . . Seven pounds was raised on my daughter's and Mary's dresses.

Horsley (who himself won a second prize) had not been misinformed. Watts's 'Caractacus', which is clearly inspired by the Raphael cartoons now in the Victoria and Albert Museum, had deservedly joined Edward Armitage's 'Caesar's Invasion of Britain' and Charles Cope's 'The First Trial by Jury' in winning a first prize. Both Armitage, who had studied under Delaroche in Paris, and Horsley were exactly the same age as Watts, and Cope was thirty-two; it was a day of triumph for the younger generation, for not one of the prize-winners was even an Associate of the Royal Academy.

The Queen went to the exhibition, which during the first two weeks attracted an average daily attendance of eighteen hundred visitors paying a shilling a head. Then entrance was made free, and crowds of 'most respectably dressed people' (observed *The Times*) thronged the Hall. Poor Haydon, who suffered from persecution mania, saw his rejection as the result of a conspiracy against him; but he put on a brave face, paid his shilling, and was 'astonished at the power displayed . . . My own [cartoon] looked grand, like the effusion of a master.' The great mistake, he considered, 'and it has been a tremendous one', was the awarding of what he calls *the* prize— in fact the top three prizes were all equal—to a man who had studied in France. 'The injury it will do is incalculable, for, instead of destroying the prejudices against British genius, it will root them deeper than ever.' A dark, tousle-headed boy of fifteen was also among the visitors. He wrote to his mother of the 'Caractacus', 'The artist is a young man by the name of Watts, who has been ever since he took to the arts, struggling with poverty. He is, however, as good as he is talented, and has been for many years the sole support of his mother.'[2] The boy's name was Dante Gabriel Rossetti.

In September Haydon removed his rejected works from

[1] Elizabeth Barrett, who married Robert Browning in 1846.

[2] Mrs Arthur Bell, *Representative Painters of the Nineteenth Century*, London, 1899 (quoted by Chapman). Mrs Watts, it will be remembered, had in fact died when George was only nine.

Westminster Hall. 'Thus ends the cartoon contest,' he wrote, 'and as the very first inventor and beginner of this mode of rousing the people when they were pronounced incapable of relishing refined works of art without colour, I am deeply wounded at the insult inflicted.' The eleven winning cartoons were purchased *en bloc* by a dealer and in due course exhibited in various provincial towns. Watts, although he had received a much better private offer for his 'Caractacus', generously allowed it to be included in the sale when told that by withholding it he would prejudice the value of the collection as a whole. He was unfortunately abroad when, later, his cartoon passed to another dealer, who without reference to him cut it up into pieces of more manageable size. Not surprisingly, he was extremely indignant when he heard what had happened. Several of the fragments have, however, survived, though it may well seem doubtful whether they will ever again emerge from the catacombs of the Victoria and Albert Museum's storerooms to receive a place on the walls where the public can see them.

It is strange that none of the cartoons was actually carried out in fresco, but perhaps they were intended to be no more than a test of strength. All the winning ones, together with ten more which had been given consolation prizes out of the money taken at the exhibition, were, however, published in lithograph. The problem of painting in fresco in England was now carefully studied and experiments made, Prince Albert putting at the disposal of a group of artists a small pavilion in the grounds of Buckingham Palace which was decorated with illustrations to *Comus*. Further competitions were held and a number of murals were eventually carried out in the Houses of Parliament, among them Watts's 'Alfred inciting the Saxons to resist the Landing of the Danes'—a winning design of the 1847 competition.[1]

From this triumph of youth we return to the tragedy of disappointed middle age.

It is marvellous to read with what a façade of zest and fortitude poor Haydon went back to his easel after his humiliation, and at the close of this bitter year he wrote in his Journal, 'This is B. R. Haydon—the *real* man—may he live a thousand years! and here he sneezed—lucky!' He fooled himself into believing that he was

[1] See p. 44.

painting better than ever, and of his latest picture wrote, 'What magic! what fire! what unerring hand and eye! what fancy! what power! what a gift of God! I bow and am grateful.' But in between creating these masterpieces for posterity he had to pot-boil literally dozens of little pictures of Napoleon 'musing' at various moments in his career (there were no less than thirteen musings on St Helena alone), to keep the wolf from the door.

Then in the spring of 1846 he staked all he had—and quite a lot that he did not have—to hire the Egyptian Hall in Piccadilly in which to display his two latest masterpieces, 'The Burning of Rome by Nero' and 'The Banishment of Aristides'. The magnificence of the conception of the former had so overwhelmed the artist that he had 'fluttered, trembled, and perspired like a woman', and finally collapsed on a chair, while blocking it in.

When the exhibition opened, the critics were surprisingly generous with their praise, that of the *Herald* urging 'every Briton who has pluck in his bosom, and a shilling in his pocket'[1] to 'crowd his works during the Easter week'. Alas! they did not; for in an adjacent room was an irresistible rival attraction: the famous American midget, Tom Thumb.[2] 'April 21st—Tom Thumb had 12,000 people last week. B. R. Haydon 133$\frac{1}{2}$ (the $\frac{1}{2}$ a little girl). Exquisite taste of the English people!' A month later Haydon 'marched out before General Tom Thumb, a beaten but not conquered exhibitor.' He had lost £111. 8s. 10d. by this rash venture, and there were other formidable debts outstanding.

In fact, this time the defeat was final, the war lost. On the morning of 22 June he made, with a trembling hand, the last entry in his Journal:

God forgive me. Amen.
Finis
of
B. R. Haydon
'Stretch me no longer on this rough [sic] world' *Lear*[3]
End of Twenty-sixth volume

[1] 'Admission 1s.; catalogue 6d.'

[2] Charles Sherwood Stratton (1838–83), known as 'General Tom Thumb'. At the age of eight he was twenty-five inches tall.

[3]
       'Vex not his ghost: O! let him pass; he hates him
       That would upon the rack of this tough world
       Stretch him out longer.'   (*King Lear*, v. iii)

A quarter of an hour later he attempted to cut his throat with a razor, and then shot himself.

Eleven Davids had floored Goliath, but it was left to a midget to deliver the *coup de grâce*.

At Tom Taylor's request, Watts later wrote an interesting appraisal of Haydon the artist, which Taylor appended to his edition of the Journal.[1] Though very conscious of Haydon's tireless struggle on behalf of High Art, Watts felt obliged to condemn his paintings:

> The characteristics of Haydon's art appear to me to be great determination and power, knowledge and effrontery. I cannot find that he strikes upon any chord that is the basis of a true harmony . . . Indeed his pictures are himself, and fail as he failed . . . They are themselves autobiographical notes of the most interesting kind; but their want of beauty repels, and their want of modesty exasperates. Perhaps their principal characteristic is want of delicacy of perception and refinement of execution. . . . To particularise—I should say that his touch is generally woolly, and his surface disagreeable . . . It is somewhat remarkable that the only man who can be said to have formed a school in England after the manner of the Italian artists, is perhaps the only artist of any eminence who has had no imitators.

Fate has not treated too kindly those English historical painters of the nineteenth century who chose to work in the Grand Manner, and for this they are themselves in part to blame. Their enormous murals, whether painted in true fresco or in some kind of tempera on the dry plaster, have mostly suffered severely from the passage of time and at the hands of bungling restorers, till some of them are now total wrecks; and it should have been obvious to these artists that their huge canvases, unless painted to decorate a particular building, might soon be rolled up and stored until doomsday in the vaults of public galleries.

For nearly twenty years Watts was to devote a large part of his

---

[1] It occurs again, in an extended form, in the second edition of Taylor's book. It will be immediately evident to anyone who has read a holograph of Watts, that Taylor has turned what Watts actually wrote into decent English. For Taylor see p. 104.

time and energy to the production of enormous paintings in the Grand Manner—and what has become of them? His forty- by forty-five-foot fresco in Lincoln's Inn Hall[1] has so darkened and deteriorated that barely a diner raises his eyes from his plate to observe its very existence. His fresco of 'St George and the Dragon' in the Houses of Parliament has perished, and his oil painting there of 'Alfred inciting the Saxons to resist the Landing of the Danes' was, perhaps fortunately, never carried out in fresco. Of the two murals he painted for Lord Lansdowne at Bowood,[2] one has been transferred to the walls of the Watts Gallery while the other, which was in oils on canvas, was ruined by flooding. His thirty-foot 'A Story from Boccaccio'[3] soon vanished from the walls of the Tate Gallery, and though briefly hung at Compton was found to be too space-consuming in a small gallery. So it returned to the bowels of the Tate, and was not even considered worthy of an airing at the big Watts exhibition organised in 1954 to celebrate the fiftieth anniversary of the artist's death. The great series of murals painted for Lord Somers in Carlton House Terrace[4] were cut from the walls in 1966 and stored in crates.

But, suddenly, for Watts the tide has turned. In 1973 the enterprising and energetic Mrs Jenny Stein cajoled the Tate Gallery into exhuming 'A Story from Boccaccio' and allowing it to be exhibited at the Watts Exhibition at the Whitechapel Art Gallery in the spring of 1974; and now comes the welcome news that it has been placed in the Hall of Keble College, Oxford. Further, as will be told later, the Carlton House Terrace murals are to be given a permanent home at Eastnor Castle.[5]

Watts has indeed been more fortunate than many. Had he not returned to the portraiture he despised and to easel picture of relatively manageable size he might, over the years, have become as forgotten as were Armitage, Cope, Horsley, and most of those others who scored brief triumphs in the various competitions organized by Her Majesty's Commissioners in the 1840s. And had he been thus forgotten, would 'Boccaccio' and the Carlton House Terrace murals have been considered worth the effort and the expense required for their resurrection today?

[1] See p. 97.   [2] See p. 100.   [3] See p. 42.   [4] See p. 98.   [5] See p. 100.

3

FRA PAOLO

WATTS WAS quite carried away by his huge and unexpected success—a success which was, incidentally,
celebrated by a whole holiday for the pupils at Wanostrocht's exultant Academy. Overnight he had not only become
almost famous, he had become almost rich. Now at last he was in a
position to make a reality of what had doubtless so far been no more
than the wildest of pipe dreams: he would go for a month or two to
Italy, the Mecca of every apostle of High Art.

At the time of the exhibition of the cartoons he had come to know
Edward Armitage,[1] painter of the prize-winning 'Caesar's Invasion
of Britain', who before his return to Paris had suggested that Watts
should break his journey to Italy there for a few weeks. Armitage
was well born, well off and much travelled. An ardent advocate of
historical painting in the Grand Manner, he was all his life to be
happiest painting walls almost the size of a tennis court (his mural
in University Hall in Gordon Square, London, is sixty feet long);
but his hobby was on a smaller scale: he collected butterflies.
Though the same age as Watts, he had had far more experience of
the world, and one may imagine that the prospect of acting as
cicerone to this agreeable, eager, talented young man appealed to
him.

Watts left England some time in July, crossing to Boulogne and
from there making the sixteen-hour journey to Paris by *diligence*. Of
his stay in Paris, where he lodged with Armitage in the Latin
quarter, we know nothing beyond what Mary Watts thought fit to

---

[1] A portrait of Armitage by Watts was in the Limnerslease sale in 1939, but it
cannot now be traced. He also posed for the baron holding the Magna Carta in
Watts's fresco at Lincoln's Inn (see p. 97).

tell us: that he 'saw something of the merry life of the young French students of the time.' That might mean anything—or nothing. Perhaps Armitage was also earnest and upright; but if he made any attempt to introduce his friend to the real *vie de bohème* or the more uninhibited night-life of the French capital, it seems unlikely that he would have met with much success. Or is it possible that we are quite wrong about Watts, and that there were once wild oats whose sowing he was naturally reluctant to discuss with his wife fifty years later? Watts's sex life is, and must always remain, a mystery, though an intriguing one; for it is hard to agree with Chesterton that an artist's private life is of no interest or importance—that 'it is vain to climb walls and hide in cupboards in order to show whether Watts eats mustard or pepper with his curry or whether Watts takes sugar or salt with his porridge. These things may or may not become public: it matters little.'

It can, however, be safely assumed that the two young Englishmen went often together to the Louvre; and it is certain that Watts was taken to see the famous 'Hemicycle' painted by Paul Delaroche in the Amphitheatre of the Ecole des Beaux-Arts, in which his favourite pupil, Armitage, had played no small part, since it was clearly in emulation of this that Watts was later to paint his fresco 'A Hemicycle of Lawgivers' in the Hall of Lincoln's Inn.

At the end of August Watts left Paris by *diligence*, his destination Florence. In these vehicles, which carried about fifteen passengers, one had the choice of a seat in the *intérieur* (hot and stuffy), in the *rotonde* (dusty), or in the *banquette* where one sat beside the driver. Watts chose the *banquette*, which had at least the advantage of providing fresh air and a view; its disadvantage was to become apparent later. Mary Watts quotes a scrap of a letter which has since disappeared, written by her husband during his journey and presumably addressed to Armitage in Paris. It tells us at least that the Watts that most people envisage—the serious and high-minded allegorist, the sober portraitist of the great—had at all events once been young in heart, indeed positively hearty:

A Frenchman and a German and myself were the occupants of the *Banquette*. I soon discovered them to be the most favourable specimens possible of the two nations, and we soon became jolly companions. Laughing, talking and singing much relieved the monotony of the journey, but I defy anything to render the *Banquette* agreeable. I never passed a more wretched night, except perhaps on my passage to Boulogne. Fancy a cold night wind and a horrid disgusting brute of a French conductor, who I had the impression was possessed with murderous monomania, who came and plumped his disgusting corpus in butcher's blouse down by my side, taking the room of six men.

We had some snatches of jollity however, and the second night we behaved so uproariously, singing in chorus the *Marseillaise* and the *Parisienne*, that the proprietors of the *Diligence* took offence at the brilliancy with which we executed some of the passages and complained—the beasts. Thus reduced to silence, we were forced to amuse ourselves by going to sleep, and as I had not slept the night before, Somnus was kind enough to squeeze his poppies on my eyelids.

Then, in the middle of the night, a thunderstorm broke, and it must have seemed to Watts that those who had preferred the *intérieur* had after all chosen wisely. True, there was a hood—of a sort; but it served little to prevent anyone in the *banquette* getting soaked to the skin.

At Chalon-sur-Saône, the battered and weary traveller, if not pressed for time, usually preferred to abandon the *diligence* and embark in one of the small steamboats that plied the Saône and Rhône as far as Avignon. Watts thankfully exchanged the misery of journey by road for the relative comfort of journey by water, though at Avignon he had again to take the *diligence* to Marseilles. Here he found a ship sailing to Leghorn, and it was probably now that he made a small but informative entry in his account book: 'Monday, September 11, 1843—A stranger and an American lent me without being asked £8.' So brief a note—and yet how much it tells us about the man who made it! Not only did people immediately like Watts, they immediately trusted him and were ready to do everything possible to help him. On board was also a General Ellice, at one time Governor of Malta, and his wife, heading too for Florence, who urged him when he arrived there to make himself known to Lord Holland, British Minister to the Court of Tuscany.

The Ellices went straight from Leghorn to Florence. But Watts, overwhelmed by the beauty of the unfamiliar countryside, and perhaps also not unmindful of the need to stretch his prize money to the uttermost, preferred to thumb a lift as far as Pisa from a peasant driving a farm cart. The sun was blazing down, and the blue wall of the Apennines barred the distant horizon. The vintage was as yet ungathered, and as the cart passed under a *treillage* he had only to stretch out his hand to pick a great bunch of purple grapes. Moreover, Wanostrocht's tuition had not been wholly in vain, for to his joy he found that he could exchange at all events a few pleasantries in Italian with the carter. It was bliss to be alive—'but to be young was very heaven'. Perhaps he was never again to be so happy or so carefree. Or so well—for even his migraines seemed to have been left behind in foggy England. A week later, proceeding by easy stages, he reached Florence.

As to how he spent his first days there we can only speculate, though Dr Macmillan is no doubt right in assuring us that everything he saw was 'a perpetual fascination' to him: 'At every step the foot trod upon some reverent history . . . Every building had some great memory of the past connected with it. The Campanile of Giotto reared its lily-like stem into the blue sky, as fresh and fair as though it were a dream of the previous night'—and so on in the same vein. But every minute of his time was precious, and it was probably in order to spare himself those social engagements that would result from leaving his card on the Hollands, that he did not follow up General Ellice's suggestion. Or is it possible that the piano-tuner's son felt rather shy at the prospect of finding himself in such grand company? Here in Italy they could hardly be expected to have been much impressed by his success at Westminster—if, indeed, they had even heard of it.

Then one morning, quite by chance, he came upon the General in the street and was sharply reprimanded. 'Why haven't you been to the Casa Feroni?' he asked. 'Lord Holland has been expecting you; he's been enquiring for you everywhere.' So now he had no choice, and meekly allowed himself to be carried off to the Hollands' house[1] in the via de' Serragli, on the left bank of the Arno not far from the Carmine church. On 3 October he dined there for the first time and made so favourable an impression that Lord Holland, hearing that he was about to leave his present lodgings, suggested that he should stay at the Casa until he had found somewhere that suited

[1] Now the Palazzo Amerighi.

him. 'We have plenty of room,' he said. They had: in the Casa
Feroni there were a hundred bedrooms.

Watts's acquaintance with the Hollands was to change the whole
course of his life.

Henry Edward Fox, fourth Lord Holland, was the son of the
third baron and his clever, eccentric, tiresome wife, who had
gathered round her at Holland House an internationally famous
circle of statesmen, wits and men of letters. Henry Edward, now
just turned forty, had been appointed British Minister in Florence
in 1838, and shortly afterwards succeeded to the barony. In 1833,
after not a few unsuccessful pursuits and broken engagements, he
had married Lady Mary Augusta Coventry, who in moments of
intimacy called her husband 'Buz'; she was ten years his junior, only
five years older than Watts, and had the tiniest feet in Europe.

In a letter written to his mother at the time of his engagement,
Henry had described Augusta (as she was always called) as very
petite, her face very beautiful—especially her eyes, but her figure
bad and her way of dressing 'worse than Cinderella. She doesn't
possess a single gown or *chiffon* of any sort that I do not look forward
to burning with great complacency.' She was intelligent and well-
educated, good-natured and cheerful, and (though one would
hardly guess it from her portraits) free from 'any shadow of affecta-
tion'. Henry had soon helped her to acquire the necessary sartorial
polish, and she now presided successfully over a salon very different
from her mother-in-law's, but one to which all visitors to Florence
were eager to be invited. One thing only was lacking at the Casa
Feroni: some special, some extra-ordinary attraction for the enter-
tainment of her guests; and now a kind Fate had brought this charming and (she was assured) exceptionally talented young artist into
her life. He came; she saw; she was conquered. Watts had been invited to stay for several days; she held him a willing captive for
several years.

Before the year was out, Watts had painted in fresco in the courtyard of the Casa 'a pretty picture of *Flora*, which people are flocking
to see and much admire', and had made a portrait of Lord Holland
and at least two of his wife. That of Lord Holland was said by a
friend to have resembled him very closely, except for the chin being
too long. 'This rather altered the character of the face, but the ex-

pression was like. It was not poor Henry's *best* expression, but it was one he often had.' This was written in 1871 when, after Lord Holland's death, the picture suffered serious damage in a fire at Holland House. 'Try oh try to do something!' the broken-hearted widow cried to Watts, adding melodramatically, 'Call picture-cleaners, picture-restorers, incur any expense—I would starve to regain that portrait.' Watts did his best, but the picture had been ruined beyond repair.

One of the two portraits of Augusta may be that which now hangs in the Watts Gallery at Compton; it shows a minx-like young woman with the vacuous gaze of a bad Romney. The other is certainly that 'in the style of the *Chapeau de Paille*' (wrote a visitor to the Casa), so called 'from some lady having in a joke put one of the country hats on [Augusta's] head. Whatever may be its other merits', he added, 'it is an extraordinary likeness.' The hat, which looks more a Chinese coolie's than an Italian peasant's, bears no resemblance to that in Rubens's 'Chapeau de Paille' in the National Gallery, London; but there can be little doubt that Watts had the Rubens in mind and was in a way attempting to challenge it. On Augusta's death in 1889 this fine picture passed by bequest to the Prince of Wales (Edward VII) and is now at Buckingham Palace.

In October, even before Watts had moved into the Casa Feroni, Lord Holland had written to his aunt, Caroline Fox, giving her his first impression of Watts:

> Mr Watts seems to me full of genius and favourable ambition, without any of the jealous, niggling, detracting vanity of his brother artists. I have seen a good deal of him, as he has made a beautiful sketch of Augusta in oil. I wish you would mention and recommend him to Lord Lansdowne. I think he will be a great painter in his day . . . He returns very soon to England to prepare for the next exhibition.

But Watts stayed on and on, and five months later Lord Holland gave his mother his more considered opinion of his now permanent guest:

> I am very much interested about Mr Watts. I think he has not only great talent, but real genius. The artists here, who are all

good judges and very parsimonious of praise, are wild about him, tho' very angry at having to acknowledge foreign merit. He is, however, terribly dilatory and indolent, and will not buckle to to study fresco painting as he ought. I have worried him into painting portraits, and he has two splendid ones of Jerome Bonaparte and his daughter, P^{ss} Demidoff, besides a full-length one of Mrs Fitzpatrick, which is extremely like, and yet will hand her down to posterity as very beautiful!!!

He would not paint portraits at first, as he aims at being more than a mere portrait painter, and indeed he has talent for really fine poetical pictures—but who in this age will order them and pay for them, among the few who have sense to hang them up!!? I like him very much . . . He is very clever, well read, and wonderfully quick and intelligent; but I fear he has not the energy and qualities to ensure his prosperity in the world.

News that Watts, who had come to Italy to learn to paint in the Grand Manner, was prostituting his talents on mere portraiture, reached Haydon in London, who wrote indignantly to a friend in Florence, the painter Seymour Kirkup:

That boy Watts, I understand, is out, and went out, as the great student of the day. Though he came out for Art, for High Art, the first thing the English do is to employ him on *Portrait*! Lord Holland, I understand, has made him paint Lady Holland!! Is this not exquisite? Wherever they go, racing, cricket, trial by jury, fox-hunting, and portraits are the staple commodities first planted or thought of. Blessed be the name of John Bull!

Watts entirely agreed—yet what could he do? Here he was, living in great comfort as a guest of the Hollands; how could he refuse to paint their portraits or, when asked, those of the distinguished men and women who came to the Casa? Lord Holland was a practical man, and all through his life Watts was at times to be obliged temporarily to set aside his great uplifting allegories, which were slow to find purchasers, and descend (as he saw it) to portraiture in order to pay the milkman and the baker. But Holland must have been wrong in calling Watts excessively idle. This was surely a case of the laymen imagining that a painter is working only when he is actually applying paint to canvas, and of his failure to understand that

Watts's refusal to make copies of the Old Masters (as was then the fashion) stemmed not from laziness but from the fact that he considered such an occupation pointless.[1] Visits to the Uffizi and the Pitti must have opened up vast new worlds to the young artist, and he needed time to reflect and to assimilate. He was not idle; he was thinking—thinking very hard. Then, in the summer of 1844, he decided to become England's Michelangelo, and that was enough to give anyone pause.

This decision followed upon a visit to Rome which Watts made with Lord Holland that August. The first sight of the Sistine Chapel, previously known to Watts only of course through inadequate line-engravings, was overwhelming. Michelangelo's 'David' in Florence had made little impression on him—indeed he had impertinently gone so far as to call it 'bad'—but as a painter Michelangelo was supreme. Pheidias remained his god where sculpture was concerned, but he now had a second deity to worship. After Rome came Naples, where they were the guests of Augusta's mother, Lady Coventry, who had an apartment in the Villa Rocella. There was the obligatory visit to Pompeii, and an expedition to climb Vesuvius when only two of the party, Watts and Lord Walpole, actually reached the summit and 'peered down the fiery throat of the crater'.

But Lord Holland was right in finding his protégé really rather tiresome about portraits. Since he looked upon portraiture as mere pot-boiling, and since he was in no need of money so long as the Hollands were providing him with bed and board, Watts stubbornly refused to accept payment for a portrait he had made of Sir Charles Bannerman, the father of one of the attachés at the Legation. 'I have scolded,' wrote Lord Holland, 'and reasoned, and for the time kept him quiet, but he vows he shall return the money and will not paint portraits for gain. I think this foolish. However, I suspect he is just now in the fever of historical painting, and will not be so unreasonable when the fit of glory and the visions of Michael Angelo shall subside a little.'

Meanwhile Augusta was each day more delighted with her latest acquisition, her household pet. He seemed to have all the virtues of the artistic temperament and none of its vices. Finding that he did

[1] He did, however, make little colour sketches, some no bigger than postage stamps, of a number of pictures.

not drop paint on the carpets or chair-covers—to do so, he once said, was 'so inartistic' and would make him feel 'degraded'—she let him paint in any room in the house. Her nickname for him was 'Fra Paolo' because a visitor—a man endowed with tact rather than artistic expertise—had announced that he found in the 'Chapeau de Paille' the influence of Paolo Veronese. 'Being young,' wrote Watts later of himself at this time, 'with a profusion of very good hair, a vigorous moustache and imperial, my appearance was not against me. In fine, I was liked . . .'

He was. He had what today is called 'charisma', and Augusta immediately fell for it. She bitterly regretted being childless, but at thirty-one she could hardly hope to make of her Fra Paolo, absurdly young though he was for his age, the son she had always longed for. Did she then hope for him as a lover? It is probable that idle gossip in Florence soon cast her in the role of Potiphar's wife, and that tongues eventually began to wag. Perhaps they would have wagged even more busily had Augusta shown visitors to the Casa (as we must presume she did not) an enchanting little sketch of her, now euphemistically entitled 'Lady Holland on a day-bed', which Watts painted during a second visit to Naples, this time with both the Hollands, in 1845. Here is a *maja vestida*; could there also have been a *maja desnuda*? The answer must surely be 'no'. Fifty years later, in reply to an inquiry as to whether a painting of Princess Mathilde Demidov in the nude was his work, Watts wrote: 'I have never painted but one portrait of the Princess Mathilde, and that was for her father. Certainly I never should at any time have painted a lady in such a state as you describe. *The picture is not by me.*'

Watts's attitude to adultery is made plain in the draft of a letter, written at a later date and presumably addressed to the English dramatist, Tom Taylor, in which he describes a curious little episode of his Florentine days. He was giving a course of drawing lessons to a married woman, an 'Italian lady of high birth . . . young, and possessed of no small personal attractions', who fell in love with him. Her attentions, he wrote, were 'anything but agreeable,' his 'English sense of propriety was shocked' and he found himself 'constantly manoeuvring to avoid situations'.

One day on his way to her house he was presented in the street with 'a little bouquet of peculiar beauty and sweetness' which, on his arrival, he rashly gave to the *signora*, who immediately tucked it

in her bosom. Watts says that he realised with horror the implica-
tions of this gesture, which one must suppose was the Italian way of
'making a pass'; but he was rescued from a fate worse than death by
the timely arrival of other visitors. Next day, however, came another lesson, and there, once again, were the flowers installed in her
bosom. Watts 'saw that the moment was come. As, with a look and
gesture I shall never forget, the flowers were drawn from their
resting-place (and not an inappropriate one) I took them from her
hand and—flung them into the fire!' Then, at a speed to be equalled
only (he thought) by a man shooting a rapid or being carried off by a
runaway horse, he fled.

This little incident, he naively suggested, might provide Tom
Taylor with the theme for a short play; but, he added, it 'may not
appear anything to you'.

For the moment, however, Augusta was happy in Fra Paolo's company, and we may picture them walking innocently together among
the fountains of the long terrace of the Villa Feroni, sitting sometimes under the shade of the famous old pine from where one could
watch the setting sun gild the red dome of the church of San Spirito,
discussing the little events of the day or the expected guests of the
evening, or visiting the room that had been allotted to him as a studio
to see what progress he had made with his latest picture.

Watts, for his part, was no less captivated by his hostess and by
the glittering court that she held in Florence. She was so witty and
so clever, and her French and Italian were at that time almost more
fluent than her English; yet one must presume that she never let her
Fra Paolo feel left out of things, or embarrassed when he floundered
with his small Italian and less French in that cosmopolitan, polyglot
society in which only the trilingual could feel fully at ease. After all,
he could do one thing which none of her other guests could: he
could paint. Indeed, Watts was soon so much at his ease that he
even went so far as publicly to snub a pompous guest. The man had
announced with obvious self-satisfaction that music had no effect
on him whatever, pleasurable or otherwise. 'What does that mean?'
he inquired of the company at large. Watts immediately accepted the
challenge. 'It means,' he said, 'a defective organisation.' Lord Holland overheard the conversation and was much amused.

Lord Holland he had charmed from the very first by his natural good manners, his simplicity and his modesty; one would never have guessed that his father wasn't a gentleman. The food at the Casa was famous (the host used to put a guinea for the chef on any dish that was returned to the kitchen empty), yet Watts preferred the plainest food. When offered wine, he asked for water. What a shame (thought Lord Holland) that this brilliant young man, who might have become another Lawrence, was so set on becoming a second Michelangelo! One had to be realistic. Patrons like Julius II or the Medici did not exist in Victorian London, and one could not transform Euston Station into another Sistine Chapel. Or could one? Watts was not so sure. Might this not be exactly what he was looking for?

Was Lord Holland jealous of the interest Augusta took in her protégé? Not perhaps at first; the young man was so ingenuous, so unlike a Don Juan. But later he may well have become a little uneasy about what others might be saying or thinking. A high proportion of cosmopolitan Florentines have always had a taste for gossip and the leisure to indulge in it; the wife of the Austrian Minister once almost precipitated an international crisis by spreading a rumour that Augusta wore a wig.

This Florentine society into which the young innocent from London had been suddenly plunged, has changed little over the years. Then as now there were the genuine lovers of art and the mere culture-vultures, the real poets as well as the poetasters; there was the genuine aristocracy, and the bogus; and among the English expatriates there were those who found England too cold for them, and those who had made it too hot for them. Worst of all was the Englishman who 'went native', of whom it was said, '*Inglese Italianizzato, Diavolo incarnato*'. There were also the birds of passage: the followers of the sun, the idly curious, the eternally restless. Watts saw them all, met and made pencil drawings or portraits in oils of many of them. The pencil drawings[1] in particular are by any standards admirable, and of such delicacy that reproduction does them scant justice. Many people, as they survey the vast allegories of Life and Love and Death, the endless Eves Created, Tempted and Repentant—the 'Mega-Wattses', as they have been

[1] More than forty of them, formerly in the collection of Lord Ilchester, have won passed to his daughter, Lady Galway.

dubbed—may well agree with Lord Holland that it is regrettable
that Watts looked upon portraiture as a 'chore', and was determined to devote so much of his time to uplifting us all in the grandest of Grand Manners.

Some of Watts's closest friends in Florence were to be found
among the resident artists and intellectuals who frequented the
Caffè Doney in the via Tornabuoni. There was Haydon's correspondent, Seymour Kirkup—a consumptive painter who as a young
man had come to Italy to die, yet lived to marry, at the age of nearly
ninety, a girl of twenty-two. Kirkup's other claim to fame was that
in 1840 he had revealed, under a coat of whitewash on a wall of the
Bargello, the portrait of Dante traditionally ascribed to Giotto, and
had surreptitiously made a tracing and a copy of it before its ruina-
tion by a bungling restorer in the following year.

Then there was the American sculptor, Hiram Powers, who had
just caused a sensation with his 'Greek slave', a marble statue of a
nude girl which was to provoke Mrs Browning to a sonnet. A brilliant mechanic also, Powers had been responsible for the horrifying
'effects' in an animated 'Dante's *Inferno*' constructed for Dor-
feuille's Western Museum in Cincinnati. This handsome, hard-
boiled and apparently level-headed American later became an ardent
convert to spiritualism.

With an artist named William Spence, well known in Florence as
a collector of and dealer in old masters, Watts was still in correspondence in the nineties. Two scraps of letters, both undated, have
survived[1] from the time they were together in Florence. The first,
from Watts to Spence, is an urgent appeal for the loan of a fancy
dress 'for the ball tonight' at the Casa Feroni. The second was
written to Spence by the artist George Wallis, whom he had taken
to see Watts's paintings. 'Without flattery—a sin I detest,' Wallis
wrote, 'I can assure you I was delighted to see so much real genius.'
It was doubly satisfactory to find an Englishman 'so different from
the dunghill race that infests Italy, without either feeling or taste
for the high and noble department of the art'.

Another friend was an Englishman, Count Cottrell, Chamber-
lain to the Duke of Lucca and for some months a fellow guest of the
Hollands at the Casa Feroni. Watts painted his portrait and also that
of the Duke, from whom the artist received his first decoration, the

[1] In copies typed for Mary Watts.

Order of San Lodovico. To Cottrell we are indebted for the preservation of a number of experimental fragments of fresco[1] and a
quantity of other work abandoned by Watts when in 1847 he 'left
Florence in a hurry [he said] intending to return, but never did'.

The fancy dress ball mentioned in Watts's letter to Spence was
probably that held in February 1845, which Augusta attended as a
Quakeress and Mathilde de Demidov so scantily dressed as *Diane
Chasseresse* that many of those present were scandalised. 'The beauty
of her legs and ankles,' wrote Holland, 'accounted for, but did not,
it seems, justify the costume.' One of the guests, exhausted by the
weight of the suit of armour he was wearing, shed it in the first
empty room he could find, which happened to be the one Watts was
using as a studio. Armour had always fascinated Watts, and next
day he made studies from it which were ultimately used in a self-
portrait that he gave to the Hollands.

'One New Year's Day'—Mary Watts does not specify the year,
but it was probably 1844—Augusta presented Watts with a gold
watch and chain, specially commissioned from a Genevan watch-
maker, and as she placed the chain round his neck she said, 'We not
only bind you to us, we chain you.' Many years later this treasured
memento was stolen. 'He could never speak of the loss without
pain,' wrote Mary, 'nor would he allow anyone to replace them.'

[1] Now in the Victoria & Albert Museum.

4

PIANO-TUNER'S SON AND BARONET'S DAUGHTER

THE SUMMER in Florence can be stifling, and soon after Watts's arrival at the Casa Feroni the Hollands had decided to rent a country house to which they could retreat when the town became unpleasantly hot or when they wanted to relax. This was the Villa Medicea at Careggi, sometimes called the Villa Careggi, and Watts was to spend a good deal of his time there— using as a studio in the summer months the enormous orangery, more than a hundred feet long, in which lemon trees and other tender plants were housed during the winter.

Bought by Cosimo de' Medici in 1417 and refashioned for him by the great Florentine architect Michelozzo, the villa had become the seat of the Platonic Academy. Here and at another Medicean villa at Fiesole Tuscan Humanism had reached its finest flowering. 'It was at Careggi', wrote Iris Origo, 'that Lorenzo [de' Medici] gave a party every year on Plato's birthday, while Pico della Mirandola and Marsilio Ficino discussed the "mysteries of the ancients".'[1] At Careggi too, Lorenzo, denied absolution by Savonarola, died in 1492 —according to tradition from poison administered by his doctor, who was thrown by Lorenzo's attendants into the well in the courtyard.

Watts had always had a strong historical sense, and the ghosts of the Medicis perpetually haunted him during the months he spent at Careggi. As, day after day, he passed by the well in the courtyard, the murder of the doctor began to take clear shape in his mind, and he determined to record it in fresco on a wall of the loggia.

[1] *Images and Shadows*, John Murray, 1970.

He had been experimenting with fresco ever since his arrival in Florence, but had not yet mastered the difficult and largely forgotten technique. In December 1843 Holland had written to his mother asking her to make enquiries about some frescoes that were being carried out at Bowood for Lord Landsdowne. 'An artist here,' he explained, 'has been making several trials with unequal success. Sometimes his labours dry quite spotty and bad, and sometimes tolerably well; but he had not been able to discover what (unless it be the changes of atmosphere) makes this variety.' Whether old Lady Holland followed up her son's request we do not know, but in July 1844, when 'The Drowning of the Doctor' was under way, he wrote again: 'Watts's fresco is not quite so flourishing as at first. It does not dry equally, and he is somewhat dispirited about it . . . He is really very busy. He and Peters are now drawing from a model for the back of the ruffian who is throwing the Doctor into the well. Watts means to make a study for each picture [figure?].' A later owner of the Villa converted the open loggia into a closed saloon, and the fresco has been preserved.

By May 1845 the 'Drowning of the Doctor' was at last finished, and in the same month Augusta wrote to her husband from Paris, where she had gone for several months for medical treatment, a letter on the subject of Watts and his future. 'He must work for his country,' she said, 'for fame, riches and position.' She continued:

I hope our home, wherever it be, may be his home occasionally, under circumstances whenever he likes, but I have a strong and determined wish to break the spell, and make him feel that he is ever a welcome guest but not a constant and *necessary* inmate. I consider this *necessary* for all parties, becoming all parties, and I feel certain it will lead to the ultimate comfort of all parties. The world is ever cold and heartless in all its judgments; and I feel unfortunately a strong conviction that Watts's prolonged *séjour* in our house will not be ascribed to its real cause—good-nature and kindness of heart on our side, want of energy, affection and gratitude on his. His idleness will be laid at our door; and we shall be accused of having been the ruin of him, lucky if both of us escape with even so mild a censure.

Two passages in this letter call for comment. When Augusta wrote with some ambiguity of Watts's 'want of energy, affection and gratitude', it was only the energy that she considered to be lacking. Then there is the final sentence: 'Lucky if both of us escape with so mild a censure.' This collective charge may refer principally to the fact that the Hollands were said to be badly spoiling the young man, though Augusta must have been aware that where she was concerned the censure might go deeper.

Lord Holland always reacted very strongly to people. As everyone could see, he had taken a great fancy to Watts, whose company he enjoyed, whose talent he recognised and by whose infectious enthusiasm he was stimulated. When in the autumn of 1844 he had paid a flying visit to London to see his much-loved aunt, Caroline Fox, who had suffered two strokes, he took Watts with him. Old Lady Holland was at that time living ('in poverty on £5,000 a year') in Great Stanhope Street; but she had strictly forbidden her son to visit Holland House in her absence, and he did not dare to enter it with Watts except by stealth and the tradesmen's entrance.

One night they both dined with the formidable old lady, who was frightened of nobody and nothing except thunder and speed (it was said that the drivers of hearses used to jeer as they overtook her dawdling carriage). Holland had warned Watts to be prepared for a bad reception, because she made a point of snubbing all his friends. However, she chose on this occasion to be particularly affable to the young artist,[1] reserving all her venom for her daughter, Lady Lilford, whom she at last succeeded in reducing to tears. Watts also saw his father for the last time; in fact, Lady Holland, Caroline Fox and Mr Watts were all to die in the course of the following year.

Charles Greville, who was present on 9 November, 1845, at the last dinner-party Lady Holland ever gave, wrote after her death, which occurred a week later:

> Though she was a woman for whom nobody felt any affection, and whose death therefore will have excited no grief, she will be regretted by a great many people, some from kindly, some from selfish motives; and all who had been accustomed to live at Holland House and continued to be her habitués will lament over the fall of the curtain on that long drama, and the final extinction of

[1] So Mary Watts; but according to Mrs Barrington, Lady Holland and Watts took a dislike to one another at sight. Mary Watts is mistaken in stating that this visit took place in 1845.

the flickering remnant of a social light which illuminated and adorned England, and even Europe, for half a century. The world never has seen and will never again see anything like Holland House . . .

It was probably on the return journey from London that Watts disgraced himself in the eyes of Lord Holland by neglecting to draw the picturesque towns through which they passed. In a letter to his wife, Holland wrote, 'Watts, since he has been in France, has only sketched a midden.[1] He says it is the best thing he has seen.' However, the artist recovered some lost ground in Milan by condescending to approve of Leonardo's 'Last Supper', though he was unable to agree with his travelling companion that it was 'the finest conception of Christ ever painted'.

Throughout the winter of 1844–45 Watts seems to have been restless and unsettled—'more maundering than ever,' wrote Lord Holland, whose work he interrupted by endlessly standing around 'see-sawing from one leg to the other'. At Careggi his fresco kept him reasonably occupied, but when in Florence he could hardly be got to his studio. Was it that he was in love? 'It was now,' wrote Mary Watts (who, needless to add, makes no mention of any idleness), 'that his picture the "First Whisper of Love" was painted, and little scraps of verse belong to this time, written to one who was fair.' No name is given; no verses remain. Possibly the girl in question was Georgy Duff Gordon, with whom he was undoubtedly more or less in love a year later. What would one not give to be able to see those papers that have disappeared over the years or that Mary and others saw fit to destroy!

At this time Watts also suddenly became interested in landscape painting. His so-called 'Fiesole'—in fact a view of the Fiesole hills as seen from Careggi—is a fine picture, much more happily composed than many of his subsequent landscapes, some of which (for example those painted in Asia Minor in the fifties and in Scotland in the late nineties) merely 'sprawl' and seem capable of indefinite extension in any direction.

[1] In 1873 Ruskin, complaining to Watts that the Old Masters were wrong because they did not paint what they saw, pointed to a scavenger's heap of muck in the gutter and said, 'Paint that as it is. That is truth.'

The Hollands, sometimes together and sometimes apart, were constantly on the move, and when, after Lady Coventry's death in the autumn of 1845, the lease of the apartment in the Naples villa was taken over by Augusta, they spent an increasing amount of time in the south. In June 1846 Holland, who had had his fill of diplomacy, finally resigned his post in Florence, though he periodically returned to the Casa Feroni, and in August the use of the Villa Medicea (with Watts thrown in for good measure) was offered for a few months to their friend Lady Duff Gordon.

Caroline, daughter of Sir George Cornewall, Bt., had married in 1810 Sir William Duff Gordon, the second baronet, by whom she had two sons and two daughters—Georgy and Alice. Sir William died in 1823, and his ample and amiable widow was now in Florence ostensibly widening the artistic and cultural outlook of the two 'girls' (as Ronald Chapman charitably calls them; Georgy was in fact twenty-eight—the same age as Watts, and her sister five years younger). But she was no doubt also hoping to marry them off to suitable parties before it was too late. Alice was the prettier: classically handsome, with fair wavy hair 'like the tendrils of a vine'; but it was Georgy who received all the proposals. A friend described the elder sister as 'the most remarkable young lady I know, very clever, very sincere, saying whatever comes into her head, very decided and active, too worldly, with not the least tinge of romance, full of spirits, with the most perfect figure in the world—altogether the person to inspire love which I much doubt she will ever feel in the same degree.' The Villa Medicea, with all its associations, was an education in itself, and Lady Duff Gordon saw at a glance that in Watts she had inherited the ideal tutor; that he might possibly also assume the role of a prospective son-in-law never of course crossed for a moment her innocent aristocratic mind.

The loving care of three women suited Watts admirably, for throughout his life he remained hopelessly unpractical. He needed mothering and cosseting and not infrequently nursing. It also pleased Lady Duff Gordon to have a man about the house again— and one who responded gratefully to the care she took to make him comfortable, and to see that he was regularly provided with the simple fare that suited him.

Naturally the two young women were given lessons by Watts in drawing and modelling, and naturally they for their part followed with an eager interest the progress of the pictures on which he was presently engaged. 'We have been most fortunate,' Georgy noted in her diary at the end of August, 'in finding Mr Watts here, who has fallen into our ways as if we had lived together all our lives and whose painting is a constant interest to us.'[1] The vast orangery, and the memories of the Sistine Chapel and the Vatican *Stanze*, were now inspiring him to paint on a heroic scale. Most gigantic of all was his 'Story from Boccaccio', a splendid canvas illustrating the eighth tale of the fifth night of the *Decamerone*. What, one may wonder, did Lady Duff Gordon feel about its nude Philomena, prancing larger than life and very provocatively from the thicket in which, although pursued by mad dogs, she had preferably remained until she had resumed her clothing? This picture, together with one or two other female nudes, was apparently erotic enough to provoke that expert in erotica, Monckton Milnes (Lord Houghton), when he saw them later in London, to a celebrated *bon mot*: 'You have heard of Watts' *Hymns*, now come and see Watts' *Hers*!'[2] To Lady Duff Gordon, broad-minded though she was, it may well have seemed that this kind of subject, appropriate enough for a Titian, hardly befitted the drawing-master of her two unmarried daughters.

Then there was 'Echo'—admittedly a more chaste-looking maiden, but life-size and what is today called a 'full frontal nude'. Probably she preferred his 'Guelphs and Ghibellines' (a mere twelve foot by eight foot six inches), or the splendid 'Peasants in the Campagna during the Vintage', pictures in which there was nothing nakeder than a baby's leg and the upper half of a child of indeterminable sex. She was very interested in art; but no doubt she was also very concerned about the moral welfare of her charges.

However, we may assume that Georgy (who had soon established herself as Watts's favourite) was little troubled by such matters. She was fascinated by the handsome, delightful, stimulating young man who passed so many hours with her in the orangery, discussing a thousand wonderful things or singing duets with her—Lady Duff

[1] The extracts from Georgy's and Lady Duff Gordon's diaries are taken, by kind permission of Sir Andrew Duff Gordon, Bt., from the Harpton Court papers, now deposited in the National Library of Wales.
[2] Sir Algernon West, in his *Recollections*, attributes the remark to Sir William Stirling-Maxwell.

Gordon mentions 'a divine Hymn of his own composing'—to the accompaniment of the guitar that he had brought with him from England. And oh! the beauty of those hot Florentine summer nights: the scented air, the plashing fountains, the galaxy of fire-flies; the moonrise over the Fiesole hills and the glitter of starlight reflected in the winding waters of the Arno! Was it surprising that before very long Watts at least realised that he was on the point of falling in love?

According to Ronald Chapman, Lady Duff Gordon realised it too, panicked and whisked her daughters away to Rome at a moment's notice; much though she may have wanted to get her girls off her hands, there were limits—and a piano-tuner's son was one of them. But in fact she always wintered in Rome, and her departure from Careggi on 17 November was routine. The same day Georgy noted in her diary:

> Our residence at dear Careggi has closed and the three happiest months I ever spent in my life (not even excepting dear old Rome) have closed for ever. It is an epoch in one's life, to look back to three months of intellectual life, without any bores or social plagues. Yesterday we parted from Mr Watts with the greatest regret; he very wisely going to Florence for a few days preferring leaving us, to being left.

Though Lady Duff Gordon may have hoped to marry her daughters off to titled owners of English stately homes, or even to relatively impoverished scions of the ancient Italian aristocracy, in the event the two sisters lived on to a ripe and eccentric old age as spinsters, Alice dying in 1901 and Georgy several years later. In their house in Mayfair they shared a single egg for breakfast, Georgy preferring the yolk and Alice the white, and of a summer evening would sit on chairs outside their front door to wave at friends as they passed.

Typed copies of a dozen or so letters, written by Watts to Georgy over the next two or three years, have survived; they all begin 'My dear Miss Duff Gordon', and contain nothing that could have given her mother, if she had any apprehensions, the slightest cause for alarm. Georgy was, it seems, ever reluctant to put pen to paper (her diary entries are very brief), and such letters as she did bring herself to write have not survived.

On 21 December Watts told her that he was glad to hear that she was still keeping up her modelling. He had hoped to come to Rome, but unfortunately he was too busy to get away. 'How goes the music?' he continued. 'Do you ever sing any of our old duets? I tried the other day our old German duet with a lady, but although she sang it as well as possible it was quite another thing, and I could not but feel how wonderfully well our voices must have suited each other. I have not touched the clay since your departure. My guitar is consigned to its case, and my music is covered with dust; and excepting upon the occasion above mentioned I have not attempted to sing a note. One does nothing alone . . .'

A month or so later he wrote again, giving her full details of the new *magnum opus* which was now occupying all his time. This was a big oil, nearly twenty feet long, of 'Alfred inciting the Saxons to resist the Danes', and he was painting it at the suggestion of Lord Holland and other friends as an entry for a further competition (actually the fourth: he had missed two others) for the decoration of the Houses of Parliament. The size of the work made it necessary for him to continue to use the orangery, which by then was so 'abominably cold' that he was obliged to spend half his time 'capering about like a *ballerino*' in an attempt to keep warm and to dodge the mosquitos that still swarmed everywhere.

Alfred (he wrote), 'long-limbed and springy', stands in the centre of the canvas, and he had endeavoured to give him 'as much dignity, energy and expression as possible without exaggeration'. Near him is an elegant young patrician 'who in his excitement rends off his cloak in order to follow his king and leader'—a rash gesture, one might think, in view of the breezy voyage that lay ahead. Other figures are described: the peasant who 'grasps a ponderous axe and threats extermination to the whole Danish race'; the distracted wife, her weeping infant at her breast, finding scant comfort in the noble gesture of her husband 'who points upwards and encourages her to trust in the righteousness of the cause and the justice of heaven (religion and patriotism)'; the 'maiden with dishevelled locks (your sister's hair)', whose lover has already embarked; and the ancient warrior, too old to enlist, baring his chest to show his war wounds as he hands his sword to the youth whose 'glowing cheek and beat-

1. *Self-portrait at the age of seventeen,* 1834
One of the first works in which Watts gives a hint of what
he is later to achieve (see p. 6)

2. Three 'muffins': a. (*ab*
Caractacus, 1843.
Engraving after a cartoo
never executed, for the 1
Houses of Parliament
competition (see p. 18)
b. (*left*) *Alfred inciting the
Saxons to resist the Landing
the Danes*, 1846/47.
Watts's entry for the 184
Houses of Parliament
competition (see p. 44)
c. (*below*) *A Story from
Boccaccio*, 1845/46.
This vast canvas, thirty f
long, is on loan to Kebl
College, Oxford (see p.

Augusta Lady Holland

by Watts

3. *Lady Holland*, 1843
Augusta, Lady Holland, wife of the British Minister in Florence, whose
guest Watts became after his arrival there in 1843 (see p. 29)

4a. *The Drowning of the Doctor* (detail), 1844
Fresco painted by Watts on the walls of the Villa Medicea at Careggi (see p. 38)

4b. *Lady Holland on a Day-bed*, 1844
Painted in Naples when Watts was there with the Hollands (see p. 32)

5. *Watts* by Charles Couzens, *c.* 1849
Watts was deeply impressed by the Elgin marbles

6. *Under a Dry Arch*, 1850
On his return from Italy in 1847, Watts's conscience was stirred
by the miseries of the poor (see p. 55)

7. *The Sacrifice of Noah*
and other studies.
Few English painters of the day
handled a pencil more
sensitively than Watts

8. *Life's Illusions*, 1849

This early allegory was greeted with ridicule when exhibited at the Royal Academy in 184

(see p. 64)

ing heart' make it plain that he will not disgrace the family honour. And so on; in this monument 'dedicated to patriotism and posterity' we are spared nothing that might be expected to stir the heart of a viewer to lofty thoughts and noble actions.

Watts concludes, 'Now I think you have an idea of what my picture is intended to be; pray give me your united opinion and criticisms. I have endeavoured to cast my figure in the most heroic mould—simple, grand and elegant. Pheidias, my adored Pheidias, shall reign throughout; my idolatry daily grows upon me! I am strongly advised to go to England with my pictures to ensure their safe arrival, and I shall probably do so.'

Meanwhile a certain Lady Boyle had come to occupy the Villa Medicea, and again Watts was included in the transaction. On hearing the news of her impending arrival Watts had, he told Georgy, torn his hair and almost determined to burn his brushes; but she turned out to be harmless enough, and with her was a lady who wanted to become his pupil. One day the famous picture-collector, Robert Holford, called with an introduction to Watts; but Holford proved more eager to discuss a Giorgione he was pursuing than to inspect the work of a living painter. In any case Watts was far from anxious to show his 'Alfred', which was, he considered going very badly—an opinion confirmed, he felt, by the praise lavished upon it by local Italian artists. Watts's meeting with Holford was, however, to bring him dividends after his return to London.

While at Careggi Watts had also been in correspondence with his first patron, A. C. Ionides:

I have been most fortunate [Watts wrote] and have made great and powerful friends. If I have not made money, it has been my own fault. With the connection I have made, if I applied myself to portrait-painting I might carry all before me; but it has always been my ambition to tread in the steps of the old masters, and to endeavour, as far as my poor talents would permit, to emulate their greatness. Nor has the sight of their great works diminished my ardour. This cannot be done by painting portraits. Cannot you give me a commission to paint a picture to send to Greece— some patriotic subject, something that shall carry a moral lesson, such as Aristides relinquishing his right to command to Miltiades, that those who look upon it may recollect that the true hero and patriot thinks not of his own honour or advantage, and is ever ready to sacrifice his personal feelings and his individual advancement for his country's good? Such subjects grandly painted would not be without effect upon generous minds. Take advantage of my enthusiasm now; I will paint you an acre of canvas for little more than the cost of the material . . .

Or stay! If you are not rich enough yourself, get up a subscription among your friends for two hundred and fifty pounds and I will paint an historical picture which will be worth six times the sum. I cannot say a less price, for the materials and models cost a good deal, and I have besides my sisters to look after . . . Don't think I offer this because I cannot get occupation. I sold a picture last year containing two half-length figures and a couple of bulls' heads for two hundred guineas, and my price for a single portrait is a hundred guineas; so you see I offer merely for the sake of gaining honour, and name a sum which will only prevent my being out of pocket . . .

Ionides consulted some of his friends, who very reasonably asked that, before committing themselves, they might see a sketch. Watts in replying added pomposity to indignation:

You speak of a sketch, as if your friends wanted assurance that I know what to do with arms and legs. Three years ago I was thought capable of doing something, and as I have since pursued my studies ever with the ardent and disinterested view of raising art to the level it attained in the great days of Greece, it may fairly be presumed that my progress has been commensurate.

As to making a sketch, the subject is one of the very highest class and would depend entirely upon grandeur of style and treatment, elevation of character, correctness of drawing; dignity and justness of expression, purity of design, colour and sentiment: it is quite impossible to express these qualities in a sketch. I might give you a dry outline of a number of figures, which would present no idea of what the picture would be, even should the general arrangement remain the same . . .

Very possibly! But this was not the way to treat potential clients, who have within reason to be humoured, and it was hardly surprising that they now backed down—all except the faithful Ionides.

A fortnight later Watts reported that he was about to 'commence making studies for the large picture, which I aspire to treat as Pheidias or Apelles would have done'; he always spoke of Pheidias as if he were painter rather than sculptor. By the end of October he was 'studying and composing my great work'; but since it was to be 'dedicated to patriotism and posterity', he now felt that he ought first to take a look at Greece—or, as he put it, 'to acquaint myself by ocular demonstration with the characteristics of the scenery, atmosphere, etc.' of that country. And, he added, could Ionides see his way to letting his two half-sisters have twenty-five pounds on account? Two months later Ionides seems to have criticised the subject Watts had chosen ('Aristides and the Generals'); but the artist was reluctant to consider changing it, being convinced that it was one 'which if properly and worthily treated could not fail to have a beneficial effect upon well-organised minds'—and, he added, could Ionides see his way to letting his two half-sisters have another twenty-five pounds — also on account, of course?

Spring came, but without there being any more talk of a visit to Greece; however, Ionides was planning to come to Italy and asked his friend's advice as to what he ought not to miss there. Watts dutifully listed for him the more obvious sights in the more obvious towns and concluded, 'Pompeii! Pompeii is the great thing of all. I was going to say, wander about it alone; but I remember you are a married man, and probably think the less imagination is encouraged the better.' Apparently in those days the conducted tourist was tactfully steered away from erotica openly displayed, whereas now he is carefully coaxed towards doors unlocked only by a golden key.

It seems that it was now agreed that there were to be *two* pictures for Greece: the big composition ('Nausicaa' or 'Aristides and the Generals'?) for Athens University, and a smaller 'Panthea', illustrating an episode from Xenophon's *Cyropaedia*, for which an additional fifty pounds was to be paid. Money was advanced, and Watts's 'Aurora' handed over to Ionides as a security for the 'Panthea'. What followed is too complicated and too boring to warrant description in detail. The big picture was never painted, and the 'Panthea', a failure, was overpainted in 1850 with the still extant 'Irish Famine'. Then Ionides quarrelled with the University, and the whole affair was dropped and forgotten until nearly thirty years later when, suddenly and without warning, Ionides demanded the return of the two hundred and fifty pounds advanced for the big picture that had never been delivered.

Watts was horrified. Some unpleasantness ensued, the result, Ionides finally admitted, of 'want of memory, the mistaken meddling of over-zealous friends, change of circumstances and times', which 'may have for a moment disturbed the even harmony of our understanding and mutual reliance on each other's honour and good-will'. But good sense prevailed. Watts made generous offers of compensation which Ionides with equal generosity declined, and the former unclouded friendship was resumed.

Entries for the Houses of Parliament competition had to be submitted in June (1847), and Watts felt that he ought to deliver his in person; but he could not bring himself to leave Italy without another sight of Georgy. Probably it was on the spur of the moment that he decided to pay a flying visit to Rome, for it is clear from Lady Duff Gordon's diary (20 March) that his arrival there was unheralded: 'Just as we were going into dinner, in walked to our amazement Mr Watts. He dined with us and took possession of Pietro's room—and belonged to us therefore. In the evening we went to Lord Ward['s][1] dancing!'

Watts spent ten happy and crowded days with the Duff Gordons, all fully recorded by his hostess. There were visits to innumerable churches and picture galleries, and while Watts was with Georgy and her mother in the Vatican Alice went sketching with Edward Lear in the Campagna. Excursions were made to Frascati, and on 27 March to Hadrian's Villa 'where we walked about, and dined, and danced, and drank Lord Ward's health as today is his birthday (30) and returned at ½ past 7, dined au grand gallop and went to a concert for the distressed Irish and Scottish, at which amateurs also performed. Mrs Sartoris[2] sang the great air in the Freyschutz [sic], and the "Casta Diva" admirably. Ld. Compton sang, Georgy also in a Trio! and six Pianofortes were played by amateurs very well—the

[1] 11th Baron Ward (1817–85), created 1st Earl of Dudley (of the second creation) in 1860. This very unsatisfactory young man had a very satisfactory private annual income of nearly £80,000. (See also p. 85.)

[2] *Née* Adelaide Kemble, later to become a close friend of Leighton's and an *habituée* of Little Holland House.

Overture to Oberon! Nearly 500 tickets at 2 scudi were sold!'

At the end of the month Watts tore himself away from Rome and shortly afterwards left Florence for England. Careggi, he told Georgy, was just 'beginning to put on all its charms'; but he sailed from Leghorn in pouring rain that helped to reconcile him for what he then believed to be only a temporary parting from his beloved Italy. He was, however, always to recall it as a land of sunshine; and when, winter after winter, he shivered in English cold, floundered through London fogs, and suffered from his asthma and his innumerable other real or imagined ailments, he looked back on his Florentine days as among the happiest in his life.

Though his hurried departure obliged him to leave some of his drawings and smaller paintings behind,[1] his baggage now included at least half a dozen gigantic or very large and carefully executed canvases: his 'Story from Boccaccio', 'Echo', 'Peasants in the Campagna during the Vintage', 'Guelphs and Ghibellines', 'Fata Morgana', the unfinished 'Alfred', and possibly a painting now called 'Diana's Nymphs'. Their total area amounts to some eight or nine hundred square feet; and if to these pictures we add his very considerable output of other works it is impossible to sustain Lord Holland's charge that Watts was idle during the three and a half years he spent in Italy.

The strangest part of the story is that all these big compositions were inspired by the painters of the Venetian rather than of the Florentine or Roman school; yet it was not until six years later that 'the Kensington Titian' (as he has also been called), though he had visited Rome and Naples, managed to reach Venice. The Raphael *Stanze* in the Vatican and Michelangelo in the Sistine Chapel had opened his eyes to painting in the grandest of Grand Manners, and of course he was able to see plenty of Venetian works in Florence and Rome; but the full splendour of her decorative art, which was what would most have inspired him at that moment, could have been understood only by a visit to Venice itself. One must suppose that Lord Holland had no occasion to visit Venice, and that Watts could not bring himself to make the not very difficult journey on his own.

[1] In a cellar in Florence. Two years later Lady Duff Gordon wrote to thank Watts for allowing her to 'steal' two of the paintings—a study of the head of an ox (for 'Peasants in the Campagna during the Vintage') and 'Judas returning the thirty pieces of silver to the High Priest'. These now belong to Sir Andrew Duff Gordon.

5

MUFFINS AND MISERY

IT WOULD appear that one of the first things that Watts did on his return to England was to get rid of his moustache and imperial. To judge from a pencil self-portrait of 1848, and more particularly from the delightful water-colour full-length portrait of him made about this time by his friend Charles Couzens,[1] the sacrifice effected a marked improvement in his appearance. We do not know for how long he remained clean-shaven; but by 1853 a modest fringed beard had returned, and a year later (as a photograph shows) he was sporting the lush growth that made so many of the great Victorians almost indistinguishable from one another and gave to their most trivial utterances the weight of major prophecy.

Watts immediately set to work to complete his 'Alfred', a task quite impossible to carry out in the humble apartment he had rented in Cambridge Street. But Holford came to the rescue by offering him the use of a large room in his splendid London home, Dorchester House,[2] and in June the painting was taken to Westminster Hall where it was awarded one of the three first prizes of £500. Armitage received another for his 'Battle of Meeanee', which was bought by Queen Victoria and is now in St James's Palace, and the third went to another now forgotten artist named Pickering.

Perhaps the public, after four such competitions, was growing rather bored with the Houses of Parliament and their decoration; at all events, the interest aroused by the first of them was not repeated. The *Athenaeum* damned Watts's entry with faintest praise, and young Rossetti, who had so admired his 'Caractacus', curtly dismissed it as 'truculent'. Then Watts, in one of his misplaced fits of

1 See p. 56.
2 In Park Lane, where the Dorchester Hotel now stands.

highmindedness, attempted to reduce the price fixed by the Fine Art Commissioners for the purchase of 'Alfred', thus causing trouble and embarrassment all round and making himself appear foolish rather than public-spirited. Lord Holland, if this ever came to his ears, would have been very angry indeed.

The work now hangs in Committee Room 10 of the House of Commons and, though grimy, is basically in a sound condition. The design is noble, the drama sustained, the canvas not overcrowded. To turn from it to, for example, the eight frescoes by Cope in the Peers' Corridor is to appreciate that there is a dignity and a simplicity in Watts's 'Alfred' which is sadly lacking in so many of the other official decorations in the building.

This and other vast paintings by Watts came to be known as 'Muffin' pictures after Thackeray had published in 1848 his amusing skit on Watts (thinly disguised as 'George Rumbold, A.R.A.') in *Our Street*.[1] Thackeray met his George in Rome, where he 'wore a velvet doublet and a beard down to his chest, and used to talk about high art at the Café Greco':

> It was in his studio that I had the honour to be introduced to his sister, the fair Miss Clara; she had a large casque with a red horse-hair plume (I thought it had been a wisp of her brother's beard at first), and held a tin-headed spear in her hand, representing a Roman warrior in the great picture of Caractacus George was painting—a piece sixty-four feet by eighteen . . . George while at Rome painted 'Caractacus'; a picture of 'Non Angli sed Angeli', of course; a picture of 'Alfred in the Neat-herd's Cottage', seventy-two feet by forty-eight; (an idea of the gigantic size and Michael-Angelesque proportions of this picture may be formed, when I state that the mere muffin, of which the outcast king is spoiling the baking, is two feet three in diameter); and the deaths of Socrates, of Remus, and of the Christians under Nero respectively . . .
>
> None of George's pictures sold. He has enough to tapestry Trafalgar Square. He has painted since he came back to England 'The flaying of Marsyas'; 'The smothering of the little boys in the Tower'; 'A plague scene during the great pestilence'; 'Ugolino on the seventh day after he was deprived of victuals',

[1] Watts also figures fictionally as 'Mr Royal' in Lady Ritchie's *Old Kensington*.

&c. For although these pictures have great merit, and the writh-ings of Marsyas, the convulsions of the little prince, the look of agony of St Lawrence on the gridiron, &c., are quite true to nature, yet the subjects somehow are not agreeable; and if he hadn't a small patrimony, my friend George would starve . . .

If Watts's 'Alfred' did not please the critics, neither did the portraits that he sent in 1848 to the Royal Academy. The *Athenaeum* found that of Lady Holland[1] 'as little remarkable as an example of feminine individuality as is the portrait of the ex-minister M. Guizot as a like-ness of the man'. The five hundred pounds had of course been very welcome; but Watts, always sensitive to hostile criticism, would gladly have sacrificed it, not for flattery but for intelligent apprecia-tion of his work. In fact, everything suddenly seemed to be turning sour for him. He had entered upon the bleakest lustrum of his life.

He was often ill. He was homeless, for his father was now dead, his unloved half-sisters had moved to the country, and his half-brother seems to have vanished. True, he went a good deal to Holland House when the Hollands were in London; he dined there and painted there, restoring the ceiling in the Gilt Room, and making a full-length (she called it 'full shortness') portrait of Augusta; there was a room set aside for his occasional use; but Lady Troubridge[2] speaks of 'a difference of opinion, or quarrel' which prevented Watts from making Holland House his home. The old intimacy had been withdrawn, and just when he most needed it. Georgy, back in Scotland, was lost to him, and now no more than a sounding-board which augmented rather than relieved the un-happiness in the letters that he wrote to her. After Florence, London was cold and hostile, and his eyes were suddenly opened to, and his social conscience stirred by the omnipresent poverty and misery which, though it existed in Italy, was in part alleviated there by the warmth of a southern sun. There was famine in Ireland and there was revolution in Europe. He was half in earnest when he told Georgy, 'I often think very seriously of Prussic acid!'

It is from his (sometimes undated) letters to Georgy, and from the subjects that he now chose to paint, that we can best gain an under-

[1] Destroyed at Holland House during an air raid in 1940.
[2] *Memories and Reflections* by Laura, Lady Troubridge, Heinemann, 1925.

standing of his condition at this time. His loneliness prompted him to write:

No doubt you are quite right in accusing me of a morbid state of feeling, but wrong in imputing it to the effect of living in an atmosphere of enchantment. I wish I could find one . . . If you will promise to look out for, and if possible find me a wife, I will promise while I am abroad[1] to work hard; upon my honour I am serious. I must have something to look forward to. You talk of Fame! I am no longer to be taken in by such pretence, but an agreeable companion in Italy would be an object worth working for.

I take a commercial and commonsense view of the subject and therefore should not risk being deceived or disappointed, and if I myself felt no violent love at least I am incapable of betraying a trust. You are probably somewhat surprised at such apparently new ideas in me, but they are not new; I have long thrown my romance to the winds.

In another letter he speaks of his disgust with the sort of life he had been leading—a life of 'occupation without an object and consequently without interest'. 'Could I begin again,' he continues,

I would (not neglecting the higher walks of my profession) seek to make money in the hope of some day sharing it with some amiable companion whose society would give a charm to my life and whose happiness and welfare would form a real and tangible object for my exertions . . . Every day I feel more and more the impossibility of living alone. I am becoming subject to frightful fits of melancholy and despondency. But there is no reason why I should bore you with my absurdity excepting that I have always looked upon you, may I say as a sister? And really with very great affection, which after all is not a thing to be despised from any-body. I could find it in my heart to wish you were an ill-used or overworked governess. Remember you once wished me raised! So you have no right to be angry . . .

Did Georgy think that Watts, in spite of the 'sisterly' relationship he alleged, was still hinting at the possibility of her marrying him? So it would seem, for Watts referred coldly to her reply as having

[1] He was still hoping to return to Italy.

'duly come to hand', adding that he was 'not indifferent to the many kind expressions of friendship and regret' that it contained. Nor did Georgy succeed in finding him any alternative wife; that was to be done for him, later and disastrously, by others.

Another of his letters will have surprised her:

What would you think [he wrote] if I have made up my mind to paint all sorts of portraits! The fact is I am beginning to look upon myself as a monster of selfishness. Objects of distress that have come under my observation during the last two or three days have induced me to reflect seriously that I have no right to throw away any means of being useful. No one has the right to censure me for not being ambitious of a trifling distinction, or for not desiring to acquire wealth, but neglecting opportunities of assisting the unfortunate is nothing less than gross selfishness on my part. The cold that nips me up makes me feel for others. I think every poor shivering wretch I meet has a right to revile me for wanting charity . . .

Today I saw a poor woman whose appearance evidenced better days, applying for relief at the Workhouse (which was refused). £20 would have gone far to set up the poor trembling brokenhearted creature, which £20 I might easily have had in my power to give her; but beast that I am, I hadn't sixpence. I am ashamed of myself when I think that I spend my time in unprofitable admiration of what is good, and make no effort to emulate what I admire. So this winter I will paint portraits in order to purchase the luxury of bestowing. I will refuse *nothing* . . . If you can put any heads in my way, do—and I'll turn them into coals and comforts for poor devils whose misery, seriously speaking, I think of with much pain.

When Georgy, anxious to help, inquired what Watts now charged for a portrait, he replied in a rambling letter which began unrealistically by stating that if anyone wanted 'a lover or a mother, a sister or a brother' painted, the pleasure he might give by doing this would be reward enough. Then suddenly he came down from the clouds and proposed a sliding tariff: forty guineas for a kit-cat, fifty for one size larger, a hundred for 'a bishop half-length' and one hundred and twenty for an entire bishop. 'So now to open my shop and ticket the articles—"Anything else today, ma'am? A very superior thing, warranted fast colour." ' He concluded, 'I feel too much of a shopkeeper, to say most sincerely yours, G.F.W.'

The misery that Watts saw everywhere around him also inspired him to paint four large melancholy realistic canvases, more interesting as autobiography and social comment than as art: 'Found Drowned', 'The Irish Famine', 'The Song of the Shirt' (also called 'The Seamstress'), and 'Under a Dry Arch'; when exhibited in 1881–82 at the Grosvenor Galleries they troubled the Victorian conscience much as did the novels of Dickens. All are now in the Watts Gallery at Compton and all—particularly the last two—are in poor condition.[1] They were mainly carried out in a big studio that Watts rented in 1849 in Charles Street, Mayfair. 'Found Drowned', which shows the body of a young woman lying under the dark arch of the bridge from whose parapet she has thrown herself into the Thames, is said to have been suggested by an incident he himself witnessed; but it would well serve as an illustration to Tom Hood's '*The Bridge of Sighs*',[2] and doubtless 'The Song of the Shirt' was related to Hood's poem[3] bearing that title.

Of 'Found Drowned', Chris Mullen has written:[4] 'The work reflects a European preoccupation with Social Realism in the late 1840's, e.g. *The Stonebreakers* by Courbet (1849) and *A Scene during the Cholera Epidemic* by J. N. Paton (1849), an artist who exhibited his paintings during the period for the benefit of the unemployed'; and A. L. Egg was later to recall 'Under a Dry Arch' when in 1858 he came to paint the third canvas of his 'Past and Present' series, now in the Tate Gallery.

'The Irish Famine', originally (and more reasonably) called 'The Irish Eviction', was painted in 1849, a year before Watts

[1] 'Under a Dry Arch' has now been successfully restored.
[2] 'One more Unfortunate,
    Weary of breath,
  Rashly importunate,
    Gone to her death . . .'
[3] 'With fingers weary and worn,
  With eyelids heavy and red,
  A woman sat in unwomanly rags,
  Plying her needle and thread—
  Stitch! stitch! stitch!
  In poverty, hunger, and dirt . . .'
[4] Notes on the Watts Exhibition at the Whitechapel Art Gallery, 1974.

accompanied his friend the Irish poet Aubrey de Vere to his family home near Cork. De Vere, writing to Watts of what he called the 'second-sight vision' that had enabled him so accurately to portray what he had not yet experienced, had proposed the visit. Possibly Watts never did see much, if anything, of the horrors left in the wake of the great potato famine, for he came back to England revived, temporarily at least, by 'many a scamper across country' and many a romp with de Vere's little niece, Mary O'Brien: riding, and fairly innocent Victorian romping with little girls, were all his life two of his preferred ways of relaxing. The highest common factor of Watts's friendship with de Vere was the spiritual crisis that each was passing through at that time. De Vere found his salvation in the arms of Rome; Watts was to seek it in the dedication of his talents to the betterment of mankind.

Watts made other friends also—some from among the Holland House circle—and his studio in Charles Street soon began to attract distinguished visitors who would hardly have found their way to remote rooms in Cambridge Street. Among these was Tom Taylor, a man of many parts who was later to play a major role in bringing about Watts's rash and disastrous marriage to Ellen Terry. Another was an old friend from his boyhood days, Charles Couzens, a miniaturist and copyist who came to occupy a studio immediately below his own; besides his already mentioned portrait of Watts, Couzens also made copies of a number of his friend's portraits of members of the Ionides family.

No doubt this *va-et-vient* of visitors to the Charles Street studio helped to alleviate Watts's loneliness, but it was not enough to dispel morbid thoughts. Misery might or might not be the result of sin; but Satan, conceived by Watts as 'a mighty power ruling over the evils which were unconnected with sin', was much in his thoughts at this time. 'Michael the Archangel contending with Satan for the body of Moses' was probably begun in Dorchester House and, though never completed, was bought by Ruskin about 1849 or 1850; and a vast and tedious Miltonic 'Satan, whither goest thou?' now lumbers the store-room at the Watts Gallery. There was also 'Satan, Sin and Death' (now vanished, perhaps prudently destroyed), and it was presumably about this time that Watts painted his only (or only surviving?) erotic picture, 'Satan and Sin'—a fumbling Etty-like sketch which might interest a psychiatrist. Watts, now in his early thirties, was not only disillusioned and often physically ill; he was also emotionally unstable, sexually frustrated, and probably sexually ignorant.

These tormented years also witnessed the painting of the first allegories, and the conception of a wild scheme for a 'House of Life' which Mary Watts has described as 'the ambition of one half of his life and the regret of the other half'. They form the subject of the chapter that follows.

6

THE IMPORTANCE OF BEING EARNEST

THE IMPORTANCE? Or should one rather say, the folly?
By 1850 Watts had reached the great watershed of his
life, from which two streams flowed. The stream which he
was passionate to follow was that of moral uplift: of high-minded
historical and mythological 'muffins', where Michelangelo and
Raphael would guide his brush and Pheidias whisper encouragingly
in his ear, 'Well done!'; of allegories whose message to mankind
would be so abundantly plain that (wrote Chesterton) 'if some
savage in a dim futurity dug up one of these dark designs on a lonely
mountain, though he worshipped strange gods and served laws yet
unwritten, it might strike the same message to his soul that it strikes
upon clerks and navvies from the walls of the Tate Gallery.' As Lord
Holland had been the first to warn Watts, and as bitter experience
soon brought home to him, the waters of this alluring stream were to
flow for long years into a penniless sea.

To Watts the other stream, that of portraiture, was murky and
polluted; but it flowed into a sea of gold. Again and again his noble
nature, which unfortunately was totally devoid of any sense of
humour (for what he believed to be this was merely a sense of fun),
made him forswear portraiture for ever; again and again he was
obliged, in order to pay for tomorrow's breakfast, or canvas and
paints or, towards the end of his life, his wife's 'very active philanthropy which sometimes outruns strict prudence', to return to what
seemed to him a prostitution of his gifts. In April 1870 he wrote to
his friend and patron, C. H. Rickards, 'I am not anxious to what is
called "*make money*", but . . . it is necessary for me to make certain
saleable pictures to provide me with the means to paint certain
other pictures for which there can be no sale . . .'

What saved him, what was to make this drudgery appear at times almost an act of piety, was the eventual realisation that by recording for future generations the great figures of his age—by creating a kind of 'House of Fame' rather than a 'House of Life'[1]—he was performing a *public service*; and to a man of Watts's lofty ideals a public service was something that he could not dismiss as unworthy of his highest effort. Watts never despised the man in the street, but it was mere (though at times unavoidable) pot-boiling to paint Mr Smith or Mrs Jones, or even some nincompoop peer or nitwit socialite; to paint Cardinal Manning or Lord Tennyson was, however, to leave to posterity not just that outward likeness of a great man but, if he could capture it—and he often did—his very soul. And in five often-quoted lines Tennyson was to embody what the painter told him was the ideal at which he aimed:

As when a painter, poring on a face,
Divinely thro' all hindrance finds the man
Behind it, and so paints him that his face,
The shape and colour of a mind and life,
Lives for his children, ever at its best.

Lady Holland once observed that she never knew her friends until Watts had painted them, and Chesterton wrote:

He scarcely ever paints a man without making him about five times as magnificent as he really looks. The real men appear, if they present themselves afterwards, like mean and unsympathetic sketches from the Watts original. . . .

Watts does not copy men at all: he makes them over again. He dips his hand in the clay of chaos and begins to model a man named William Morris or a man named Richard Burton; he is assisted, no doubt, in some degree by a quaint old text-book called Reality, with its stiff but suggestive woodcuts and its shrewd and simple old hints. But the most that can be said for the portraiture is, that Watts asks a hint to come and stop with him, puts the hint in a chair in his studio and stares at him. The thing that comes out at last upon the canvas is not generally a very precise picture of the sitter, though, of course, it is almost always a very accurate picture of the universe.

*   *   *

[1] See p. 65.

On the outbreak in 1854 of the Crimean War Watts was seized with patriotic zeal. To his friend Lord Somers he wrote in a letter that bears no date:

> I had seriously thought of going to the Crimea though it is not quite the place to winter in; but in addition to the intense interest I feel in what is going on I am sure the occurrences of the excitement would afford an artist effects and produce impressions no imaginings could shadow out or even suggest. Indeed I had a scheme and hoped to be able to induce a few young men of my acquaintance to go out and be useful in many ways, by carrying out clothing, carrying out friendly faces and perhaps even rendering assistance in the field. I feel so impressed with the greatness of the struggle that I do not think a man should stay at home who is not called upon to remain by duties. If we fail our decline as a nation will be frightfully rapid, and our own hope of success lies in the greatness of our efforts.

He was right: the Crimea in mid-winter would not have suited him, and he was wise to decide to fight there by proxy. Instead, England's Michelangelo sensibly chose to devote the fifties to decorating Lord Somers' dining-room and other large open spaces with enormous historical or allegorical murals, and to dream of painting yet larger ones.

Watts's main corpus of allegories dates from the second half of his life; but his earliest essays in this field were undertaken soon after his return from Italy. On the subject of allegory in general and of Watts's attitude to it in particular, Chesterton writes with his customary wit:

> The real objection to allegory is, it may roughly be said, founded upon the conception that allegory involves one art imitating another. This is, up to a certain point, true. To paint a figure in a blue robe and call her Necessity, and then paint a small figure in a yellow robe and call it Invention; to put the second on the knee of the first, and then say that you are enunciating the sublime and eternal truth, that Necessity is the mother of Invention, this is indeed an idle and foolish affair. It is saying in six weeks' work with brush and palette-knife what could be said much better in six words.

Many allegories of the past were of this kind:

Of such were the monstrous pictures of Rubens, which depicted a fat Religion and a bloated Temperance dancing before some foreign conqueror; of such were the florid designs of the eighteenth century, which showed Venus and Apollo encouraging Lord Peterborough to get over the inconvenience of his breastplate; of such again, were the meek Victorian allegories which showed Mercy and Foresight urging men to found a Society for the Preservation of Young Game. Of such were almost all the allegories which have dominated the art of Europe for many centuries back . . .

But Chesterton absolves Watts absolutely from the charge of painting allegories of this nature. And so does Watts! 'Allegory,' he said to his wife in 1895, 'is nonsense! George III on a horse and a naked woman blowing is meant to represent Fame!' He went still further: 'I don't like my work to be called allegorical,' he added, 'I never mix the real and the unreal.' Yet 'allegorical' was the very word he himself had used, and for want of a better one we must continue to use it.

Watts's allegories, said Chesterton, were not 'mere pictorial forms, combined as in a kind of cryptogram to express theoretical views or relations'. They were not 'proverbs or verbal relations rendered with cumbrous exactitude in oil and Chinese white'. They were not 'merely literary'. However, they too deal for the most part with 'eternal truths': with innumerable permutations and combinations of Love, Life, and Death; with Hope, Humanity, Peace, War and Time; with the Spirits of Progress and Non-Progress—with abstract concepts given corporeal form. Indeed, on occasions the distinction between the allegory as defined by Chesterton and as interpreted by Watts is undeniably slight. Watts's 'Greece in the lap of Egypt' may not, like Chesterton's fictitious 'Necessity is the Mother of Invention', illustrate a proverb; but it illustrates in a very similar way the historical fact that Greek civilisation owed a debt to that of Egypt.

Mary Watts and others were at pains to discover concealed allegory in 'The Wounded Heron', but it is generally accepted that Watts's immense 'Time and Oblivion' of 1848 was his first allegory proper. Though the artist liked to maintain that his allegories were self-explanatory many in fact were not: how often has 'Hope' been mistaken for 'Despair'? He frequently provided, in exhibition catalogues or elsewhere, a verbal explanation. Of 'Time and Oblivion', for example, he wrote for the catalogue of his exhibition at the Grosvenor Gallery in 1881–2:

The forms of Time and Oblivion, rising above the sphere of the terrestrial globe, are poised in mid-air betwixt the orbs of day and night. Time, as the type of stalwart manhood gifted with imperishable youth, holds in his right hand the emblematic scythe, while Oblivion, with bent head and downcast eyes, spreads her ample cloak and speeds swiftly towards the tomb.

Elsewhere he made a further comment on his conception of this design:

It is human in form and human in characteristics because my language appeals to the mind through the medium of the eye; but it is not human in detail . . . I endeavoured to make it noble and elevated for I wished to stimulate the mind and awaken large thoughts. It is solemn, sad and hard, for solemn, sad and hard are the conditions: an organ chord swelling and powerful but unmodulated.

Fifty years later, as he came away from the New Gallery where 'Time and Oblivion' was among the works exhibited, he remarked of the picture, 'I think Pheidias would have said, "Go on, you may do something." I never did anything better; but discouraged by those who alone regarded art seriously, I did not go on working in the way that I believed in. I lost many years of my life for this reason.' And to Mary he said, 'Those Pre-Raphaelites played the devil with me! . . . I hadn't their strength . . .'

Ruskin, who had called on Watts soon after the latter's return from Italy, wrote to a friend in 1849:

Do you know Watts? *The* man who is *not* employed in Houses of Parliament[1]—to my mind the only real painter of history or thought we have in England. A great fellow, or I am much mistaken—great as one of these same Savoy knots of rock—& we suffer the clouds to lie upon him, with thunder & famine at once

[1] Not at that moment. He had painted his 'Alfred' and was later to paint a 'St George'.

in the thick of them. If you have time when you come to town, &
have not seen it, look at the *Time & Oblivion* in his studio.

Ruskin was so taken with the picture that he borrowed it and
hung it for a while in his house in Park Street; but as he fell increasingly under the influence of the Pre-Raphaelites[1] it ceased to
please him and he returned it to the artist. It was exhibited at the
Royal Academy in 1864, where it was mysteriously described in the
catalogue as 'A design for sculpture, to be executed in various
materials'. Later it was bought by Lord Somers and now hangs,
together with a small sketch for the design, in Eastnor Castle.

In *The Stones of Venice* (1851–53) Ruskin had written: 'We have
as far as I *know* at present among us, only one painter G. F. Watts
who is capable of design in colour on a large scale. He stands alone
among our artists of the old school in his perception of the value of
breadth in distant masses and in the vigour of invention by which
such breadth must be sustained; and his power of expression and
depth of thought are not less remarkable than his bold conception
of colour effect.' The two men continued to correspond over the
years; but the arrogant schoolmaster in Ruskin could never long be
contained, and when he lost faith in Watts the artist he became
frankly offensive. On 13 February 1873 he wrote to Watts:

> You yourself were paralyzed for years by your love of the Greek
> style—you never made an entirely honest, completely unaffected
> study of anything. You drew [illegible] for instance—trying to
> make an angel of her—she was not an angel, by any means—The
> soft chalk translation of her did you deadly mischief at every
> touch—in the deliberate falsification. You fancy you see more
> than I do in nature—you still see life—for I, long ago, learned
> how impossible it was to draw what I saw—you still struggle to
> do so, that is to say, to draw what you like in what you see with-
> out caring what others like—or what God likes . . .

In old age, however, they came together again in spirit, and it was a
source of deep regret to Watts, as also to 'your lovingest J. Ruskin',
that a projected visit to Brantwood in 1893 to paint his 'dear old
friend, master and best teacher' was prevented by Watts's ill health.

*   *   *

[1] The Pre-Raphaelite Brotherhood (P.R.B.) had been formed in 1848, its three
principal members (of seven) being D. G. Rossetti, Millais and Holman Hunt.

'Life's Illusions', painted at Dorchester House in 1849 and shown that year at the Royal Academy, is the perfect example of the Watts allegory at its most foolish—and, incidentally, its most literary; when it was hung on the walls of the Grosvenor Gallery in 1881, even those critics most favourable to his work in general pounced on it and tore it to shreds. That of the *London Quarterly Review*, though unreservedly (and very properly) praising the much later 'Love and Death', found 'Life's Illusions' badly designed and frankly ridiculous. After dismissing the message of another allegory, 'The Spirit of Christianity', as incomprehensible, he continues:

Let us turn to an earlier work, *'Life's Illusions'*. Here there is no room for doubt as to the painter's meaning. He himself furnishes an explanation which occupies nearly a page of the catalogue. The 'design' is 'allegorical', 'typifying the march of human life'. To the left is a swirl of upfloating figures, of flesh and drapery and garlanded flowers. These are 'fair visions of beauty, the abstract embodiments of divers forms of hope and ambition' that 'hover high in the air above the gulf which stands as the goal of all men's lives.' To the right, 'upon the narrow space of earth that overhangs the deep abyss' and quite heedless of the 'abstract embodiments'—though these are large, substantial and very obvious—are a 'knight in armour' who 'pricks on his horse in quick pursuit' of a bubble, 'an aged student' who is so absorbed in his book that the next step will take him over the edge of the precipice, a pair of lovers, a child pursuing a butterfly. The ground is all bestrewn with bones, and scattered gold, and sceptres and crowns.

And here again, one feels that the inspiration from which the work has sprung is literary rather than artistic. The picture has no coherence. Its parts do not hang together. Its composition is confused. The little plateau on which all these incidents are crowded is obviously too small. Images which in poetry or impassioned prose are admissible, and even striking, become almost mirth-inspiring when presented to the eye in form and colour. None but a very foolish old gentleman persists in reading a book at the edge of a very steep cliff. When we *read* of the soldier

Seeking the bubble reputation
Even in the cannon's mouth,

our imagination never presents to us an actual bubble. Shakespeare did not mean that it should. The 'bubble' here is merely a very vivid kind of adjective qualifying reputation and imparting to it, in a particularly striking manner, certain attributes of lightness, prismatic beauty, evanescence. But show us a knight, of mature years, armed for fiercest strife, and riding madly in a very confined space, after a soap-bubble, and the image loses its magic altogether. Art is trying to do the work of literature, and doing it badly.

Yet Watts clung doggedly to his belief that in spite of a 'strong disposition today [he was writing in 1868] to pooh-pooh allegory', it was by his allegories that posterity would (he hoped) judge his claim 'to be considered a real artist; and it is only by these that I wish to be known.' The time did eventually come when the public allowed the Grand Old Man to have his way, and many a bereaved mother found comfort in his conception of Death as 'the kind nurse who was putting the children to bed'. But today his allegories are largely forgotten; by the public he is known through his portraits of the famous, by artists also as one of the finest pencil draughtsmen of his generation.

*   *   *

Watts's vast murals of the fifties will be dealt with in their proper place; but his 'House of Life'—his 'Sistine Chapel in the air'—may, since it was conceived in the late forties and never carried out, be considered here.

The information concerning it is derived from two drafts in Watts's handwriting, both undated[1] and both incomplete, which Mary Watts has combined, edited, repunctuated, and in places misread. Since, however, her version conveys the gist of what her husband wrote, it is for the most part retained in what follows:

> The ceiling to be covered with the uniform blue of space, on which should be painted the Sun, the Earth, and the Moon, as it is by their several revolutions and dependence upon each other that we have a distinct notion of, and are able to measure and estimate, the magnitude of Time. The progress of Time, and its

[1] The sheets bear the watermark 1837, but the writing would suggest a date at least ten years later.

consequent effect, I would here illustrate for the purpose of conveying a moral lesson—the design of Time and Oblivion would be exactly in its place. To complete the design, the Earth should be attended by two figures symbolic of the antagonistic forces, Attraction and Repulsion.

I would then give, perhaps upon one half of the ceiling, which might be divided by a gold band on which the zodiac might be painted, a nearer view of the earth, and by a number of gigantic figures stretched out at full length represent a range of mountains typifying the rocky structure or skeleton. These I would make very grand and impressive, in order to emphasise the insignificance of man. The most important (to us) of the constellations should shine out of the deep ultramarine firmament. Silence and Mighty Repose should be stamped upon the character and disposition of the giants; and revolving centuries and cycles should glide, personified by female figures of great beauty, beneath the crags upon which the mighty forms should lie, to indicate (as compared with the effect upon man and his works) the non-effect of time upon them.

A couple of little sketches (a mere ten feet in length) for these giants have survived;[1] one is in the store-rooms of the Tate Gallery, the other on the walls of the Watts Gallery. Watts entitled them 'Chaos', but later regretted that he had not called them 'Cosmos'—further evidence that his allegories cannot dispense with verbal explanation. Our English Michelangelo continues:

Then I would begin with man himself, trace him through his moral and political life; first the hunter stage, gaining, through the medium of his glimmering yet superior intelligence, advantages over the stronger yet inferior animals, almost his equals. Next the pastoral state, his intelligence further developed to the consequent improvement of his condition: serviceable animals domesticated, reclaimed by his thoughtful care, the stronger and fiercer subdued by the force of his will, aided by all-conquering intelligence. This is the Golden Age of poetry . . . In this period of the history of society it is probable the human animal enjoyed the greatest possible amount of happiness, equally re-

[1] There are other still smaller sketches, one also at Compton.

moved from the penalties of ambition, and from the degradation of a precarious and merely animal existence. There would be a great choice of exquisite subjects to illustrate this epoch, and here might be introduced the episode of Job.

The final paragraph of one of the two drafts now follows exactly as Watts wrote it, so that the reader may the better appreciate what he has elsewhere been spared:

Next should be man the tyrant, the insiduous oppressor, & the slave, the dweller in cities, the Egyptians should raise their Piramids, illustrate its story of Joshep & his brethren, from Egypt we would accompany the Jews of Palestine until the history becomes identified the Assyria, history of that country principal illustration, fall of Nineveh & Sardinapalus, history of Persia, principle illustrations Cyrus and Creasus;—India its mythology animals & . . .—Africa, mythology; general history, principal illustration, building of the Parthenon, portraits of the principal heroes. Rome, history; illustrating Scipio, habit, maners, orations, combats of gladiators, & wild animals in the amphithreher, Achitenters, Naval archtecter seafight, Antony & Augustus,—Founding of the Christian era treated simply as a matter of history setting up the cross:—destruction of Jerusalem, General history during the domination of the Popes, Goths, invasion of Rome, Mahomet,—Saracens history of Gaul—France, England, Peter the Hermit, crusades, middle ages,

Such was Watts's stupendous project to decorate a vast building with 'a history of the progress of man's spirit'. Stupendous—but quite unrealistic; for he was born in the wrong age, or at all events in the wrong country. Had he been a Bavarian, might not Ludwig II, another sufferer from the *folie de grandeur* (but one with the means to indulge it), perhaps have taken him up and employed him to decorate some fantastic Hall of Valhalla on the shores of the Chiemsee? Admittedly Watts would always have preferred 'Tom Bowling' to Walther's 'Prize Song'; but his 'Chaos' would have served admirably as an illustration to *Das Rheingold*.

It has more than once been stated in biographies of Watts that the artist intended to convert the great hall of Euston Station into his

House of Life;[1] but though his 'Chaos'—obviously a multi-purpose design—might today be quite appropriate for the decoration of a London railway station, in fact his wild project to fresco the hall was quashed before it had reached the stage of deciding upon a subject.

Watts was perpetually searching for a suitable wall on which to unburden, while his 'House of Life' was taking shape in his mind, some of the noble thoughts which were for ever welling up within him; and the great hall at Euston seemed the very thing. He therefore appealed to his friend Frank Charteris (Lord Elcho), whom he had known when in Florence, to approach the Chairman of the London and North-Western Railway on his behalf; if the Company would cover the cost of his paints and the erection of scaffolding, then he would offer his services free. Probably Elcho realised that he was dealing with a Don Quixote; but out of friendship he agreed to do what was asked of him. Not surprisingly, the Chairman threw up his hands in horror at the suggestion, and the architect declared that he and the directors would probably be stoned if such an outrage were committed.

So the scheme was abandoned, and the world thus deprived of 'Patience in the Lap of Unpunctuality' or whatever allegories Watts might have considered appropriate to soothe the ruffled traveller or fill his mind with lofty thoughts as he awaited the delayed departure of the Edinburgh express.

[1] See, *Annals* i, 132, and the myth still propagated by Chris Mullen in his Introduction to the catalogue of the Watts Exhibition held at the Whitechapel Art Gallery in 1974.

7

THE SEVEN PATTLES

THE SEVEN PATTLE SISTERS!
They sound like a turn in the big tent, and there was indeed something rather theatrical about these remarkable young women, two at least of whom were to play a not unimportant role in Watts's life; in fact Sara, the third of the brood, was to 'mother' him for more than twenty years, to regulate it and at one moment to come dangerously near to wrecking it.

It must have been some time in the year 1849 that a man named Fleming, one of the Holland House circle, mentioned to Watts the startling beauty of a certain Miss Virginia Pattle. She lived, he said, with a sister and brother-in-law, Mr and Mrs Thoby Prinsep, in Chesterfield Street in Mayfair, and he offered to bring together the talented artist and what he believed to be the perfect subject for his brush. But Watts declined. He was, he said, in no mood to paint portraits; still less was he eager to enlarge his circle of acquaintances. Further, he was especially busy at that moment, being just on the point of moving from Cambridge Street to his big new studio in Charles Street.

Now Charles Street and Chesterfield Street adjoined, and it was therefore inevitable that sooner or later the paths of Watts and Virginia Pattle would cross. Fleming must have described her appearance exactly (which was not difficult), for the moment Watts saw two women and a small boy coming towards him in the street he recognised the younger woman as Virginia. She was tall, and dressed with striking unconventionality in a long grey cloak; further, she was, to use a word that was about to become fashionable with the Pre-Raphaelite painters, a 'stunner'. Watts went straight home and

69

penned an urgent letter to Fleming that was soon to win for him the entrée to 9 Chesterfield Street.

These Pattle girls—Sir Henry Taylor used to refer to them collectively as 'Pattledom'—were the daughters of James Pattle, a rich Indian civil servant, and his French wife, and it may perhaps be convenient to introduce them and their husbands in tabular form.[1] They were:

ADELINE (1812–36), m. 1832 General Colin MACKENZIE (1806–81)

JULIA MARGARET (1815–79), m. 1838 Charles Hay CAMERON (1795–1880)

SARA(H) (1816–87), m. 1835 Henry Thoby PRINSEP (1793–1878)

MARIA ('MIA') (1818–92), m. 1835 Dr John JACKSON (1804–87)

LOUISA (1821–73), m. 1838 Henry Vincent BAYLEY (1815–73)

VIRGINIA (1826–1910), m. 1850 Charles, Lord EASTNOR, later 3rd Earl SOMERS (1819–83)

SOPHIA (1829–1911), m. 1847 Sir John Warrender DALRYMPLE 7th Bt. (1824–88)

It was, incidentally, Sophie Dalrymple who had the happy idea of calling Watts 'Signor'; it seemed impossible to call him 'George', still more so 'Fred'.

James Pattle—known to his friends as 'Jim Blazes' and to his enemies as 'the greatest liar in India'—had married the daughter of the Chevalier de l'Etang, page to Queen Marie Antionette and her fellow prisoner in the Conciergerie. After the Queen's execution, the Chevalier counted himself lucky to escape with life and wife to banishment in Pondicherry. Pattle died in Calcutta in 1845, leaving behind him in India a widow and his two youngest daughters, both still unmarried. The extraordinary story of what then ensued first appeared in print in 1919 in Dame Ethel Smyth's *Impressions that Remained*, since when it has been constantly reprinted, usually with embellishments and without acknowledgment.[2] The reader must judge for himself how much of it is credible.

[1] Three further children died at birth or in infancy.

[2] See also under Bell, Benson, Fitzpatrick, Hill, and Dalrymple-Champneys, in the Bibliography.

Dame Ethel relates what she heard her father, General John Smyth, tell Sir George Henschel one evening after what may well have been a very good dinner. Jim had left instructions that his body was to be taken to England; his widow therefore had had it put in a barrel of rum—appropriately enough, since he had died of drink—which was deposited in the room next to her bedroom till there was a vessel ready to sail:

'Well, in the middle of the night there was a loud explosion; she rushed into the room and found the cask had burst . . . and there was her husband half out of it! The shock sent her off her head then and there, poor thing, and she died raving . . .

'All the same his friends thought they'd better carry out his last wishes, so they had him put up again and taken down the Ganges. The sailors hadn't the most distant idea what they'd aboard, and thinking the cask was full of rum, which was the case, they tapped it and got drunk; and by Jove, the rum ran out and got alight and set the ship on fire! And while they were trying to extinguish the flames she ran on a rock, blew up, and drifted ashore just below Hooghly. And what do you think the sailors said? that Pattle had been such a scamp that the Devil wouldn't let him go out of India!'

What at all events might possibly be true is that two young girls, still in their teens and conversing together more readily in Hindustani than in English, had the macabre and perhaps unique experience of arriving in England with luggage consisting principally of the corpses of both their parents. But Brian Hill throws doubt even on this, considering it more probable, on the evidence available, that James Pattle's corpse caught an earlier boat and that his widow's was committed to the depths of the Indian Ocean. Thus does research conspire to demolish a picturesque legend!

All the Pattles were almost embarrassingly devoted to one another; but Sara Prinsep was the most maternal of them, and it was only natural that she was the one to provide a home for Virginia and Sophia. Then Sophia married, and it was Sara and one of her three sons whom Watts had seen with Virginia in the street of Mayfair on that fateful day.

Sara was not beautiful (Lady Troubridge speaks of her as 'only comely'), and the unconventional clothes that were a part of the Pattle way of life—the long cloaks (when crinolines were the fashion), the hair-nets and the tinkling Indian bangles—made her look, and sound, affected rather than distinguished. But Virginia wore hers like a queen. Yet it was the perfect oval of Virginia's face that people first turned to admire; then the dark, heavily-lidded eyes and the raven hair parted in the centre. Edward Lear called her 'certainly the handsomest living woman . . . I think her expression of countenance is one of the most unmitigated goodness I ever contemplated.' Passers-by stopped dead in the street to stare and to worship; and Lady Troubridge recalls an occasion when so great a crowd collected outside an Oxford Street store which Virginia had entered, that she was obliged to leave by a side door. As for her smile,—there must have been something refulgent about it, for another friend reported that it 'lighted a room', while yet another, indulging in almost oriental imagery, compared her to 'a splendid full moon, so radiant and benignant was she'. Yet she once told Thackeray that it 'broke her heart' that people cared more for her beauty than for her soul.

Goethe said that all men and women are born to be either anvils or hammers—'*Ambos oder Hammer sein*'. Watts was one of Nature's anvils, while Sara Prinsep might fairly be described as a sledge-hammer. She had married a man more than twenty years older than herself, a former Indian Civil Servant and now, at the age of fifty-seven, a director of the East India Company. An American friend of the family, Mrs Edward Twisleton,[1] describes Thoby Prinsep in 1853 as 'a great six footer, not fat, with a fair complexion, grey hair, and a good broad forehead and a generally sunny expression. He is a generous, affectionate person who appreciates his wife, and likes to have her do as she pleases and to have everybody at their ease and at home in his house.' Mary Watts, who can only have known him at the very end of his long life, writes of him as 'large and philosophic in mind, grand in his stature, his learning, his memory, his everything, even to his sneeze! (once received with an *encore* from the gallery of a theatre), child-like in his gentleness and in the sweetness of his nature'. Watts called him 'an encyclopedia of valuable in-

[1] *Letters of the Hon. Mrs Edward Twisleton written to her Family, 1852–62*, John Murray, 1928—an invaluable source of information about the Prinseps and their circle.

formation on any sort of subject. It was just like turning the pages of a delightful book, and, like it, open if you wanted it and shut when you did not.' Thoby already had several distinguished books to his credit, and was currently engaged on a work dealing with Tibet, Tartary and Mongolia.

Though at one time a very rich man, repeated unsuccessful attempts to enter Parliament had left him no more than well-off. We may safely infer that he was another anvil, now happiest when in his study and among his books; but Sara, already renowned in India as a hostess, saw to it that he was always at hand to be winkled out of his scallop-shell of quiet and pressed into service to add lustre to the social, intellectual and artistic gatherings that were her whole life.

For Sara was at once a sledge-hammer and a lion-hunter, and it must have been an unforgettable moment for her when the handsome and brilliant young artist first crossed the threshold of her house in Chesterfield Street. Before long the two sisters were to be found constantly in and out of Watts's studio, on whose walls hung the thirty-foot 'Story from Boccaccio', his 'Echo', and other of his recent finished and unfinished paintings. There could be no doubt that she and Virginia had discovered a genius. 'I was never dazzled by any other painter's brush', Virginia declared later. 'All other brushes were like boot-brushes to me.'

Like so many formidable women, Sara Prinsep had a heart of gold: dare one call her a 'sledge-hammer with a soft centre'? Though only a year older than Watts, her attitude towards him was protective rather than amorous; it was what Mary Watts called 'her large mother-heart' that went out to him. He was so frail-looking, so obviously in need of care and cosseting, and some melancholy very recent paintings spoke only too clearly of the morbid state of his mind. In fact, during the following winter Watts was to be seriously ill with a 'nervous fever with a threatening of paralysis . . . His old enemy of headache and nausea had returned, and so violent were these attacks that, while they lasted, he would lie quite motionless for hours, with almost the look and the pallor of death upon his face.'

A sick lion-cub, and at her very door: it was almost too good to be true! Sara, who had a 'genius for all sorts of confections in the way of delicate foods', was all over him, feeding him and tending him and putting cold compresses on his brow, while Virginia, so much younger and so very much prettier, paid periodic angelic visitations that made his heart beat dangerously fast. Before long he was convalescent, and when pronounced fit to travel he was ordered by Sara to Malvern to consult Dr Gully, the hydropathist who had made Malvern famous. On his way there he stayed several days with old Lord Somers at Eastnor Castle,[1] where soon Virginia was to reign as hostess.

It was said that Lord Eastnor—heir to the second Earl Somers, whom he was to succeed in 1852—had fallen in love with Virginia after seeing a portrait of her in Watts's studio, no doubt the over-lifesize standing figure now at Eastnor Castle.[2] So had Thackeray, who was soon obliged to admit that 'she never cared $2\frac{1}{2}$d for me'. Indeed, Virginia had every eligible bachelor in London at her feet: 'Oh, how in love with her we all were!' Lord Aberdare once exclaimed, and it was Sir Charles Newton's opinion that she ought not to marry 'any *one*'. Among her most ardent worshippers was Watts; but what hope had a sick, neurotic, impoverished artist, however brilliant and handsome, to compete with the rich heir to an earldom? Chichester Fortescue, after spending an evening at the Prinseps' with Henry Phillips, the fashionable portrait-painter, noted in his diary for 8 May 1853, 'On our way back Phillips talked of Ly. Somers; said her marriage had been a tremendous blow to Watts, who worshipped her in a way that Somers has never done.'[3] It was the misfortune of Watts always to be moving in a circle 'above his station'; he never came across piano-tuners' daughters.

Later Fortescue again refers to 'that clever little man, Ld. Somers, with his beautiful little wife, whom he is tolerably indifferent about'. Certainly Somers, though described as 'listless' by one who knew him well, was both clever and enterprising. In spite of suffering all his life from injuries received from a fall from his horse when a young man, he travelled extensively and audaciously, accompanying Layard (who called him his 'dearest and truest friend') to Athos in

[1] Those who saw 'The Pallisers' on television may be interested to know that the exterior views of Gatherum Castle were photographed at Eastnor.
[2] According to the *Birmingham Evening Dispatch* of 8 August 1904, 'The portrait of Mrs Prattle [sic] impressed [Watts] so deeply that he sought her personal acquaintance, and soon made her his wife'!
[3] '. . . *and Mr. Fortescue*'. *A Selection from the Diaries from 1851–1862 of Chichester Fortescue, Lord Carlingford, K.P.* edited by Osbert Wyndham Hewett, John Murray, 1958. There is a little-known portrait of Watts by Phillips (*c.* 1850) in the National Portrait Gallery.

the autumn in 1843 and also visiting Greece with Robert Curzon, for whose *Monasteries of the Levant* (1849) he provided a frontispiece.[1] He was, indeed, a very competent artist, a friend of Ruskin and Turner and perhaps a pupil of Lear; there are some twenty of his topographical water-colour drawings at Eastnor Castle.

Somers shared the tastes of Robert Holford of Westonbirt for both Italian art and arboriculture; he purchased Italian paintings (mostly now dispersed), introduced the Atlas cedar into England and planted it and other conifers extensively in the grounds of his castle. He was a pioneer photographer, and it may well have been he who inspired his sister-in-law, Julia Margaret Cameron, to take up photography. We have only Fortescue's word for it that matrimony was not his forte, and he did at least sire two daughters— Isabella (the ill-starred Lady Henry Somerset) and Adeline, Duchess of Bedford.

It was now Watts's turn to be of service to the Prinseps. Sara had come to the conclusion that her house in Chesterfield Street was an unsatisfactory setting for her rapidly expanding intellectual-bohemian salon. It was too small; it lacked character; it had no garden where there could be tea on the lawn for the grown-ups and romping in the shrubbery for her four children and their friends. It so happened that at this moment Lord Holland chanced to mention to Watts that he was looking for a tenant for Little Holland House, a kind of dower-house on his estate; did he happen to know of anyone who might be interested? Watts told Sara, who had no difficulty in persuading her amenable husband that it was just what they needed. In December 1850 a twenty-one years' lease was signed, subsequently extended by four years, and a month later the Prinseps took possession.

Poor Watts, now a couple of miles rather than a couple of minutes' walk from his ministering angel (in the singular, for Virginia had just married), was bereft and wretched; but as soon as Sara had settled in she invited him to stay. In her own words, which are true enough in general for some mild exaggeration to be excused, 'He came to stay three days; he stayed thirty years.'

[1] According to Edward Lear, Somers paid a further visit to Athos, this time *with his wife*! 'It seems that she, S[omers] and Coutts Lindsay really landed at Athos, and lived there 2 months! in tents, various mucilaginous monx coming now and then to see them.'

8

LITTLE HOLLAND HOUSE IN THE FIFTIES

IF THE Prinseps' house in Chesterfield Street was commonplace, Little Holland House most certainly was not. It was rambling and haphazard, and though only two miles from Hyde Park Corner it was in the depths of the country. It had character, charm, historical associations. It had what the Germans call, and we have no word for it—'*Stimmung*'. Here Lord Camelford had been carried to die after his duel in 1804 with Captain Best. Here, for more than forty years, lived Caroline Fox, whom Lord Holland had hastened from Florence to visit in 1844; she called the house her '*Paradisino*' —her little paradise. True, old Lady Holland had once dismissed it as 'swampy, damp and unwholesome'; but this had not prevented her from establishing herself there on several occasions as Miss Fox's uninvited guest and making herself a good deal more than at home. Many of the Holland House circle came to see dear old Miss Fox: Jeremy Bentham came—with an offer of marriage wisely rejected; and no doubt her great admirer, George IV, passed more than once through its low thatched porch. 'Miss Fox,' the King once said, 'is right, and by G-d it is a *vary coorious* fact, I just never knew her wrong in the whole course of my life. By G-d, I always agree with her.'

We know the exterior appearance of Little Holland House from two old photographs,[1] taken by Charles Dixon, which served for the pen-and-ink 'reconstructions' (in fact, little more than copies) made by F. L. Griggs to illustrate Mary Watts's *Annals*. Of the interior, an anonymous author wrote:

To eyes accustomed to early Victorian wall-papers and carpets,

[1] Reproduced in Schleinitz (see Bibliography).

how describe what was the refreshment and delight of those matted rooms, with cool green walls against which hung paintings glowing with Venetian colour, and the low ceilings, painted a dusk harmonious blue? In the principal drawing-room, where stood the piano, the planetary system was traced in gold upon the deep-blue ceiling. Bedrooms and all were in this scheme of colour, with lattice windows framed with creepers, through which one saw the waving trees. The walls of the long narrow dining-room were entirely painted by Watts . . .

A vivid account of its inhabitants and of the ebb and flow of life there will be found in *A Painter of Dreams*—a biography of Roddam Spencer Stanhope by that remarkable old lady Mrs A. M. W. Stirling, who died in 1965 in her hundredth year. Though not an eye-witness of what she describes, she came later to know most of the Little Holland House circle. Of Sara Prinsep's famous Sunday afternoon 'at homes' she wrote:

A breezy Bohemianism prevailed. That time of dread, the conventional Sunday of the early Victorian era, was exchanged for the wit of cynics, the dreams of the inspired, the thoughts of the profoundest thinkers of the age. Throughout the sunny summer afternoons, under the shade of the fine old trees, were placed big sofas and seats, picturesque in their gay coverings, and the desultory talk round the tea table was varied by games of bowls and croquet on the lawn beyond. But by and by, as the light faded and all who were mere visitors departed, those who belonged to the more intimate coterie of friends remained on to an impromptu dinner-party. The seats were carried indoors, the lights within gleamed in rosy cheerfulness, and conversation flowed into fresh and delightful channels.

'They talked,' we are told, 'of things that belonged to no date, their subjects would have interested men of any age.' For while those without that charmed circle spoke sneeringly of 'Mrs Prinsep's tea gardens', of the parties where she and her husband —'her dog Toby' as he was facetiously called—entertained a medley of cranks, among the habitués of Little Holland House were Carlyle, with his rugged genius, Tennyson, Thackeray, Dickens, Rossetti, Burne-Jones, Browning and a score of others whose names now enrich the sun of England's greatness . . .

The young painters collected there were to form that celebrated pre-Raphaelite brotherhood, with Watts. Stanhope writes, 'I have to go to Little Holland House every day, lunch and paint with Watts. One of the great secrets that make Little Holland House so charming is that there are no books there,[1] and everybody has to talk or make an effort to do so, and that is why those great literary swells go there.'

One 'literary swell' who had first-hand knowledge of Little Holland House was John Ruskin, who in 1859 wrote two interesting letters to his friend Margaret Bell:

You must have heard people speak of Watts—He's named with Rossetti sometimes in my things—the fresco painter—a man of great imagination & pathetic power:—he is painting Tennyson's portrait[2]—both staying at the pleasant house of a lady to whose kind watching over him in his failing health, Watts certainly owes his life . . .

One of the scenes that perhaps you and one or two other people would have liked to have sketched was this—Watts lying back in his arm chair—a little faint—(he is still unwell) with Tennyson's P.R.B. illustrated poems[3] on his knee. Tennyson standing above him—explaining over his shoulder why said illustrations did not fit the poems, with a serious quiver on his face—alternating between indignation at not having been better understood & dislike of self-enunciation:—I sitting on the other side of Watts— looking up deprecatingly to Tennyson—& feeling very cowardly in the good cause—yet maintaining it in a low voice—Behind me as backer [Burne] Jones, the most wonderful of all the Pre-Raphaelites in redundance of delicate & pathetic fancy . . . laughing sweetly at the faults of his own school as Tennyson declared them and glancing at me with half wet sparkling eyes, as he saw me shrink—A little in front of us—standing in the light

[1] But Thoby Prinsep must have had a good library.
[2] Watts's second (and so-called 'moonlight') portrait of Tennyson. At the time Watts spoke of it as 'the greatest work of his life', and was afraid he might die before he had finished it; Tennyson therefore, though longing to return home, stayed on in London. The picture is now at Eastnor Castle.
[3] *Poems by Alfred Tennyson*, London, 1857, published by Edward Moxon, with illustrations by Rossetti, Millais, Holman Hunt and others.

of the window Mrs Prinsep and her sister [Virginia?]—two, certainly of the most beautiful women in a grand sense—(Elgin marbles with dark eyes)—that you could find in modern life— and round the room Watt's [sic!] Greek-history frescoes.

Tennyson's face is more agitated by the intenseness of sensibility than is almost bearable by the looker on—he seems almost in a state of nervous trembling like a jarred string of a harp. He was maintaining that painters ought to attend to at least what the writer *said* [—] if they couldn't, to what he meant—while Watts and I both maintained that no good painter could be subservient at all: but must conceive everything in his own way,— that no poems ought to be illustrated at all—but if they were— the poet *must* be content to have his painter in partnership—not a slave . . .

Of Watts himself he wrote:

. . . Watts is very ⟨pale &⟩ thin—long faced—rather bony & skinny in structure of face features—otherwise sensitive in the same manner as the Tennysons, of course in less degree the thinness being evidently caused by suffering both of mind & body; but not involving any permanent harm to health—no [illegible]—Dark hair—Eyes ⟨bright⟩ clear & clean, but not in any way noticeably brilliant or beautiful—and rather small. His smile very sweet: but firm—not going far. Jones's face melts all away into its smile like a piece of sugar candy . . .[1]

A young woman, Lady Constance Dawson-Damer, wrote of the impact of Little Holland House on one who was totally unsophisticated. Her fiancé, (Sir) John Leslie, took her one day in 1856 'to what was to me a new world—something I had never imagined before of beauty and kindness. I was a very ignorant little girl, and oh how proud I felt, though rather unworthy of what seemed holy ground. The Signor came out of his studio all spirit and so delicate, and received me very kindly as John's future wife. Thackeray was there with his young daughters, Coutts Lindsay, Jacob Omnium, and Lady Somers, glorious and benevolent. Signor was the whole object of adoration and care in that house. He seemed to sanctify Little Holland House.'

[1] *The Winnington Letters*, edit. by Van Akin Burd, Allen and Unwin, 1969.

A more sophisticated picture is drawn by George du Maurier, who describes the adoration shown by Mrs Prinsep and her sisters to the great who frequented their salon. Cups of tea were

> handed to them by these women almost kneeling. Watts, who is a grand fellow, is their painter in ordinary; the best part of the house has been turned into his studio, and he lives there and is worshipped till his manliness hath almost departed, I should fancy . . .
> After the departure of the visitors we dined; without dress coats—anyhow, and it was jolly enough—Watts in velvet coat and slippers. After dinner, up in the music room Watts stretched himself at full length on the sofa, which none of the women take when he's there. People formed circle, and I being in good voice sang to them the whole evening, the cream of Schubert and Gordigiani—*c'était très drôle*, the worship I got. I wonder if they are sincere. At eleven we left, and Mrs Prinsep almost embraced me . . .

But our most valuable observer of life at Little Holland House in the fifties is undoubtedly Mrs Edward Twisleton (*née* Dwight)— 'dear, diamond-eyed little Mrs Twisleton,' as Mrs Carlyle called her —and no excuse is needed for quoting freely from the lively letters that she wrote to her three sisters in America. This young Bostonian had married in 1852 a younger brother of Lord Saye and Sele, 'Twisty' or 'Mr T' to his friends, who was twice his wife's age and passionately in love with her. He knew everyone in London, and one evening at a party he introduced her to Mrs Prinsep, who, wrote Ellen Twisleton, 'struck me most agreeably. She was so cordial and smiling and sunny that it was really delightful to speak to her . . . She had with her, too, a beautiful younger sister, a Mrs Dalrymple, who is the second handsome woman I have seen in England—i.e. handsome enough to be called a beauty.' This was in the summer of 1852, and soon afterwards the Twisletons went abroad for some months; but one June afternoon a year later they

> drove out to little Holland House to see Mrs Prinsep, who is the greatest cordial you can imagine. I never saw such exuberant cheerfulness and beaming kindheartedness in anyone as her manners express—she is rather stout and not handsome, but

delightful to look at, and the sort of person one would like to live under the shadow of, or rather bask in the sunlight of. I am so tired of the formality of the greater part of the people I have to do with, and of the sensation of being forever a stranger, that when I see a person who makes me feel at home with her, it is difficult to go away again.

Mrs Prinsep has taken into her house and home a poor forlorn artist, with great talents and weak health, which is just like her, and in consequence her house is full of his pictures—one was a portrait of her, and of her beautiful sister, Mrs Dalrymple . . . Some others by the same person, Mr Watts, struck me as much.

Before the month was out, the visit was repeated:

In the afternoon, we drove out to Mrs Prinsep's, who had met Edward one day last week, and begged him to come, and bring me that she might introduce us to her sister, Lady Somers . . . Out we went therefore, I too pleased to have the chance to see her and found Mr Vaughan, Mrs Grote and some persons I did not know, already there, at a sort of luncheon—that is, straw-berries, etc., were on the table, but there were three rooms, and people in all of them, and nobody was bound to eat anything, if they didn't want it . . .

[Mrs Prinsep] lives quite out of London, in a place called Little Holland House, which is just beyond Holland House itself, and where everything is free and green, and beautiful, with trees and flowers and a beautiful garden—the house was an old farm-house, and has had another house, as it were, built on to it, so that the rooms are low and large, and wainscotted, and oddly placed in relation to each other, and then there are long passages, and out you come again into rooms where you don't expect them. So when I first went in, she wasn't in that room, but Mr Vaughan promptly went and got her, and she came and greeted us, in her own dear, delightful way, and carried me off to introduce me to her sisters, Lady Somers and Mrs Jackson.

Lady Somers is fair, and round, and sweet, and Mrs P's 'dar-ling', as she says, and looks as if she might be any one's darling, but really not so charming to me as Mrs P herself, as is often the case with such warm-hearted people's idols. Mrs Jackson is a tall, striking person, who has been a great invalid, and lives in complete retirement, near Mr Vaughan, at Hampstead. She has been a great reader, and has the greatest refinement and charm of manner—very quiet, not like Mrs P, but equally attractive, in another line. So, first Lady Somers talked to me, Virginia, and then Mrs Jackson, Maria, and then Mrs Prinsep came again, and took both my hands in hers, and said she was so glad to see me with her sisters and that I must learn to call them all by their names, and not Mrs and they were so sweet with each other, and so sweet to me, and overcame me so, with every kind of loving-kindness, that I was really upset, and fairly cried in Mrs P's face . . . When I found my best kid gloves and my best white bonnet-strings, and my best company face, all in danger of being flooded so unexpectedly, I got up and rushed off with Mrs Prinsep, and she took me into such an artist's studio, and kept on being perfectly lovely to me, while I wiped up, dreadfully ashamed of myself, as fast as I could.

The studio belonged to Mr Watts, an artist of positive genius, I think, whose portrait of the beautiful Mrs Dalrymple I spoke to you of, in my last letter. The family had known him a long time, and Mrs Prinsep found him living in London in uncomfortable quarters, and fighting with poverty and ill-health, and so took him home to her own house, and gave him friends and plenty of every description, and there he lives and paints; and as a reward, paints nothing but idealised figures and faces of herself, and her sisters, and their children. In this studio was a picture of 'The Good Samaritan', an illustration of the 'Song of the Shirt', and a companion to it, of a poor woman cowering under the arch of a bridge by night, for shelter, a picture of St George and the Princess painted for the House of Lords, a picture of Echo, and of the Angel of Death, which were most striking—and all full of imaginative power of a very high order. He has been a very thorough student and draws quite faultlessly, while his eye for colour is uncommonly fine.

Mrs Twisleton was then taken to see, in a room known as 'the upper dining-room', a series of frescoes by Watts showing 'Greece in the Lap of Egypt', 'Assyria and Hindustan', 'Time unveiling Truth', 'Peace and War', and so on, for many of which various Pattle sisters had served as models. When in 1875 Little Holland

House came to be demolished, Watts's friend Mrs Charles Wylie had them cut from the walls and stored in crates. They were later given by Watts to his future biographer, Mrs Barrington, who reproduces some of them in her book. Mrs Twisleton was, of course, duly impressed; but, to judge from rather inadequate photographs, it is hard to believe that their loss—for they appear to have perished—is very great. Mrs Twisleton continues:

> Mr Watts is a peculiar, eccentric person, always dissatisfied with and destroying what he does, living on nothing, not caring even to sell his pictures, much—and has quite given up sending anything to the exhibitions, because his pictures were not well-hung and not appreciated. Pray don't tell anyone else that I think I have discovered a genius . . . I daresay he will never do enough to distinguish himself, as it needs industry and patience as well, and only his gratitude to Mrs Prinsep, I suppose, prevailed with him to finish this series. He takes, also the most beautiful likeness in crayon, and has just finished one of Mr Vaughan, which is extremely admired. I saw what he could do, in his portrait of Mrs Dalrymple.
>
> Dear girls, nobody since I left home has treated me as these people did, so lovingly, so frankly—neither looking at me formally, because I was a stranger, nor curiously, because I was an American, but heartfully, and sympathetically, and I had never seen any of them before except Mrs Prinsep, and her, only twice . . . I only wish I lived next door to them all.

Here and there among Ellen's letters are scattered other observations about subsequent visits to Little Holland House. She met Tennyson, who 'has a fine forehead, and calm, good eyes—and a face of great sensibility; but he keeps himself rather shaggy, and his complexion has rather the look of the inveterate smoker, which he is.' There was a dinner-party 'wonderful with calves-heads and lobster curries and odd sort of dishes, all first-rate'; and after dinner, while she talked with Watts, Twisty 'pitched into East Indian politics with Mr Prinsep'. Another evening she met Ruskin, whom she found less attractive than his books: 'I don't know that he is bad in any way, but he is very odd. He is separated from his wife, because he treated her with such absolute indifference . . .'

All this social round—this 'ringing perpetual door-bells and leaving perpetual little pieces of pasteboard'—was exhausting for even a young American, and by 1855 Ellen reported that she was in danger of becoming 'clean tuckered out'. Perhaps it was this weariness that caused the almost complete cessation of her correspondence from this time until her sadly early death seven years later. Therefore nothing survives—or at all events, nothing has been published by the editor of her letters—to explain in detail the 'complete disillusionment' she suffered in 1861 about the ladies of Little Holland House. At the root of it (her editor informs us) was an unfortunate love affair between the Mr Vaughan already mentioned—a great friend of both the Twisletons and the Prinseps—and a relation of Ellen's. Vaughan, as the Twisletons saw it, behaved disgracefully, and presumably the Prinseps took his side. Pattle charm, we are told, had blinded Ellen at first to 'grave defects, which, when recognised, inevitably brought about a separation'.

Ellen Twisleton was not the only person to believe, rightly or wrongly, that the bohemian atmosphere of Little Holland House was unhealthy and dangerous. Lord Holland's great friend, Edward Cheney, spoke of the place as a 'hornets' nest', and George du Maurier wrote, 'Somehow in the very delightful atmosphere of this house I seem to perceive a slight element of looseness, *hein*? which I don't sympathise with—when I say delightful, it isn't enormously so to me but could be if I were a "gay" young bachelor.'

Another critic was Lady Charlotte Schreiber,[1] who wrote in her Journal for 13 June 1859, 'I know there cannot be a worse place to go alone than Little Holland House, amidst artists and musicians, and all the flattery and nonsense which is rife in that otherwise most agreeable society.' She had a particular cause for concern in that Merthyr Guest, the second son of her first marriage, had become infatuated with a certain Georgina Treherne, a young lady of great charm but dubious morals who had been taken up by the Prinseps— and, indeed, by Lady Charlotte herself, who had presented her at court. But it was a visit to Little Holland House, paid without parental permission by Lady Charlotte's twenty-two-year-old daughter Katherine, that had been the immediate cause of the above outburst.

[1] Married first to Sir John Guest, Bt., and after his death to Mr Charles Schreiber. She was famous as a collector of china, fans, etc.

An account of the extraordinary life and career of Georgina Treherne, afterwards Mrs Harry Weldon, must be read elsewhere.[1] She had been brought up in Florence, and in view of her subsequent reputation it is amusing to learn that as a girl she had not been allowed by her father to set foot in the Casa Feroni because of the 'gossip that was afloat concerning Lady Holland'. Arriving in England at the age of nineteen she soon found her way to Little Holland House, where Watts fell for her ripe beauty and lovely voice (which also charmed Gounod and Mr Gladstone), writing her a number of letters[2] and painting at least two splendid portraits of her. He called her his *'Carissima Bambina'*, assured her he was her 'best friend' and, declaring himself to be a man who knew the world intimately, offered her copious, high-minded, unwanted, unheeded advice on the conduct of her affair with Merthyr. He seemed quite unaware of the fact that Georgina knew more of the world at twenty than he would know at eighty, and was merely using him as a go-between and cat's-paw.

But it did not take Lady Charlotte long to see Georgina in her true colours. On 3 June 1858 she wrote, 'I had already begun to have my eyes opened about the young lady's duplicity and flightiness'; and ten days later, when visiting Mrs Prinsep, she learnt that Georgina was at that very moment 'closeted with Lord Ward alone in Watts' studio, Watts being absent at Bowood.' Before July was out, Merthyr's eyes had been prised open by his mother, who reported, 'I am most thankful that the young lady's character has been unmasked in time, and that my dear son has been saved.'

After her marriage in 1860 to Harry Weldon, Georgina, who had received endless kindness from Sara Prinsep, began to abuse her in letters to Watts. This was more than he could stand, and while still calling himself her 'best friend' he replied with a sharp rebuke. Once he had said to her, 'When any slander Little Holland House, judge it according to your knowledge of it'; now she too had gone over to the enemy.

Yet another cry of alarm about the goings-on at Little Holland

---

[1] E. Grierson, *Storm Bird: The Strange Life of Georgina Weldon,* Chatto and Windus, 1959.
[2] Sold at Sotheby's, 29 April 1969.

House was uttered by Lady Elizabeth Stanhope,[1] whose son, Roddam Spencer Stanhope, had been taken up by Watts. 'Roddy', a Commoner of Christ Church and very bored there by the philistinism of his fellow undergraduates, had come to Watts in 1850 with a desire to learn to paint and a letter from Dr (later Sir Henry) Acland, Ruskin's lifelong friend, recommending him as 'an agreeable addition to the solitude of the Long Vacation'. Acland particularly lauded Roddy's 'simplicity and bonhomie'; he really meant that the boy was very young for his age and rather 'hearty'.

Watts, after the usual preamble about their being 'fellow-students' rather than 'teacher and pupil', began his course of instruction with 'drapery studies'—that is to say, meticulous pencil drawings of 'a towel scattered in a picturesque way upon the floor', which were intended to help the tyro to become a second Pheidias—and before long Roddy was considered sufficiently advanced to lend a hand with some murals in Chesterfield Street and subsequently with those at Little Holland House. They rode together (with 'lots of jumping, some of it rather stiff'), romped together, talked for hours on end about High Art and Life, so that soon Roddy was reporting to his mother that 'Watts, now I know him, is a glorious companion, and the Prinseps very jolly people.' In another letter he wrote, 'On Thursday evening I went with a huge party of Pattles to see a Diorama of Calcutta;[2] Lord and Lady Eastnor, Mr and Mrs Prinsep, Mrs Dalrymple, Mrs Jackson with a daughter, and Watts and myself completed the party. We had very good fun, the chief amusement of the ladies being to bully poor Watts, who was in a very High Art mood at the time. We ended up with tea at the Eastnors. She is certainly A1 for beauty . . .'

The more enthusiastic Roddy's letters became, the more Lady Elizabeth's suspicions were aroused. As a boy at Rugby he had dabbled in art—'a sad waste of time,' she had then written, 'but he is happy, and it is at least harmless.' But was it? 'Art' might be harmless; but how about artists, and those who frequented artists? When in London she had no doubt heard the current gossip about Little Holland House and its circle; was the real attraction of the place

[1] Youngest daughter of the famous 'Coke of Norfolk', first Earl of Leicester of the second creation.
[2] A moving panorama painted by W. C. Stanfield and the animal painter J. F. Herring.

some scheming and highly unsuitable young woman, and all Roddy's 'gush' about Watts just a blind? Or could it be even worse? The word 'homosexual' had not yet been invented and Oscar Wilde was not even born, but possibly she could not quite dismiss the feeling that it was queer (though she would hardly have used that word) for a bachelor in his middle thirties to be showing so marked an interest in her good-looking boy. 'I mean to satisfy myself when I go to town,' she wrote, 'what is his influence, *moral as well as artistic*'.

Lady Elizabeth (a formidable woman) arrived from Yorkshire with her elder son, William, to be greeted by Roddy who 'had made an illumination ready for us, on the mantelpiece, of five hand-candles and two others, and was as pleased with it as any schoolboy. Obviously *he has nothing on his conscience*! I hear there is a merry-go-round in the garden at Little Holland House, and the three Prinsep boys and their tutor, with Roddy and Watts, go round and round on it till they are quite exhausted. *Very innocent!*' The boy was 'crazy about Flaxman' (Watts's current god) and 'at his High Art' even before breakfast; but though she 'questioned him closely' she could not discover even the hint of any impropriety. He might be rather silly but, thank God! he was pure.

So Watts's *moral* influence was beyond reproach. But not, curiously enough, his *artistic* influence; for the more Lady Elizabeth, who herself dabbled in art, saw of Watts's paintings, the more convinced she became that he simply did not know how to draw! 'Though Roddy has done wonders,' she wrote, 'I still have my doubts, as his drawing is decidedly wrong, and so is Watts's, with all his genius. I wish you could see the horrible, naked, mutilated figures from the Elgin marbles with which he intends to *decorate the Governesses' Institution*. There is one as large as life, I think it is the Theseus—enough to frighten them all out of their wits.' Nonetheless, in 1852, at Roddy's urgent request though with some misgivings, she invited Watts to stay with her at her London house in Harley Street and to use, whenever he liked, one of its rooms as a studio. Since Watts had just given up his house[1] in Charles Street, and the studio that was being built for him at Little Holland House was not yet ready, this suited him admirably. Lady Elizabeth found him to be 'quiet as a mouse, working from morning to night', and

[1] It became the famous Cosmopolitan Club, of which Watts was a member.

doubly acceptable in that he was 'not an expensive guest, as he drinks nothing but water'.

Roddy, though he had an excellent sense of colour (Burne-Jones called him 'the finest colourist in Europe'), was never to reach the top of his profession, and some were to blame Watts for not having made him study drawing thoroughly enough. But all Old Marlburians will remember with nostalgia, and many with affection, the series of decorative panels that he painted for the School Chapel.

Two at least of the three Prinsep boys mentioned by Lady Elizabeth need introduction. They were Henry, Valentine ('Val') and Arthur, aged (in 1852) sixteen, fourteen and twelve respectively; and there was also an eight-year-old daughter, Alice. Henry, though he was on one occasion with Watts in Italy, spent almost the whole of his life in India and hardly concerns us. Val, destined for the Indian Civil Service, fell under the influence of Watts, became his pupil and adopted painting as a career. Writing in 1857 to Lady Duff Gordon, Watts said:

> I have conscientiously abstained from inoculating him with any of my own views or ways of thinking, and have plunged him into the Pre-Raphaelite Styx. I don't mean to say that I held the fine young baby of six feet two by the heels, or wish to imply the power of moulding his opinions at my pleasure; but I found him loitering on the banks and gave him a good shove, and now his gods are Rossetti, Hunt and Millais—to whose elbows more power! I don't know whether you are an admirer of the school— perhaps not. I confess I rather am, and think they have begun at the right end. The said Master Val, commonly called Buzz by reason of his hair which is this sort of thing [a scribble follows], has made most satisfactory progress, and has distinguished himself by painting a picture at Oxford fourteen feet long with figures ten feet high—a muffin!

This picture at Oxford was one of the murals painted in the Union by a team of artists (including Roddy Stanhope) under the direction of Rossetti and Morris. Val, described by du Maurier in 1861 as a 'tender rollicking Hercules . . . six foot one, twenty-three years of age, not an ounce of fat but weighs sixteen stone six, was the original of Taffy in *Trilby*. He became an A.R.A. in 1878 and an

R.A. sixteen years later; but it was Watts's opinion (he was writing in 1885) that Val, in spite of his 'unusual abilities . . . let slip his best opportunities from indifference and idleness.'[1]

Arthur, with his mop of fair hair and his deceptive expression of gentle wistfulness, was clearly Watts's favourite. In the winter of 1855–56 the painter took the 'boy of fifteen, full of spirits and fun, and needing some handling',[2] with him to Paris, where they found a studio in the Latin Quarter. Unlike the teenagers of today, Arthur was longing to be rid of his girlish locks; but Watts bribed him to retain them while he made several drawings which were later to serve him for his 'Sir Galahad', 'Aspiration', 'Hyperion' and 'Una and the Red Cross Knight'. The full-face drawing used for 'Aspiration' was subsequently borrowed by Holman Hunt for his 'Christ among the Doctors'. It has often been stated that Ellen Terry was the model for 'Sir Galahad', but the existence of the drawing of Arthur proves this to be untrue.[3] We can only conclude that Watts found this particular type attractive in both sexes.

The Hollands were in Paris at the time, and it was partly at their suggestion that the visit had been made. Doubtless it was they, too, who arranged for Watts to paint portraits of M. Thiers, Prince Jerome Bonaparte, and Princess Lieven. But how, one may wonder, did poor Arthur pass the long days while Watts was tied to his easel? His French, in spite of French grandmother, was presumably minimal, and probably he had no one of his own age to go about with. Further, Watts was far from well for much of the time, and this boisterous youngster often got on his nerves. Many years later, Arthur told Mary Watts that Watts's 'If you do that I shall have a headache' was all that was necessary to reduce him to silence.

[1] Whistler wrote a very feeble Limerick about Val Prinsep:

> There is a creator named God
> Whose doings are sometimes quite odd,
>   He made a painter named Val,
>   And I say—and I shall—
> That he does no great credit to God.

This is quoted by William S. Baring-Gould in his *The Lure of the Limerick* (Rupert Hart-Davis, 1968), who failed to identify 'Val'.

[2] Mary Watts, *Annals*. Arthur became sixteen in January 1856 while they were in Paris.

[3] Nor, as is often alleged, was the picture painted to illustrate Tennyson's poem, which Watts had not yet read (MS. note in the Watts Gallery archives).

Only one of Watts's letters from Paris survives; it was addressed to a new friend, Jeanie Senior,[1] to whom, over the years, he was often to pour out his heart. She became his safety-valve; and perhaps he was hers too, for Ellen Twisleton describes Mr Senior as 'an intelligent, active-minded, talkable person, but not one of the souls that Nature tried her finest touches on. At the bottom of everything there is a little coarse commonplaceness about him, such as you like to shake hands with at arm's length.' Watts tells Jeanie that he is always grateful for her affection and kindness, but is doubly so when he is ill, as he is at the moment: 'Every day I feel more and more the truth spoken in the beginning of things, "It is not good for a man to be alone". Every day I conclude more and more that life cannot be a pleasure to me—that it is better to die than to live . . . You think me better than the generality of persons; it is simply that I am less interested, looking forward to nothing! I have neither vanity, ambition nor religion—at least in the ordinary acceptation . . . Poor Arthur must find me a sorry companion for his youth . . .'

But poor Arthur's youth was almost over. Before the year 1856 had run its course he had shorn off his locks, entered the Bengal Cavalry and sailed for India, where he joined his eldest brother and was just in time to become involved in the Mutiny. Sara Prinsep was in an agony of mind; but both her sons survived (though Arthur was wounded), and both were decorated. Probably few of those who admired Millais's 'Bubbles' on the walls of the Royal Academy in 1886 saw in the child who posed for it a future admiral; and perhaps not many of those Etonians who pass Watts's 'Sir Galahad'[2] as they enter their Chapel are aware that this epicene youth, so unmilitary-looking in spite of his armour, ended a distinguished career as a Lieutenant-General in Probyn's Horse. In fact, a certain Head Master of Eton who long clung tenaciously to the Ellen Terry theory, when finally convinced that it was untenable hazarded the guess that Arthur's regiment must have been the Middlesex.

Lastly there was the Prinseps' only daughter, Alice—youngest of the brood—married first, at the age of seventeen, to Charles Gurney

[1] The wife of Mr Nassau Senior and sister of Tom Hughes, the author of *Tom Brown's School Days*. She became the first woman Inspector of Workhouses in 1873, and died in 1877 at a comparatively early age.
[2] This version was painted in 1897—thirty-five years after the first, which is now in the Fogg Art Museum, Cambridge, Mass.

خَيْرُ الْكَلَامِ مَا قَلَّ وَدَلَّ

April 5. 1865

Little Holland House

Dear Lady Lothian

I send you the head of Lord Shrewsbury which ought to have been sent long ago. I have often thought of you in Scotland with an extra shiver during the bitter winter, I hope you & Lord Lothian have succeeded in weathering it

I have seen Lord Clanwilliam several times he has given me news of you, but I should like to be honoured with some from yourself.

Poor Lord Clanwilliam finds it difficult to shake off the effects of his attack. I am afraid he is

An example of Watts's writing. The letter refers to the portrait of Lady Lothian's father, Lord Shrewsbury, reproduced as Plate IV. The Arabic tag, which is printed embossed in blue, reads, 'The best sentence is one that is brief and to the point'— sound advice which Watts took all too rarely. Perhaps the writing-paper belonged to Thoby Prinsep, for Watts often drew on his official 'India Office' stationery.

and soon 'to achieve the dubious distinction of being one of the scores of young married women with whom the Prince of Wales was closely associated'. This dubious distinction was also to be achieved in due course by her younger daughter, Rachel.[1]

The visit to Paris was not the only foreign journey made by Watts in the fifties. In the autumn of 1853 he had gone to Italy for a few weeks with Henry Prinsep and Roddy, now seeing Padua and Venice for the first time. Of his travelling companions he tells us nothing; but he wrote ecstatically to Ruskin about Titian and Giorgione, and elsewhere of the 'glories of that Golden House, the Cathedral of St Mark's—more, to my thinking (no critic as I am), like a house not made with hands than anything I ever saw.' The Giottos at Padua, so 'Pheidian', were an almost greater revelation, and he accepted Haydon's wild surmise that 'some wandering artist had made [Giotto] acquainted with either some fragments or drawings from the Panathenaic procession'.[2]

A second and more adventurous journey was made in the autumn of 1856. After his return from France that February Watts had continued ill for much of the spring and summer, and Dr Gully strongly urged him to accept an offer from the distinguished Greek archaeologist, (Sir) Charles Newton, to join the staff of an expedition he was directing to excavate at Budrun in Asia Minor. Watts, accompanied by Val and Roddy, sailed in mid-October in the steam corvette H.M.S. *Gorgon*, and was away for eight months.

Watts had known Newton for some years, and in 1852 the latter, at that time Vice-Consul at Mitylene, had written to him:

Why are you not here? If you could but see my cave by the sea-shore where I lie all through a summer's day and read Shelley, all nature shut out by the overhanging rock except one blue bit of the Mediterranean which comes in little summer waves plashing at my feet! All through my siesta I hear the monotonous murmur which has continued to lull weary mortals to sleep since the time when in these islands was the cradle of Greek civilisation. I am getting very fond of the place; it would suit you exactly . . . I

[1] Rachel Gurney married the second Earl of Dudley, son of the Lord Ward previously mentioned.
[2] A fuller account of Watts's impressions of Venice and Padua will be found in Mary Watts's *Annals*, vol. I, pp. 144–50.

feel that the landscape before my eyes is the landscape which Homer saw and has described in his similes, and which Pheidias turned into beautiful impersonations in sculpture . . . When will you come out to me?

Watts had been sorely tempted; but four years were to pass before he finally succumbed to the call of the sirens.

Life on board the *Gorgon* was enjoyable—so long as the sea remained smooth and his migraines left him in peace. At first he was lucky; but in mid-Mediterranean, he told Jeanie Senior, they struck a 'most tremendous storm which kept us knocking about outside Malta for nearly two days and nights. I have been very ill indeed—a wretched creature; I shall never be fit for anything. I pine dreadfully for some tender mind and hand; it is not good for man to be alone'; by 'alone' he meant, of course, without some female ministering angel at his constant beck and call. After picking up Newton at Smyrna they sailed south to Budrun, to take part in the excavation of the great Mausoleum—one of the Seven Wonders of the Ancient World—erected in the middle of the fourth century B.C. by Artemisia in honour of her late husband (and, incidentally, brother) King Mausolus of Caria.

Newton, an officer in the Royal Engineers and four Sappers encamped on shore; but Watts, his friends and the staff remained on board, where Christmas was celebrated in the traditional English manner with the crew 'dancing and making merry'. There was a ship's concert, too, at which Watts (nicknamed 'Betty' by all on board) sang 'Tom Bowling' with such effect, wrote Mary Watts, 'as to reduce the bluejackets to tears'.[1] How gladly would we exchange a whole acre of Watts's allegorical vapourings for one or two witty pen-and-ink sketches '*à la* Dicky Doyle' of Watts and those one hundred and fifty tear-drenched tars, or indeed all his self-pitying letters to Jeanie, for a racy account, in the manner of Kinglake's *Eothen*, of the events of that long winter in the Levant!

Newton was particularly anxious to carry away with him some lions' heads—'Greek, and of the school of Scopas'—that he had discovered the previous year built into the walls of a medieval tower by the Knights Templar. For this a firman was necessary, and he therefore despatched Watts to Constantinople to ask the help of

[1] Mr Gladstone used to score similar triumphs with 'The Campdown Races'.

Lord Stratford de Redcliffe, the British Ambassador to the Porte, in obtaining one. The Turks created innumerable obstacles and delays; but these gave Watts the chance to get to know the city, and to paint two portraits (one not completed until many years later) of Lord Stratford, whom he described as the most indiscreet public figure who ever sat to him. Watts was also able to cruise briefly in H.M.S. *Swallow* among the Greek islands and to visit Athens. It was Lord Lyons, acting as Commander-in-Chief of the Mediterranean Fleet, who arranged this VIP treatment for the artist, to whom he 'playfully said, "I put you in command" '. Watts, in return, painted two portraits of him.

The delaying tactics of the Porte had been carefully calculated, but Watts arrived with the firman just in time to prevent the lions' heads being carried off by the Turks in a caique. On New Year's Day 1857, after some exploratory digs, the excavation of the principal site was begun, and the magnificent results of Newton's work here and elsewhere in the Levant are now in the British Museum, where in 1861 he became its first Keeper of Greek and Roman Antiquities. Newton makes no mention of Watts, Val or Roddy in his published account of the excavations at Budrun. Perhaps he came to regret having invited them, though (according to Hugh Macmillan) all reports confirm that Watts was the life and soul of the party, 'being full of spirit and enthusiasm, not unmixed with the saving grace of a quiet and genial humour'. And one would have thought that Val at least would have earned his keep by helping to shift the larger stones. Heaven knows what Watts did all day, for his total haul at Budrun seems to have been a couple of harmless little landscapes and one or two portrait studies. However, the impressions that he received that winter were to bear fruit later in such paintings as 'The Genius of Greek Poetry', 'The Island of Cos', and 'other works of imaginative beauty'.

Watts, wrote Mary Watts, 'was much attracted by the men of the place. The Dragoman, with his good looks and Eastern gift of good manners—"such a gentleman", as Signor used to say—sat to him for studies more than once.' Watts was also, he told her, greatly impressed by the fact that Moslems did not smoke between sunrise and sunset during *Ramadan*, although the Prophet had been in no position to prohibit a pleasure not as yet invented; an earnest Roman Catholic convert, on the other hand, who happened later to

be sitting to Watts during Lent, remarked as he lit his pipe how
glad he was that tobacco had not been discovered when the fast was
instituted. It is, perhaps, worth mentioning that Watts was not at
Budrun during *Ramadan*, which in 1857 fell in June.

Watts and his two companions sailed for home in May in a man-
of-war, leaving Newton behind to continue his work. Watts was as
melancholy as ever; from Smyrna he wrote to Jeanie, 'My last regret
will be that I have no child; yet God knows that it is not a subject for
regret unless it would have been very different from me . . . How
happy could I have been out here! What sights! What glories!
Sweet nature I adore; but still there was something wanted, something more than sky and cloud and sea and mountain could afford: a
society, friendship and love, "divinely bestowed upon man".' The
mood of gloom and self-pity continued after his return. 'What is the
use of life?' he wrote. 'At least, what's the use of mine, with a
second-rate intellect and no stamina at all!' Autumn came, and he
would like to 'settle down in some nice warm place for the two
worst months [of the winter] in the house of some professor of
music and do nothing from morning to night but strum away on
the piano . . .'

But that would hardly have helped, and perhaps it was now that
Watts first clearly understood that what he really needed was a wife.
If so, it was to take him another four or five years to acquire—the
wrong one!

9

THREE ACRES AND A BRUSH

IT MIGHT at first seem that the fifties could hardly have been for Watts a time of much artistic productivity. There was the ceaseless *va-et-vient* at Little Holland House; there were his three trips abroad, and then there were his recurrent bouts of illness and melancholia. Moreover, the Prinseps had now taken to spending several months every winter with a widowed sister of Thoby's at Esher, and Watts usually went with them. Here he hunted on his filly, 'Undine', with the Surrey Union Foxhounds or the duc d'Aumale's Harriers,[1] fraternised with the Orléans princes, held forth to all who would listen on the 'brutal fashion of docking horses . . . a disgrace to our civilisation,' and, according to Thoby, did little else beyond 'laying in a stock of health and fresh air for the coming year's work'. So it is surprising to find Mary Watts listing, in her very far from complete manuscript catalogue of her husband's pictures, more than fifty portraits painted during this decade, and still more surprising to learn that his major activity was not portraiture but a series of enormous murals in the Hall of Lincoln's Inn, at the Somers' town house (7 Carlton House Terrace), and at Bowood—Lord Lansdowne's country house in Wiltshire.

It was Jesse Collings, the enthusiastic advocate of land reform, who was to coin the slogan 'three acres and a cow'; Watts cried out for three acres (of wall space) and a brush. As Roddy wrote, 'He has taken up a crusade against bare walls, and intends painting everything that comes his way'. His decorations in Chesterfield Street and at Little Holland House had merely been intended to keep his hand in while he looked around for a suitable wall and a well-

[1] The duc d'Aumale, inviting him to hunt, writes, 'Cher Monsieur—Aimez-vous toujours l'air de la campagne and a good ride across the country? . . .'

disposed patron. He was not demanding, for he was prepared to do the work for no more than his expenses; and after all, if the worst came to the worst, a mural could always be painted over. Many years later, William Morris, hearing that 'that fellow Watts' (with whom he had by then quarrelled) had been 'daubing over' the walls of some old house or other, remarked acidly to Wilfrid Scawen Blunt[1] that 'a coat of whitewash would soon set that right'.

The new Hall at Lincoln's Inn, built by Philip Hardwick in the forties in the 'collegiate gothic' style, had a wall forty-five feet wide and forty feet high that was simply crying out for a mural; in June 1852, therefore, Watts seized his quill and addressed one of his typically grandiloquent letters to the Benchers. It begins, 'Believing that no man of liberal education denies or undervalues the importance of art, at once the test and record of civilisation . . .', and after a good deal more in this vein concluded with the plain offer to paint in fresco, in return for the cost of his materials, 'any part or the whole of the Hall'. The offer was accepted and work begun in the following year; but since Watts could use the Hall only when the courts were not sitting, and since he was also intermittently ill (and even apparently idle: Roddy wrote that he and Val Prinsep had at times to *force* him to work), it was not until 1859 that the fresco was finished.

The subject chosen—and in choosing it he was no doubt also recalling Delaroche's mural in Paris—was 'Justice: a Hemicycle of Lawgivers'; it was carried out in true fresco—that is to say, in tempera colours with egg medium on the fresh plaster. The design, which was unashamedly based on Raphael's 'School of Athens' in the Vatican and suffers from the comparison, includes more than thirty gaily-attired heroic figures, presided over by Truth, Mercy and Justice, subfusely semi-draped. Studies of various friends were used for the Lawgivers:—Val Prinsep (Servius), Thoby Prinsep (a Druid), Holman Hunt (King Ina), Charles Newton (Edward I), Roddy Stanhope (Solon), Lady Lilford (Alfred), Tennyson (Minos), Sir William Harcourt (Justinian), Sophia Dalrymple (Theodora), and Lord Lawrence and Edward Armitage (Barons).

[1] Poet, traveller and anti-imperialist, and a cousin of the author. When sitting to Watts in 1899 he boldly announced that he would sooner be painted by him than by Rembrandt.

It was Watts's intention that his painting should 'pervade, so to speak, the building like a strain of Handel's music, becoming one with the architecture'; this it certainly does. He once spoke of it as 'perhaps the best thing I have done or am ever likely to do', yet on another occasion he termed it a failure—not 'a disgraceful or a mean failure; but it is a failure'. In general, however, it was warmly acclaimed, and even Rossetti was this time enthusiastic. *The Times* was appreciative, and also published a long letter from Sir Henry Layard in which he 'even ventured to say' that the 'upper line of seated figures will bear comparison with the greatest works of the old masters'. He admitted that the painting was not wholly free from faults; nor were Raphael's frescoes in the Vatican, in one of which 'an angel may be detected with three legs and an apostle with six fingers'. But trifling blemishes of this kind could not, he maintained, impair the overall greatness of the achievement of either artist.

The Benchers, whose patience had been tried by the innumerable delays (for which Watts had duly apologised), were also well satisfied. They entertained the artist to a dinner—'an honour', observed *The Times*, 'before conferred on no other painter except Hogarth, who dined there in the year 1750'—and presented him with a purse containing five hundred pounds, and an ornate silver-gilt cup which after Watts's death was returned by his widow to the Benchers. But fresco is no medium for the English climate; almost before the dinner had been digested the Lawgivers began to deteriorate, and in 1882 the art critic of *The Times* described the colour as 'sombre to the verge of dirtiness' and the general effect as 'far from cheering'. By 1890 its condition was such that Professor Church was called in to deal with it. Other restorations followed, and one weary restorer calculated that in the course of his labours he had ascended and descended ladders to the equivalent of twice the height of Everest. Today the gloom still prevails. The fresco is so withdrawn, that it may well be doubted whether many Benchers even remember that it is there, while still fewer look up from their soup to seek inspiration from this *magnum opus* of England's Raphael.

The murals for Lord Somers in Carlton House Terrace were carried out in the mid-fifties, at those times when the Hall at Lincoln's Inn was inaccessible.

Watts's first idea had been to use designs of his talented friend

Louisa, Marchioness of Waterford, 'and paint them on a scale in accordance with their grand character, thinking them greater than any things that have been produced since the time of Michel Angelo. It will gratify me much to make an offering of that amount of labour which a lady cannot undertake . . .'.[1] However, in the event he used his own, taking for his theme 'The Elements' and turning to Greek mythology to illustrate it; some at least of the nine designs are associated with his never-realised 'House of Life'. The influence is for the most part Venetian, one figure in the largest of the paintings (which is more than twenty feet long) being clearly based on Titian's Bacchus in his 'Bacchus and Ariadne'; but Michelangelo is there also (in a quite unintentionally indelicate male nude), together with much that is pure Watts at his best. The colour throughout is rich and splendid.

Considering how important these frescoes are, it is strange that there is only a brief mention of them in the *Annals*, and even less in Watts's correspondence. One letter to Jeanie Senior survives, in which, as he is needing a model for a limb, he reminds her of her promise 'to lend me your hair . . . and a hand or an arm occasionally', since he finds himself obliged to call upon his friends 'for whatever they can with a perfect sense of propriety contribute'; but that is all. Young George du Maurier who dined (in evening clothes borrowed from Whistler) with the Somers' in Carlton House Terrace on 9 April 1862, does not even mention the frescoes, being more concerned with his host and hostess:

Milor [he wrote to his mother] is a jolly sort of little fellow with a squeaky voice; Miladi very handsome woman; but she and all the women were *décolletées* in a beastly fashion—damn the aristocratic standard of fashion; nothing will ever make me think it right or decent that I should see a lady's armpit flesh folds when I am speaking to her . . . Nobody tried to be swell except an imperious old maid Miss Duff Gordon . . . Jolly Mrs Prinsep drove me nearly home though quite out of her way; so droll—she and Dicky Doyle in the back seat, Val Prinsep and I on the other smoking two enormous cigars we had stolen from Milor . . . I'm

[1] Undated letter to Lady Somers. Impressive murals by Lady Waterford, painted between 1861 and 1882, may be seen at Lady Waterford Hall, Ford, Northumberland.

getting amazingly fond of Mrs. P who seems to be getting deuced fond of me . . .

In 1927 the Duke of Marlborough, then the occupant of the house, drew the attention of the Crown Estate Commissioners to five of the frescoes—all that were at that time visible.[1] Sir Charles Holmes, Director of the National Gallery, examined them and pronounced them to be 'among the artist's very finest works . . . constituting one of the most important surviving records of English work in the grand style'. Some restoration was then carried out by Professor Tristram. In 1936, while the house was occupied by the German Embassy, Ribbentrop reported to the Commissioners the discovery of four further frescoes that at some time or other had been boarded over. In 1966, when the house and its neighbours, which had also been a part of the Embassy, were being reconstructed internally to make a new headquarters for the Royal Society, the frescoes were condemned; they were therefore removed from the walls in small sections and stored in cases, at a cost to the Commissioners of over £5,000. One alone was spared: of two life-sized figures not apparently associated with the 'Elements' series; this has now been transferred to the wall of the staircase at 13 Carlton House Terrace, the head-quarters of the Commissioners. The remainder languished—and it looked like being for ever—in a warehouse in northern England. But now, as already mentioned, comes the welcome news that they are about to be installed in Eastnor Castle.[2] No more appropriate home could have been found for them.

Lord Lansdowne was an old friend of the Hollands, and in 1858 Watts agreed to paint two frescoes for him at Bowood. The first illustrates an episode from the *Iliad*: Achilles watching Briseis being led away from his tent by the messengers of Agamemnon; it was carried out very rapidly, Watts sometimes working twelve hours a day if the weather prevented him from riding over the Wiltshire downs. Various members of the house-party were pressed into service as models; Virginia Somers posed for Briseis, and Janet Ross (Georgy and Alice Duff Gordon's sixteen-year-old niece) recalls that

[1] Evelyn Waugh, after dining with the Duchess of Marlborough in June 1930, wrote, 'Sat next to Edith Sitwell. The dining room was full of ghastly frescoes by G. F. Watts. Edith said she thought they were by Lady Lavery.'
[2] see p. 23.

she 'stood for Petroclus, dressed up in a magnificent suit of armour, which hurt my shoulders. As a recompense, "Signor" gave me the study of my head.'[1] When the present Lord Lansdowne demolished the Victorian wings at Bowood he offered this fine eighteen-foot-long fresco to the Trustees of the Watts Gallery, and with the assistance of the National Art-Collections Fund it was transferred in six pieces to Compton.

A long letter to Jeanie, written by Watts from Bowood in 1858, survives. She had presumably asked him to recommend an artist to design a stained glass window, for he replies, 'There is at this moment staying at L.H.H. with Val the very man you want—Jones by name: a real genius! really a genius!' It was Rossetti who had first brought Ned Burne-Jones to Little Holland House. 'One day,' Burne-Jones wrote, 'Gabriel took me out in a cab—it was a day he was rich, so we went in a handsome, and we drove and drove until I thought we should arrive at the setting sun—and he said, "You must know these people, Ned; you will see a painter there—paints a queer sort of pictures, about God and Creation". So it was he took me to Little Holland House.'

After the recommendation of Burne-Jones, Watts's letter breaks off abruptly in the middle of a sentence, then continues on a new sheet:

I was obliged to tear off the half sheet, for coming back from my ride and sitting down to finish my letter, by degrees such a fit of the blues came over me that I wrote things I should be sorry for you or anyone else to see. The misery and despondency that often fall upon me make my life a burden. I am constantly so nervous that I am afraid almost of mounting the stairs and really quite alarmed at the idea of getting on my horse. Then it is I feel the horror of being alone, yet the dread of seeing anyone . . .

He found, however, some consolation in the fact that King Alfred— 'great, good, dear Alfred!'—suffered in the same way.

It was in part his health, in part the necessity to paint a few portraits to make a little money, and in part the urgent call of the Benchers at Lincoln's Inn to complete the fresco there, that delayed for a couple of years the execution of the companion picture at Bowood. Perhaps Watts had by then become disillusioned about the use of fresco in England, for he now chose to work in oils on canvas.

[1] *The Fourth Generation* by Janet Ross.

Presumably Lord Lansdowne had chosen the subject—Coriolanus allowing himself to be persuaded by his family to abandon his attack on Rome—for Watts wrote that it was 'impossible to invest the figure of Coriolanus with dignity, since indecision is not noble, and the space does not lend itself to picturesque general treatment which might compensate for want of grandeur.' The painting was carried out in the summer of 1860, but was later damaged beyond repair in a flood; about thirty years ago, however, four fragments of the full-sized cartoon turned up in a furniture dealer's shop in Woking, and in 1969 these were acquired by the Watts Gallery. Smaller sketches for both murals are also extant.

Lastly there were the portraits. Among the finest of those painted in the fifties must be counted that of Mrs George Cavendish-Bentinck and her children; of Mary Fox, the seven-year-old adopted daughter of the still childless Hollands, later Princess Liechtenstein, with her immense dog; of Jeanie Senior[1] and Mrs Louis Huth—both life-sized and splendid; and two of Panizzi, the Librarian of the British Museum. Two portraits—those of Mrs Hughes (Jeanie's mother) and Aileen Spring Rice—show Watts as a potential Pre-Raphaelite. Various Pattles and Ionides also sat, and there is an interesting though unsuccessful self-portrait in a red robe. Both Gladstone and Tennyson posed twice, and the latter again on several subsequent occasions; these were among the earliest of those portraits which were to constitute Watts's 'House of Fame', his invaluable record of the great men of the second half of the nineteenth century.

It was also in the fifties that Watts first met 'a delightful young painter' just back from Rome with his 'Cimabue's Madonna' for exhibition at the Royal Academy of 1855. This was the brilliant twenty-five-year-old Frederic Leighton with whom he was to enjoy 'forty years of unbroken friendship, and of whom he was once modestly to say, 'Nature got tired when she was in the middle of making me, left off, and went away and made a Leighton.' Each admired in the other the qualities that he himself lacked, and when the latter died in 1896 Watts said, 'Half my life is gone with Leighton.'

[1] Exhibited at the R.A. in 1858, together with two other portraits, under the pseudonym 'F. W. George'—'owing to a sort of curiosity to see whether his manner was recognisable or not' (*Annals*). Of course it was.

10

A CRAZY MARRIAGE

MOST MEN, by the time they have reached their middle forties, are either married or have decided to remain single for life. Some, it is true, succumb in late middle or old age to a marriage of convenience which may be little more than the acquisition of a nurse-companion-housekeeper who cannot easily give notice, and Watts's second marriage was to be of this kind. But in the early eighteen-sixties Watts was a man who had tasted loneliness to the dregs; a man who, though living surrounded by friends who watched over his health and catered for his every need, knew that there was still something lacking. He knew that he needed a wife. 'I think nature intended me to shine under similar circumstances,' he wrote to Tom Taylor (of whom more in a moment) when congratulating him in 1861 on the birth of a 'bouncing boy'. But Georgy had eluded him and Virginia Pattle had married another; where was he to turn?

The story of the marriage of this 'middle-aged, lukewarm gentleman'[1] to the sixteen-year-old actress Ellen ('Nellie' or 'Nell') Terry has been told a hundred times in 'ways ranging from cautious suppression to garrulous mendacity'; she herself said that she had never troubled to contradict inaccuracies 'so manifestly absurd'. Her own brief account in *The Story of My Life* is unbiased and, though incomplete and in places contradicted by what she wrote elsewhere, is of great value and not intentionally misleading; and recently our knowledge has been extended by the researches of David Loshak and Roger Manvell.[2]

[1] Bernard Shaw's description of Watts at the time of his marriage to Ellen.
[2] See the Bibliography. I acknowledge with gratitude the use I have made in this chapter of Mr Manvell's book and Mr Loshak's article.

The legend, widely disseminated, is roughly as follows. Mrs Prinsep, deciding that marriage was the only cure for Watts's unhappiness, conspired with Tom Taylor to marry Watts to a very promising young actress named Kate Terry. Kate was therefore carefully briefed and then despatched to Little Holland House, where Watts was to paint her portrait, fall in love with her, and propose. However, it was not for Kate that Watts fell, but for her younger sister, Ellen, who had accompanied her in the role of chaperon. Much of this has now been shown to be untrue.

It was certainly Tom Taylor who was responsible for bringing the two Terry girls to Little Holland House. Watts had known him for many years, and had often visited him and his warm-hearted but rather formidable wife, Laura, at Lavender Sweep, their home in Wandsworth. Taylor, who was exactly the same age as Watts, was brilliant, versatile, and a tornado of energy: at one time or another a Fellow of Trinity College, Cambridge; a barrister of the Inner Temple; Secretary to the Board of Health, and Professor of English Literature at London University; a playwright, author and critic; and finally the Editor of *Punch*. Chapman describes him as a 'short little man with small lensed spectacles, rather like Mr Pickwick', whose eyes 'would gleam kindly from behind them at the guests seated at his hospitable table. He still wore breeches and a long coat of velveteen and continued to do so long after they had gone out of fashion. Taylor knew everybody, was kind to everybody who needed help, and Lavender Sweep became a pleasant bourgeois refuge for artists in difficulties or actresses in need of advice . . .'

It was probably in the spring of 1862, the year that Watts was painting his first big 'Sir Galahad', that Taylor introduced the two Terry girls to the artist. They were the eldest daughters of the vast family of Ben and Sarah Terry, and like their parents they were already on the stage; Kate was at this time eighteen, her sister three years younger, and it is alleged that Watts had already seen Kate in some production or other. Taylor seems to have had no ulterior motive in effecting this introduction; the girls were extremely pretty, and he thought he would be doing a friendly turn to both parties by bringing them together for the purpose of a double portrait. 'The Sisters' was in fact painted, though never completed, and now belongs to the Hon. Mrs Hervey-Bathurst.[1] It is a charming work in

[1] Though Mrs Hervey-Bathurst is the daughter of the 6th Lord Somers, she is

which it is not difficult to see that for the artist Ellen was the principal attraction.

In fact, so far from the match being the result of a Prinsep-Taylor conspiracy, it would appear that Watts himself was the promoter of it; for in a letter written some time in 1862 to his confidant, Lady Constance Leslie, he tells her that he is 'determined to remove the youngest [i.e. the younger of these two Miss Terrys] from the temptation and abominations of the stage, give her an education and if she continues to have the affection she now feels for me, marry her.' He is also said to have added, 'To make the poor child what I wish her to be will take a long time and most likely cost a great deal of trouble, and I shall want the sympathy of all my friends.' He was clearly enlisting Lady Constance's support should the dragon of Little Holland House, Sara Prinsep, raise objections to her protégé marrying an actress. According to Roddy Stanhope, there was at some time or other the possibility of adoption rather than marriage. Watts said to a friend, 'I am thinking of adopting Ellen Terry; what do you think of this?' 'I think she is too old.' Later Watts reverted to the subject. 'I have thought over your advice and I am thinking of marrying Ellen Terry—what do you say?' 'I think she is too young.'[1]

The marriage took place at St Barnabas' Church, Kensington, on 20 February 1864; the bridegroom was nearly forty-seven, the bride a week short of her seventeenth birthday.[2] In spite of the disparity of age, Nell was 'delighted, and my parents were delighted . . . It all seemed like a dream—not a clear dream, but a fitful one which in the morning one tries in vain to tell.' But Lady Constance, as she watched the slow and ponderous progress of the 'atrabilious' bridegroom up the aisle and the 'radiant child bride dancing up it on winged feet', trembled for what might lie in store for them. Another Ruskin and Effie?

The day of my wedding [wrote Nell] it was very cold. Like most

---

not descended from Virginia Pattle (Countess Somers) but from the eldest Pattle daughter, Adeline Mackenzie.

[1] Mrs A. M. W. Stirling, *Life's Little Day*. An obvious slip has been corrected.
[2] For some unaccountable reason Ellen went through life under the impression that she was a year younger than she actually was, and it is often stated that she was only *fifteen* at the time of her marriage.

women I always remember what I was wearing on the important occasions of my life. On that day I wore a brown silk gown which had been designed by Holman Hunt, and a quilted white bonnet with a sprig of orange-blossom, and I was wrapped in a beautiful Indian shawl. I 'went away' in a sealskin jacket with coral buttons, and a little sealskin cap. I cried a good deal, and Mr Watts said, 'Don't cry. It makes your nose swell.' The day I left home to be married, I 'tubbed' all my little brothers and sisters and washed their fair hair.

Aladdin entering the magic cave can hardly have been more astonished than was Nell when for the first time she set foot in Little Holland House. 'It seemed to me a paradise,' she wrote, 'where only beautiful things were allowed to come. All the women were graceful, and all the men were gifted.' Till then she had known little beyond her squalid home knee-deep in little squalling Terrys, a succession of hideous theatrical lodging-houses in provincial cities, and an equal number of drab dressing-rooms in provincial theatres; even the Taylors' bourgeois comfort at Lavender Sweep, even the fashionable Mayfair drawing-rooms where she sometimes performed, had not satisfied her thirst for beauty. Only at the house in Bristol of her friend Edward Godwin, the architect, had she seen beautiful things. Now, at Little Holland House, she had found them in still greater measure; but that she might one day become a part of them can never at first have crossed her mind.

Then there was that angel of light, Mrs Prinsep—not yet revealed in her true colours—and the constant ebb and flow of her innumerable sisters and their innumerable famous friends. Mrs Prinsep was known as 'Dash', Lady Somers as 'Beauty', and Mrs Cameron as 'Talent'. But above all there was Watts, godlike, closeted in his big studio beyond the red-baize-covered door and surrounded by his glowing canvases. One day, perhaps when Kate was out of the room, he kissed her . . .

More than thirty years later, Nell wrote to Bernard Shaw:

I'll never forget my first kiss. I made myself such a donkey over it, and always laugh now when I remember. Mr Watts kissed me in the studio one day, but sweetly and gently, all tenderness and kindness, and then I was what they call 'engaged' to him and all the rest of it, and my people hated it,[1] and I was in Heaven for I knew I was to live with those pictures. 'Always' I thought, and to sit to that gentle Mr W. and clean his brushes, and play my idiotic piano to him, and sit with him there in wonderland (the studio).

Then I got ill and had to stay at Little Holland House—and then—he kissed me—*differently*—not much differently but a little, and I told no one for a fortnight, but when I was alone with Mother one day she looked so pretty and sad and kind, I told her —what do you think I told the poor darling? I told her I *must* be married to him *now* because I was going to have a baby!!!! and she believed me!! Oh, I tell you I thought I knew everything then, but I was nearly 16 [sic] years old then—I was *sure* THAT kiss meant giving me a baby!

Was the short-lived marriage ever in fact consummated? Chapman boldly asserts that it was not, Loshak no less boldly that it was —and unreasonably rebukes Chapman with a 'how can he possibly know this?' It has also been suggested—again without a shred of real evidence—that Watts was impotent. Though gossip once circulated that on her wedding night Nell was found weeping bitterly on the stairs outside the nuptial bedroom, all speculation is vain; their secret has gone down with them into the grave.[2]

Little Holland House was an early example of communal living. Pattles and miscellaneous lame ducks came when they liked and stayed as long as they liked; two of Sara's grandchildren, Laura and Rachel Gurney, made it their home when the Gurney Bank failed, and an orphaned great-niece, Blanche Clogstoun, was later to live there and to become Watts's legally adopted ward.[3] So it had been ordained by Sara, and very likely with the approval of both Watts and Ellen, that the newly-married couple would live at Little Holland House. Watts had little money, and lacked the desire, as also

[1] But in her autobiography she wrote that her parents were 'delighted'.
[2] In a letter to the author (6 January 1964) Mr Chapman stated that his evidence was based on 'a completely private conversation which was repeated to me. I cannot at present give the source.' If the evidence was derived, either directly or indirectly, from Mary Watts, I am not prepared to accept it without confirmation.
[3] Mary Watts says that the ten-year-old child immediately 'made her way to Signor's side, found him to her liking, jumped upon his knee, and so into his heart.'

at this time the guile, to commercialise his talent; and Ellen would of course be quite incapable at first of running a house, of coping with her husband's odd diet, his migraines and his melancholy. But not long after the wedding, Watts, Ellen and the Prinseps went to the Isle of Wight to stay for some weeks with the Camerons at Dimbola, their house at Freshwater; the visit may have been envisaged as a kind of honeymoon under suitable surveillance.

Dimbola—named after one of the estates which the Camerons had bought in Ceylon—was at that time acquiring (wrote Loshak) 'the character of a Little Holland House-on-Sea'. Charles Cameron had retired in 1848 after a distinguished legal career in India and returned to England with his wife, Julia—the second, the plain, but by far the most remarkable of the seven Pattle sisters—who in middle age had recently embarked upon the photography that was to make her name immortal; she deserves, and in due course shall have, the best part of a chapter to herself. Nell was of course obliged to pose for her—and no doubt many times; one portrait, made in the bathroom of the Camerons' near neighbours at Farringford, the Tennysons, is among the loveliest of all her wonderful photographs.

To her surprise, Nell found that the Laureate was gentle, paternal and not in the least alarming:

> The first time I saw him he was sitting at the table in his library, and Mrs Tennyson, her very slender hands hidden by thick gloves, was standing on a step-ladder handing him down some books. She was very frail, and looked like a faint tea-rose. After that one time I only remember her lying on a sofa.
>
> In the evenings I went walking with Tennyson over the fields, and he would point out to me the differences in the flight of different birds . . . He taught me to recognise the barks of trees and to call wild flowers by their names. He picked me the first bit of pimpernel I ever noticed. Always I was quite at ease with him. He was so wonderfully simple.

Many years later she recalled the hat that she wore at the time—'a brown straw mushroom with a dull red feather round it. It was tied under my chin, and I still had my hair down.' No doubt it was Mrs Prinsep, jealous perhaps of those lovely golden tresses, who soon ordained that they should be gathered up and pinned.

And then sometimes Tennyson would recite—Browning's 'How

I. *The Wounded Heron*, 1837
Shown at the Summer Exhibition of the Royal Academy in 1837, when Watts
was twenty

IIa. *Freshwater in Spring*, 1874
A view from the house which Watts built for the Prinseps at Freshwater, in the
Isle of Wight, when (old) Little Holland House was demolished

IIb. *A Story from Boccaccio* (detail), 1845/46
The largest and most important of the paintings made by Watts in Italy.
(For the whole design see Plate 2c)

III. *Choosing* (Ellen Terry), 1864
Ellen, wearing the brown silk wedding-dress designed for her by Holman Hunt,
trying to decide between the rival merits of a showy, scentless camellia and the
humble but fragrant violets held close to her heart

IV. *Lord Shrewsbury*, 1862
This portrait of the 18th Earl of Shrewsbury is said to have been painted at
Blickling Hall at a single sitting to give Louisa, Lady Waterford the pleasure of
seeing paint handled 'with absolute directness'

V. *The Cedar Tree*, 1868/69
Mary Prinsep, Thoby Prinsep's niece, with her dog in the garden of (old) Little
Holland House. Watts gave the picture to her and her husband, Andrew Hichens,
for their silver wedding, November 10th 1899

VI. *The Recording Angel*,
1888 and later
Watts kept this sketch alw
beside him in his studio

VII. *Mother and Child*, 1903/04
Painted by Watts at the age of eighty-six. In his treatment of the child the artist
seems almost to anticipate the 'shelter' drawings of Henry Moore

VIII. The Watts Mortuary Chapel, Compton
Designed by Mary Watts and carried out from 1896 onwards by her and the
villagers of Compton

they brought the Good News from Ghent to Aix' as well as his own poems, making the words of the former 'come out sharply like hoofs upon a road. It was a little comic until one got used to it, but that fault lay in the ear of the hearer.'

But fortunately for Nell, there was also youth at hand:

At Freshwater I was still so young that I preferred playing Indians and Knights of the Round Table with Tennyson's sons, Hallam and Lionel, and the young Camerons, to sitting indoors noticing what the poet did and said. I was mighty proud when I learned how to prepare his daily pipe for him. It was a long church-warden, and he liked the stem to be steeped in a solution of sal volatile, or something of that kind, so that it did not stick to his lips. But he and the others seemed to me very old. There were my young knights waiting for me; and jumping gates, climbing trees, and running paper-chases are pleasant when one is young.

Not a word, it should be noticed, about her husband, who was no doubt lumped anonymously with those others who seemed so 'very old', for later she described him as 'old for his age, . . . nervous about his health and always teetering about in galoshes.'

Back at Little Holland House the trouble—the inevitable trouble—began almost immediately. 'I was so ignorant and young,' she wrote later, 'and he was so impatient.'

Sara Prinsep, too, who had seemed so charming as a friend, now assumed the more menacing role of a kind of resident mother-in-law. When distinguished visitors called, wrote Nell, 'I sat, shrinking and timid, in a corner—the girl-wife of a famous painter. I was, if I was anything at all, more of a curiosity, a side-show than hostess.' She soon realised that the part allotted to her for the present in the tragi-comedy of Little Holland House was a vegetable one: she was to be a lily, silent, beautiful and immobile until such time as Sara had completed her education, moulded her to her satisfaction and rendered her fit to join in cultured conversation with the members of her coterie. Did Shaw ever think of her when he was writing his *Pygmalion*?

And thus, at first, she sat—a dumb but shrewd observer of the great who came and went. There was Gladstone—'like a suppressed volcano. His face was pale and calm, but the calm was the grey crust of Etna. To look into the piercing dark eyes was like having a glimpse into the red-hot crater beneath.' There was Disraeli, wearing a daringly bright blue tie and looking 'the great Jew before everything. But "there is the noble Jew", as George Meredith writes somewhere, "as well as the bestial Gentile".' He so fascinated her that later she one day deliberately bumped into him in Piccadilly—'it was a *very little* bump! My elbow touched his, and I trembled. He took off his hat, muttered, "I beg your pardon", and passed on, not recognising me, of course . . . His straggling curls shook as he walked.' There was Browning, too, 'with his carefully brushed hat, smart coat, and fine society manners,' the man 'far more incomprehensible than his poetry'.

And then, of course, there was Watts, and perhaps she was happiest when posing for the countless paintings and drawings that he now made of her. 'Choosing', in which she is wearing her weddingdress, shows her trying to decide between the rival merits of a showy, scentless camellia, and the humble but fragrant violets in her hand; it is one of the loveliest things he ever painted, and hardly inferior, though less well known, is the eager portrait of her now in the National Portrait Gallery. She posed for him, hour after weary hour but uncomplaining because she knew that she was playing a part in the creation of beauty; 'I was happy,' she wrote, 'because my face was the type which the great artist who married me loved to paint.' She posed as Ophelia—prophetically, for it was a role that she was to play in Irving's production of *Hamlet* at the Lyceum season of 1878–79. She posed in dreadfully heavy armour for 'The Watchman'—'a sad face in steel armour' someone called it—till finally she fainted and fell forward against the arm of the painter, who had been too pre-occupied with the picture to give a thought for the model; and to this day there remains the dab of carmine that his brush involuntarily made on the canvas. In 1880, that grand climacteric year which so often reawakens bittersweet memories of the past, Watts made a replica of this picture, unsuccessfully reworked his 'Ophelia', and at about the same time sent Nell the portrait of her that now belongs to the nation.

After the breakdown of his marriage Watts destroyed many of his portraits of Ellen. Even 'Choosing' narrowly escaped the holocaust, as Mrs Marion Rawson relates:[1]

[1] In a letter to the author, 4 May 1974.

My grandfather [Mr Eustace Smith] saw the painting on one of his visits to Watts' studio, and at once asked if he could buy it. Watts agreed, and my grandfather took out his cheque book and paid for it, but Watts asked if he might keep the picture for a time—probably because he wanted to send it to the forthcoming Royal Academy Exhibition. Some time later my grandfather received a note from Watts saying he wished to withdraw the picture from his agreement to sell it, and intimating that Ellen had left him and that he was destroying all the paintings and studies he had made of her. My grandfather ordered up his carriage and hurried round to Little Holland House to claim the picture as rightfully his. Watts was naturally forced to accede to his request and to relinquish it.

Sara Prinsep had been under the delusion that Ellen would be as clay in her hands: a gentle child as eager to learn as to obey; she was soon to discover her mistake. Neither she, however, nor any of the others of her coterie then had the least idea that in Ellen was a potential genius that was one day to make her as famous as the beloved painter himself.

It could only be a matter of time before Ellen asserted herself, and Mrs Stirling is our authority for, though not an eye-witness of an ominous scene which took place at the house of her uncle and aunt, Roddy and Lilla Spencer-Stanhope, at Cobham. Not long after its return from Freshwater, the Prinsep-Watts caravan had migrated to Thoby's sister at Esher, and from there a contingent had gone over to lunch at Cobham:

My aunt [wrote Mrs Stirling] described Ellen as strikingly lovely, with brilliant eyes and very beautiful hair, but quite a schoolgirl and a decided tomboy. After luncheon, while my uncle and Watts paced to and fro in the garden talking, my aunt remained with Mrs Prinsep and Ellen in the drawing-room. Suddenly the latter, with an air of supreme boredom, leant back over the arm of the chair in which she was seated, and, shaking her head to and fro, loosened the pins from her hair which tumbled about her shoulders like a cloak of shining gold.

My aunt could only gaze in delight at the beauty of the girl as she sat there swaying her head gently from side to side while the mass of shimmering hair shrouded her and swept the floor. But Mrs Prinsep was horrified. 'Ellen! Ellen!' she cried, 'put your hair up instantly.' And Ellen, flashing a wrathful glance at her tormentor, grasped the waving mass of gold, coiled it carelessly upon her head, and, stabbing it with pins, sat there looking lovelier than ever, a petulant, scolded child.

It is clear, from a letter written by Lady Lothian[1] to Watts on 21 September 1864, that already within seven months of his marriage there was serious trouble between husband and wife. Presumably Lady Lothian, a very close friend of Watts, had heard a rumour that all was not well, and by a tactful letter had elicited the *cri de coeur* that provoked the following reply:

Newbattle Abbey, Dalkeith

Dear Mr Watts,

I cannot say how touched I feel at your writing to me as you have done. I only regret if my importunity was the cause of your writing what was painful to you. I feel glad tho' that if what is painful exists you cd so far honour us with so much confidence about it. I feel so deeply sorry that I cannot be of any help or use to you, for perhaps friends like myself and my sisters might have helped to soothe away any excitement and win confidence more than much older and more sensible people. I felt from the first to warm to Mrs Watts, from hearing the story of her attraction and affection, and do trust that where there is warmth of heart and such great youth that the good and the steadiness may predominate some day and that comfort may grow out of it again.

Of course I speak in the dark and only generally, but I think I have seen that the first year of marriage is sometimes a trying one. People often have not quite [come] to understand each other at first and they grow in time to know each other's ways. In your case perhaps this would be more likely than with anybody as your own way of life has been rather an exceptional one, and so perhaps has hers. Forgive me, if I am saying anything impertinent or foolish. I think I seldom felt so sorry or so much touched as I did by your letter today. I hope you will let me write again to you sometimes. In our very quiet life it is most pleasant to have a talk with those we are not likely to see much. I shd not expect an

[1] Constance, second of the four daughters of Lord Shrewsbury.

answer always but I shd like to know sometimes if you have any thoughts in your head for pictures, or about books.

Yours most truly

C. H. Lothian

Ld. L wrote of course before your letter came.

When, how, and by whom the decision was finally taken that Watts and Nell should part is not known for certain, though there is no lack of gossip. According to Lady (Lucie) Duff-Gordon,[1] there was a scandal when Nell, who had gone to visit her old friend Edward Godwin (whose mistress she later became), found him very ill and innocently stayed the night to look after him. She alleges that Ellen herself told her this, and that the charitable act had led to an unjust accusation of infidelity; but Lady Duff-Gordon is demonstrably unreliable in other matters, and for various reasons it is very doubtful whether Godwin could have been the person involved in whatever took place. According to another account, an undisclosed incident, said to have been discreditable to Watts and to have been 'hushed up by the Little Holland House court', precipitated the separation. Possibly the two accounts refer to the same episode.

Edith Craig and Christopher St John[2] provide a more melodramatic dénouement in which the high-spirited girl, provoked beyond endurance, played to perfection the role of the *enfant terrible*. One evening, when the Prinseps were entertaining some of their distinguished guests to dinner, Ellen suddenly 'bounded into the room . . . dressed as Cupid (Cupids in those days were dressed, not undressed).' According to Ronald Chapman (who does not give his source), 'In the nineties the incident was pleasingly embellished by the wits and prudes into Nell appearing naked from her bedroom and dancing on the dinner table before an assembly of confused and astonished bishops.' It sounds a little too good to be true.

At all events, by the end of the year it had become obvious to everybody concerned that what Nell calls 'the natural, almost inevitable catastrophe' could not long be postponed. She spent Christmas with her parents but without her husband, and Lewis

---

[1] *Discretions and Indiscretions*, New York, 1932. Lady Duff-Gordon, in spite of her hyphen, was a connection by marriage of Georgy's. She is best known as 'Lucile', the dressmaker.

[2] *Ellen Terry's Memoirs*, edited by E. Craig and C. St John, Gollancz, 1933.

Carroll, who came to the house and met her for the first time, thought that her gaiety was 'partly assumed'. No doubt it was: five weeks later, on 26 January 1865, a deed of separation was drawn up. Watts was to pay Ellen £300 annually 'so long as she shall lead a chaste life . . . unless he shall be prevented by permanent ill health from following his profession of an artist'; but if she returned to the stage the sum was to be reduced to £200. Other financial conditions were laid down in the event of Watts predeceasing her. They were not legally divorced until 1877.

It may not have been Mrs Prinsep who brought about the marriage, but Roddy Stanhope was indubitably right in maintaining that it was she who wrecked it: 'She never ceased to treat Ellen as a naughty child who must be scolded and made obedient, and a high-spirited, unconventional girl naturally resented this treatment, while Watts, absorbed in his art, was little aware of the mischief which was preparing.' So Mrs Stirling; and Ellen herself was later to write to a friend, referring undoubtedly to Mrs Prinsep though she mentions no name, 'God forgive her, for I *can not* . . . What have I done that she should use me so!'

Ellen frankly confessed that when her new life, which she 'worshipped because of its beauty', suddenly came to an end, she was

thunderstruck, and refused at first to consent to the separation, which was arranged for me in much the same way as my marriage had been. The whole thing was managed by those kind friends whose chief business in life seems to be the care of others. I don't blame them. There are cases where no one is to blame . . . There were no vulgar accusations on either side, and the words I read in the deed of separation, 'incompatibility of temper'—a mere legal phrase—*more* than covered the ground. Truer still would have been 'incompatibility of *occupation*', and the interference of well-meaning friends . . .

'The marriage was not a happy one', they will probably say after my death, and I forestall them by saying that in many ways it was very happy indeed. What bitterness there was effaced itself in a very remarkable way.

So Nell, 'miserable, indignant, unable to understand that there could be any justice in what had happened', went back to the dreary overcrowded house in Stanhope Street to which a tenth and eleventh (and mercifully the last) Terry infant had meanwhile been added:

> I hated going back to live at home [she wrote]. Mother furnished a room for me, and I thought the furniture hideous. Poor mother! For years Beethoven always reminded me of mending stockings, because I used to struggle with the large holes in my brothers' stockings upstairs in that ugly room, while downstairs Kate played the 'Moonlight Sonata' . . . This was the period when I hated my life, hated every one and everything in the world more than at any time before or since.

What, apart from mending stockings, poor Nell did for the next two years it is not easy to say. She visited old friends, especially the Taylors. Laura Taylor 'had rather a hard outside . . . and I was often frightened out of my life by her; yet I adored her.' There was a short trip to Paris at Easter 1866 with an unspecified 'friend' (Godwin?), and she appeared on 20 June in Sheridan Knowle's *The Hunchback* in a benefit performance for her sister, Kate; but it was not until 1867 that she made her full return to the stage. While she had been with Watts she had 'never had one single pang of regret for the theatre. This may do me no credit, but it is *true*'; and even now she was 'practically *driven* back by those who meant to be kind—Tom Taylor, my father and mother, and others. *They* looked ahead and saw clearly it was for my good. It *was* a good thing, but at the time I hated it.'

In the summer of 1868, after a single and far from successful season, Nell suddenly again abandoned the stage to set up house with Godwin, now a widower, in darkest Hertfordshire. This 'living in sin' led to a break with her family and in due course to the birth of two children, Edy and Teddy. For a time she was blissfully happy; but by 1873 she and Godwin, as the result of his neglect of her, were gradually beginning to drift apart. Godwin was also soon in financial difficulties, the house mortgaged and the bailiffs at the door; when, therefore, Nell received a tempting offer to return to the stage, she felt that for the sake of the two children she could not afford to refuse.

It was a chance meeting with her old friend Charles Reade, novelist and dramatist, the author of *The Cloister and the Hearth,* that brought about this invitation. Reade admired Nell greatly but saw her clearly, and in his notebooks there is a description of her appearance and character as a young woman that cannot be bettered:

> Ellen Terry is an enigma. Her eyes are pale, her nose rather long, her mouth nothing in particular. Complexion a delicate brick-dust, her hair rather like tow. Yet somehow she is *beautiful*. Her expression *kills* any pretty face you see beside her. Her figure is lean and bony; her hand masculine in size and form. Yet she is a pattern of fawn-like grace. Whether in movement or repose, grace pervades the hussy.

Her character he described as 'soft and yielding on the surface, egotistical below. *Varia et mutabilis*, always wanting something "dreadful bad" today, which she does not want tomorrow, especially if you are weak enough to give it her, or get it her. Hysterical, sentimental, hard as a nail in money matters, but velvet on the surface. A creature born to please and to deceive. *Enfant gâtée, et enfant terrible*.' Later he admitted that this judgment had been made 'while she was under the influence of ——. Since then, greatly improved; the hardness below is melting away. In good hands a very amiable creature but dangerous to the young. Downright fascinating. Even I, who look coldly on from senile heights, am delighted by her.'

So Nell went back to the stage; the great romance of her life was over, and after so many false starts her triumphant career as an actress was about to begin. Godwin and Nell parted finally in November 1875, and two months later he married a young girl named Beatrice Phillips, who after his death in 1886 became the wife of James McNeill Whistler.

'I saw Mr Watts but once face to face after the separation,' wrote Ellen. 'We met in the street at Brighton, and he told me that I had grown!' This was probably in 1872; and about ten years later, when she happened to be visiting the house[1] next to that in which he was then living, he saw her through the hedge. He had always had a nagging conscience over the way he had treated her, and he now wrote asking her to forgive him—or, as he put it, to shake hands with him in spirit: 'What success I may have will be very incom-

[1] No doubt Mrs Barrington's.

plete and unsatisfactory if you cannot do what I have long been hesitating to ask. If you cannot, keep silent. If you can, one word, "Yes," will be enough. I answered simply, "Yes." '

They continued to correspond until 1886 when, no doubt as the result of Watts's marriage to Mary Fraser-Tytler, the letters suddenly ceased. But a single page of a letter from Ellen to Lady Constance Leslie, undated but written not earlier than 1889, tells that she still thought of him:

> Now this is *very* private. See Mr W. (the dear Signor) for me, and say, he, from first to last, has been a beautiful influence in my life, and that I pray God bless him. She too I bless for going into his life and cheering it. I have always had a great desire to tell her so, but feared it might not have been seemly in her eyes.

We may safely assume that the second Mrs Watts, jealous by nature, would not have welcomed the blessing of her predecessor. Indeed, in her thousand-page three-decker biography of her husband the whole episode of Watts's first marriage is dismissed in a single though not unfriendly sentence: 'To what is well known I wish to add nothing; all who have heard his name know also that a beautiful young girl who, with her yet undeveloped genius, was later to fascinate and delight thousands of her generation, came into his life, that they were married in February 1864, and were parted in June [sic] 1865, and, excepting for the accident of one chance meeting in the streets of Brighton, never met again, the marriage being dissolved in 1877.'

In the spring of 1865, after Nell had passed out of Watts's life, the daily round was resumed at Little Holland House. But it was no longer quite the same, for some of the coterie, rightly blaming Sara Prinsep for much of what had happened, now stayed away. Then came a further blow: in 1867 Kate Terry left the stage to marry a very rich and cultured silk mercer, Arthur Lewis, who had established at Moray Lodge, just round the corner from Little Holland House, a rival and glittering salon which soon attracted Leighton, Millais, Tom Taylor and others of Sara's circle as well as the cream of high society. Of one of Lewis's parties in 1863 George du Maurier had written to a friend, 'His evenings are getting more and more gorgeous; half the peerage will be there tonight and very likely the Prince of Wales'.

A decade passed, and in 1876 Watts filed his petition for divorce, citing Godwin as co-respondent. If Watts is to be believed, the Godwin affair must have been discreetly kept from him, for he stated that it was 'only just before instituting the case' that he had learned of it. Had Nell, we may wonder, been continuing all these years to receive the alimony to which she was entitled only so long as she remained 'chaste'?

Watts's evidence for the divorce proceedings, which was first published by Loshak, reads in part:

That although considerably older than his intended wife he admired her very much and hoped to influence, guide and cultivate a very artistic and peculiar nature and to remove an impulsive girl from the dangers and temptations of the stage . . .

That the conditions of his life were perfectly well known and entirely acquiesced in by the Respondent before his marriage and it was understood that nothing was to be changed.

That very soon after his marriage he found out how great an error he had made. Linked to a most *restless and impetuous* nature accustomed from the very earliest childhood to the Stage and forming her ideas of life from the exaggerated romance of sensational plays, from whose acquired habits a quiet life was intolerable and even impossible, demands were made upon him he could not meet without giving up all the professional aims his life had been devoted to.

That he did not impute any immorality at that time but there was an insane excitability indulging in the wildest suspicions, accusations and denunciations driving him to the verge of desperation and separation became absolutely necessary unless he gave up his professional pursuits which was out of the question as he had no independent means and it was arranged by his friends and those of his wife that a separation should take place. That separation took place within a year of his marriage.

That he was willing to take all the blame upon himself (excepting of course charges of immorality if any had been made against him but none were made and there could have been no sort of foundation for them).

That the matter pained him very much and that he refused to go into Society altogether and gave himself up entirely to study and close pursuit of his profession.

A decree nisi was granted in March 1877 and made absolute on 6 November. A fortnight later Nell married Charles Wardell, an actor who used the stage name of Charles Kelly. This must surely establish beyond all reasonable doubt that it was Nell who, with a second marriage already in mind, took the initiative by providing Watts with the evidence which led to the institution of the divorce proceedings. What prompted Watts to act (for at this time he had of course no thought of marrying again) were a rather guilty conscience, genuine compassion, and enough money for what was in those days an expensive business. So, after thirteen years, came the legal end of a marriage which had irretrievably broken down in a matter of months.

Godwin, when registering the birth of his son Teddy, had facetiously entered the mother as 'Eleanor Alice Godwin, formerly Watkins'; but on her marriage to Charles her two children adopted the name of Wardell. During a visit to Scotland, however, she had seen the rock called Ailsa Craig and had been so struck by the theatrical potentials of the name that in 1887 (two years after Wardell's death), when Edy and Teddy were baptised and confirmed, they formally became Edith Geraldene Ailsa Craig and Edward Henry Gordon Craig.

The valuable and entertaining *Memories and Reflections* of Lady (Laura) Troubridge, the elder of the two Gurney girls previously mentioned, provides a tail-piece for this chapter. In the early 1880s, when she was in her teens, Laura was taken on a number of occasions by her grandmother, Sara Prinsep, to see Ellen Terry in her seasons with Irving at the Lyceum. Sara used to apply direct to Ellen for a box for the first night, and a ticket would arrive with a friendly message. Then, after the fall of the final curtain, came the eagerly-awaited visit to Ellen in her dressing-room. 'In spite of everything,' Lady Troubridge wrote, 'or rather perhaps, *because* of the past, Ellen and my grandmother remained friends to the day of her death.'[1]

[1] Sara Prinsep died in 1887.

'Remained friends'? This cannot be credited. One can only conclude that when the famous theatrical partnership of Ellen and Irving made Ellen the greatest and the best-loved actress of her generation, Sara found it convenient to invoke their former friendship, and that Ellen, generous always, did not repel her advances.

11

FRESHWATER: LARGELY A DIGRESSION[1]

IT MAY be remembered that the Prinseps' lease of Little Holland House, signed in December 1850, was for twenty-one years; in 1867, therefore, when Watts wanted to build an additional studio in which to carry out a piece of sculpture that had just been commissioned,[2] he asked Lady Holland (since the death of her husband in 1859 the owner of the property) if the lease could be extended for a further ten years. Lord Holland had had a sentimental affection for the old dower house, saying that he could never bring himself to demolish it; when, therefore, Augusta pooh-pooh'd the idea that any legal agreement was necessary, Watts, too trusting, went ahead with the building.

Augusta had always been extravagant—besides Holland House she had a house in central London and apartments in Paris and Naples—and before long she was forced to recognise the unpalatable fact that she was no more enormously rich, merely rich. Then the dowry that she had to provide on the marriage in 1872 of her adopted daughter, Mary Fox, together with a loss incurred upon the death a year later of her brother, further reduced her income by some £3,000 a year. After taking legal advice and consulting her friend Edward Cheney, she agreed to save the estate as a whole by selling the reversion of it at her death to a third cousin of her late husband's, the Earl of Ilchester. She herself was thus able to live on in the big house, but some of the land that lay at a discreet distance

---

[1] This chapter owes much to the books by Virginia Woolf and Helmut Gernsheim listed in the Bibliography. Brian Hill's admirable *Julia Margaret Cameron and her Sisters* (Peter Owen, 1973) appeared only after I had written my rough draft, but I then consulted it with profit.

[2] The Thomas Cholmondeley memorial (see p. 190).

from it was to be disposed of for development. This included the site of Little Holland House, a building now found by Cheney to be so 'discreditable and ugly that nothing can be worse' and condemned to be demolished. The Prinseps, who since 1871 had been occupying it on an annual lease, were politely but firmly told to go.

It was a severe blow, and Watts in particular, who had spent a good deal of his own money on building his studio, was justifiably indignant; some unpleasantness ensued which of course made him ill. When he heard that Augusta had received an offer of about £40,000 for the Little Holland House site, he informed her that he withdrew any suggestion that might 'interfere with her prudential arrangements', and that so far as he was concerned Little Holland House had in the long term 'practically ceased to exist'. He added that he was now doomed to waste much valuable time painting portraits in order to raise enough money to build elsewhere.

Apparently he had foreseen the possibility of trouble, for he had already, at Tennyson's suggestion, bought a plot of land near his friend's house at Freshwater, in the Isle of Wight, where the air (wrote the poet) was 'worth sixpence a pint'. The Prinseps had lost money through the failure of the Ceylon coffee crops, and it was now Watts's turn to repay many years of hospitality by making a new home for them and for himself. But in order to have a London house he also rented from Val Prinsep a part of some land in Holland Park Road on which his friend had built. In due course there arose a new Little Holland House,[1] approached from the recently-constructed Melbury Road, which added yet another to what it pleased Lady Holland to call those 'dreadful houses' at the bottom of her garden. These became the nucleus of a colony of successful Victorian academicians.

The Briary at Freshwater—'a three-storied building in red and white, half villa, half cottage, yet wholly delightful'—was designed by Philip Webb and provided with two large studios; it was completed by the end of 1873. Work on 6 Melbury Road (designed by Frederick Cockerell) was, however, so much delayed by the 'drunkenness, idleness and dishonesty' of the builders that it was not ready

[1] Writing to Gladstone in May 1876, Watts said that it was 'about a hundred yards beyond the old place and is the only house finished on the new road'. All references to Little Holland House after 1876 are to 6 Melbury Road, which in spite of many protests was demolished in 1965.

until February 1876; therefore until demolition began, Watts continued to work when in London at old Little Holland House. Thoby Prinsep, now over eighty, marked the gift of a painting of his much-loved home by some well-turned if conventional verses:

Where now five villas their broad fronts present
And to the world are offered at a rent,
Stood heretofore a nest of gables, built
Each to supply a want as it was felt;
And shaded lawns, mown carefully and rolled,
Provided pastime for the young and old;
Here grew to manhood youths of honoured name,
And here their mentor *Watts* achieved his fame . . .

The poem concludes with a reference to an inscription which was perhaps placed on one or more of the new houses:

In lasting memory of days so dear
A friendly hand has placed these tablets here:
We greet the vision and suppress the tear.

Watts, the Prinseps and their *protégées* were installed in the Briary by the spring of 1874, but Watts had to continue to spend about half his time in London to be within reach of his sitters. The Camerons had been at nearby Dimbola since 1860, and the Tennysons at Farringford, ten minutes' walk down an elm-shaded lane, since the early fifties. 'It was a splendid exclusive society which circled more or less round Tennyson', wrote Sir Edmund Gosse. 'They lived in a radiance of mutual admiration. Mrs Cameron saw them in a sort of vision "standing in a circle in the High Hall, singing with splendid voices". ' Such distinguished residents invariably made Freshwater a place of cultural pilgrimage: 'Is there *nobody* here who is commonplace?' a commonplace visitor once sadly inquired. Perhaps not; but a writer who compared Freshwater to Athens in the time of Pericles was surely guilty of some exaggeration.[1]

Freshwater was still remote. The railway had not yet reached it,

[1] In 1923 Virginia Woolf wrote a short play, *Freshwater*, dealing with the remarkable fauna of that village in the 1870s; Duncan Grant took the part of Watts, Virginia's sister Vanessa Bell that of their great-aunt Mrs Cameron, in a unique amateur performance of a revised version of it at 8 Fitzroy Street in 1935. The uncontrollable hilarity of the audience brought it to a premature conclusion.

and visitors were conveyed there in a two-horse coach from Yarmouth, where on their return they were directed to the steamer with a cry of 'This way for England!' Tennyson remained, of course, the principal attraction; but Mrs Cameron, the second of the seven Pattle sisters and now in her sixtieth year, was in many ways the most remarkable member of the colony. Mary Watts wrote that she 'baffled description', possessing a double share of all those qualities that made the Pattle family so exceptional—all but the quality of beauty, none of which had come her way; and Watts spoke of her 'noble plainness'. Benjamin Jowett, for whom she built a little cottage nearby, described her as 'a very honest, really kind, enthusiastic person: perhaps she has a tendency to make the house shake the moment she enters, but in this dull world that is a very excusable fault.'

She could also shake chapels, and Thackeray's daughter Anny (Lady Ritchie), whom Mrs Cameron had persuaded to buy a cottage at Freshwater, recalls an embarrassing occasion when she was taken by Mrs Cameron to hear the famous Rev. William Brookfield preach at the Berkeley Chapel, Mayfair:

> Mrs Cameron led the way into the gallery and took up her place in front exactly facing the pulpit. When Mr Brookfield appeared climbing the pulpit stairs to deliver his sermon, his head was so near us that we could have almost touched it. Mrs Cameron chose this moment to lean forward and kiss her hand to him repeatedly. Poor Mr Brookfield sank suddenly down upon his knees and buried his face in the pulpit cushion.

Mrs Cameron was wildly and eccentrically generous. To Tennyson's elder boy, Hallam, when at death's door with congestion of the lungs at Marlborough, she despatched post-haste 'a pair of Oriental loose silk trousers of purple and gold, a dove-coloured jacket, a roll of flannel, two Japanese tea-cups, a hot-water plate and a teapot.' Her friend the poet Sir Henry Taylor, a regular visitor to Dimbola, who with his wife 'suffered the extreme fury of her affection', wrote, 'She keeps showering on us her "barbaric pearls and gold", Indian shawls, turquoise bracelets, inlaid portfolios, ivory elephants.' Nor might gifts be refused. When on one occasion Lady Taylor sent back a particularly valuable shawl, Mrs Cameron sold it and with the proceeds bought an expensive invalid sofa which she presented in

Lady Taylor's name to the Putney Hospital for Incurables.[1] 'Julia is slicing up Ceylon', poor old Cameron would say—half sorrowfully, half admiringly—when he found his wife embarking on yet another extravagance. She ordered every detail of his daily life, and when ill he would meekly submit to her current (and usually nauseous) treatment—at one time 'Ten drops of Jeremie's opiate every morning, a dose of creosote zinc and gum arabic before his meals and a dose of quinine after.'

Mrs Cameron always acted on an impulse. Hearing her husband complain one day that too much of the garden was given over to vegetables, she had a fine lawn laid down overnight by an army of labourers working by the light of lanterns; and on another occasion, to surprise Sir Henry Taylor, she added the day before his arrival a bay-window to the bedroom he was to occupy. There were dances, picnics and excursions at Dimbola, and impromptu plays in a little theatre that she had built. At Dimbola you never knew what was going to happen next, only that Mrs Cameron would be the begetter and stage manager of it.

An observant little girl, her great-niece Laura Gurney, was later to leave a most valuable account of this formidable yet fascinating creature as seen through the eyes of a very sophisticated eight-year-old:

> To me, I frankly own, she appeared as a terrifying elderly woman, short and squat, with none of the Pattle grace and beauty about her, though more than her share of their passionate energy and wilfulness. Dressed in dark clothes, stained with chemicals from her photography (and smelling of them, too), with a plump, eager face and piercing eyes and a voice husky, and a little harsh, yet in some ways compelling and even charming, my first sight of her was in her studio at Dimbola, the little cottage home at Freshwater, about a quarter of a mile from the sea; and immediately we, Rachel [her sister] and I, were pressed into the service of the camera. Our *roles* were no less than those of two of the angels of the Nativity, and to sustain them we were scantily clad, and each had a pair of heavy swan's wings fastened to her narrow

[1] It should be borne in mind that of all the stories about Mrs Cameron endless variants exist.

shoulders, while Aunt Julia, with ungentle hand, touzled our hair
to get rid of its prim nursery look.

No wonder those old photographs of us, leaning over imaginary
ramparts of heaven, look anxious and wistful. This is how we felt,
for we never knew what Aunt Julia was going to do next, nor did
any one else for the matter of that. All we were conscious of was
that once in her clutches we were perfectly helpless. 'Stand
there,' she shouted. And we stood for hours, if necessary, gazing
at the model of the Heavenly Babe (in reality a sleeping child
deposited in a property manger). The parents, anxious and uneasy, were outside, no more able to rescue their infant until Aunt
Julia had finished with it, than we should have been.

Mrs Cameron's brother-in-law, Lord Somers, was, as has already
been said, a keen amateur photographer, and she was probably
already interested in the subject when in 1863 the gift from her
daughter, Julia, of a camera had transformed her whole life. She
was not the kind of woman to do anything by halves, and photography immediately became an obsession. In her *Annals of a Glass
House* she wrote: 'I turned my coal-house into my dark-room, and a
glazed fowl house I had given to my children became my glass
house [i.e. studio]! . . . The society of hens and chickens was soon
changed into that of poets, prophets, painters, and lovely maidens
. . . I worked fruitlessly but not hopelessly . . . I longed to arrest
all the beauty that came before me.'

'Arrest' is the operative word. From her window, which overlooked the path down to the landing-stage of the ferry, Mrs Cameron
would watch for the arrival of photogenic victims, and anyone who
attracted her was immediately pounced on and kidnapped for her by
one of her maids and compelled to pose motionless for what seemed
like hours on end. If the need arose, a model might be subjected to
quite rough treatment; for example, an unfortunate girl chosen to
pose for 'Despair' was locked in a cupboard for a couple of hours in
order that she might acquire a suitable expression. 'Her sitters came
at her summons,' wrote Lady Ritchie. 'They trembled, or would
have trembled, could they have dared, when the round black eye of
the camera was turned upon them. They felt what consequences,
what disastrous waste of time and money and effort might ensue
from any passing quiver of emotion', for in those days Mrs Cameron

had to make her own plates. The very young and the very old appealed to her most; 'No woman,' she once said, 'should ever allow herself to be photographed between the ages of eighteen and eighty.'

Besides those unknown captives unwittingly immortalised by Mrs Cameron there were, of course, the famous who were cajoled or bullied into posing for a House of Fame that was to rival Watts's. Old Sir Henry Taylor, whom she idolized in a manner bordering on the ridiculous and referred to as 'my peculiar friend', was constantly victimised. 'She is a sort of hero-worshipper,' wrote Jowett, 'and the hero is not Mr Tennyson—he only occupies second place— but Henry Taylor.'[1] 'I don't see what you mean by his extraordinary beauty,' Tennyson once cried after he had been subjected to yet another exhausting eulogy of Taylor; 'why, he had a smile like a fish.' 'Only when the Spirit of the Lord moved on the face of the waters, Alfred,' replied Mrs Cameron.

The ordeal of posing for Mrs Cameron as 'Zenobia' was described by 'a lady amateur' in the *Photographic News* for January 1886:

The studio, I remember, was very untidy and very uncomfortable. Mrs Cameron put a crown on my head and posed me as the heroic queen. This was somewhat tedious, but not half so bad as the exposure. Mrs Cameron warned me before it commenced that it would take a long time, adding, with a sort of half groan, that it was the sole difficulty she had to contend with in working with large plates . . . The exposure began. A minute went over and I felt as if I must scream; another minute, and the sensation was as if my eyes were coming out of my head; a third, and the back of my neck appeared to be afflicted with palsy; a fourth, and the crown, which was too large began to slip down my forehead; a fifth—but here I utterly broke down, for Mr Cameron, who was very aged, and had unconquerable fits of hilarity which always came in the wrong places, began to laugh audibly, and this was too much for my self-possession, and I was obliged to join the dear old gentleman . . . When Mrs Cameron, with the assistance of 'Mary'—the beautiful girl who figured in so many pic-

---

[1] Watts said of him that he had 'that directness which sometimes made him say what other people only thought. I remember him saying to poor Lady Lilford after she had been singing and out of tune, "I advise you never to sing".'

tures, and notably in the picture called the 'Madonna'—bore off the gigantic dark slide with the remark that she was afraid I had moved, I was obliged to tell her I was sure I had . . .[1]

The history of this 'Mary' appears to have been as follows. Mrs Cameron, when driving one day on Putney Heath, had been accosted by an Irish beggar-woman and her daughter Mary, a child of about eleven. Struck by the girl's beauty, she took them under her wing and gave them employment, educating Mary with her own sons and then appointing her parlourmaid with subsidiary duties as photographic assistant and model. 'Mary Madonna' (as Mrs Cameron instantly renamed her, since she was destined to pose for religious subjects) proved in every way a treasure. An exhibition of photographs of her was held at Colnaghi's Gallery in Bond Street, with Mary in person in charge of the catalogues. A visitor to the gallery, a rich young bachelor named Henry Cotton, fell not only for the photographs but also for the model, to whom, with Mrs Cameron's blessing and in full knowledge of the girl's history, he was in due course very happily married.

Many photographs of Mary Madonna were included in the albums that Mrs Cameron broadcast among friends and acquaintances both high and low, the Crown Prince of Prussia and her gardener being alike recipients. Watts received one inscribed 'To the Signor to whose generosity I owe the choicest fruits of his immortal genius I offer these my first successes in my mortal but yet *divine* art of Photography'. A particularly sumptuous example was that given to Lady Ritchie, on the first page of which the photographer had written in her big bold hand, '*Fatal* to photographs are cups of tea and coffee, candles and lamps, and children's fingers'.

Tennyson, though a reluctant sitter, was also made to pose innumerable times, his favourite portrait being that which he called the 'dirty monk' and in which he certainly looks not unlike Rasputin. At Tennyson's suggestion Mrs Cameron made a series of illustrations for *The Idylls of the King*, for which all and sundry, including complete strangers, were pressed into service. The Yarmouth porter proved an admirable King Arthur, and his Guinevera, a girl abducted on the beach, was once discovered in a state of com-

[1] See also Lewis Carroll's satirical parody, *Hiawatha's Photographing*, which is reprinted in Brian Hill's *Julia Margaret Cameron*.

plete exhaustion after sprawling for two hours on the floor, clutching his heel and much breathed upon, to illustrate the lines: 'And while she grovell'd at his feet, she felt the King's breath wander o'er her neck . . .' One day when she was with Tennyson in London, Mrs Cameron noticed a young priest previously unknown to her. 'Alfred,' she cried, 'I have found Sir Lancelot!' Tennyson replied, 'I want a face well worn with evil passion.' The priest was the future Cardinal Vaughan.

It was Tennyson who brought Longfellow to the torture-chamber, leaving him there with the words, 'You will have to do whatever she tells you. I will come back soon and see what is left of you.' Rossetti, the bravest man in all England, alone refused to obey her summons, but Browning was another and a terrified victim. Abandoned in a posture of extreme discomfort while the absent-minded photographer went off in search of some missing piece of equipment, he was not remembered and rescued, more dead than alive, until some two hours later.

So keen was Mrs Cameron to photograph Garibaldi, who had come to Farringford to see Tennyson, that she fell on her knees at his feet and, being innocent of Italian, made a gesture of supplication; but Garibaldi, mistaking her for an old beggar-woman who had strayed into his host's garden, brushed her aside. Darwin—the only sitter known to have *paid* for being immortalised—inscribed beneath his portrait, 'I like this photograph very much better than any other which has been taken of me,' and Carlyle commented on his, 'It is as if suddenly the picture began to speak, terrifically ugly and woe-begone, but has something of a likeness; my candid opinion.' As a reward for posing, Mrs Cameron sent him a prayer-book; 'Either the Devil or Julia Cameron must have sent me this,' cried Carlyle when he opened the parcel.

Ruskin, Holman Hunt, Sir John Herschel (the astronomer)[1], Thomas Huxley, Lord Dufferin, Palgrave, Lecky . . . Mrs Cameron's bag was almost as rich and as varied as Watts's. And Watts, too, was of course made to pose often, and often to give artistic advice. His encouragement, she said, gave her 'wings to fly with'. On receiving a batch of her most recent photographs he wrote, 'All the heads are divine, and the plates very nearly perfect; the tone, too, is excellent.

[1] Herschel was the recipient of one of Mrs Cameron's albums. It realised £52,000 at Sotheby's in October 1974.

If you are going on photographing your grandchild, and he is well worth it, do have a little shirt made of some yellowish material; the blot of white spoils the whole picture. What would not do in painting will not do in photography, but otherwise I am delighted with the amount of gradation you have obtained . . .' Beneath one of her photographs he wrote, 'I wish I could paint such a picture as this.'

A final tribute comes from Roger Fry, who wrote almost prophetically in 1926:

> Mrs Cameron's photographs already bid fair to outlive most of the works of the artists who were her contemporaries. One day we may hope that the National Portrait Gallery will be deprived of so large a part of its grant that it will turn to fostering the art of photography and will rely on its results for its records instead of buying acres of canvas covered at great expense by fashionable practitioners in paint.

*   *   *

The veterans of Freshwater were Thoby Prinsep and Charles Cameron, aged (in 1875) eighty-three and eighty respectively; Henry Taylor (who looked a hundred) was in fact only in his mid-seventies, and a frequent visitor (he lived for a part of the year at Bournemouth) rather than a resident; Tennyson was sixty-six and Watts a mere fifty-eight. Tennyson would walk over almost every day from Farringford to chat with Thoby, now half-blind but uncomplaining and still with all his wits about him. Watts was much more attached to Thoby than to Sara—something hardly to be wondered at in view of the part she had played in the breakdown of his marriage. Lady Troubridge wrote that after Thoby's death in 1878 the artist's links with the Briary grew weaker, and it was only his 'chivalrous wish to help and his love for his adopted daughter Blanche' that prevented them from breaking. Moreover, there were by this time in London two very demanding women who were beginning to play a large part in Watts's life: Mrs Russell Barrington and Mary Fraser-Tytler—the future second Mrs Watts.

Charles Cameron, once described by Tennyson as 'a philosopher with his beard dipped in moonlight', had had a very distinguished career. He had become one of the four Members of Council at

Calcutta—a post which made Julia Cameron second only to the wife of the Governor-General in the European society in India. Now a recluse and a good deal of an invalid, he never stirred outside his own garden, where he pottered 'in a picturesque dressing-gown, over the blue and crimson of which his white locks flowed', or his house, in which he might sometimes be heard reciting long passages of Homer. A visitor to Dimbola recalled being taken by Mrs Cameron up to the bedroom to which her husband had escaped for a siesta; 'Behold!' she cried as she flung open the door—'Behold the most beautiful old man on earth!'

Mr Cameron took—was, no doubt, obliged to take—a deep interest in his wife's work. 'My husband,' she wrote, 'from first to last has watched every picture with delight, and it is my daily habit to run to him with every glass upon which a fresh glory is newly stamped, and to listen to his enthusiastic applause. This habit of running into the dining-room with my wet pictures has stained such an immense quantity of table linen with nitrate of silver, indelible stains, that I should have been banished from any less indulgent household.'

But Tennyson of course was, and had long been, the lion and the oracle of Freshwater. He adored his wife, Emily, of whom he said, 'The peace of God came into my life when I married her'; and in a letter to Lord Carlingford, Edward Lear (who, incidentally, could not stand Mrs Cameron and the 'odious incense, palaver and fuss' that surrounded her) wrote: 'I should think, computing moderately, that fifteen angels, several hundreds of ordinary women, many philosophers, a heap of truly wise and kind mothers, three or four minor prophets and a lot of doctors and school-mistresses, might all be boiled down and yet their combined essence fall short of what Emily Tennyson really is . . .'. Though he remained utterly devoted to Emily Tennyson, Lear came eventually to find Tennyson self-centred and tiresome.

Tennyson's grandson, Sir Charles Tennyson, recalls a little episode which illustrates Emily's utter trust in her husband:

I remember when a small boy seeing my grandfather returning, hatted and cloaked from his morning walk, carrying a basket of prismatically-coloured fungi which, in the face of universal protest, he bade be cooked for luncheon. As he ate them in silence, everyone at the table and the servants waiting were in an agony, expecting some awful fate to befall him—everyone, that is to say, except my grandmother at the head of the table. There she sat as ever serene: as ever her faith in the Poet was absolute: if he said Fungi were edible, they were.

At first, Tennyson's 'bad hat and unusual ways' had perplexed the local inhabitants, who maintained that he wrote his poetry while mowing his lawn. But soon he was being consulted by the public on every imaginable subject, 'from a clergyman who had lost his faith, to a father who wanted a name for his new-born child'. Carlyle's famous word-portrait of him as a younger man is as vivid as are the portraits of the bearded Laureate painted by Watts:

> One of the finest-looking men in the world. A great shock of rough, dusky, dark hair; bright, laughing hazel eyes; massive, aquiline face, most massive yet most delicate; of sallow, brown complexion, almost Indian looking; clothes cynically loose, free, and easy; smokes infinite tobacco; his voice is musical, metallic, fit for laughter and piercing wail, and all that may lie between; speech and speculation free and plenteous; I do not meet in these last decades such company over a pipe.

It is impossible to resist quoting, and at some length, from a twenty-page letter which Mrs Cameron had written to her husband as far back as May 1860, for it throws light not only on the writer and on the beauties of Freshwater in spring, but also on the character of Tennyson, with whom she was probably staying while three rose-covered cottages were being united and converted into Dimbola. Mrs Cameron was an indefatigable correspondent. 'She wrote letters till the postman left,' said Virginia Woolf, 'and then she began her postscripts. She sent the gardener after the postman, the gardener's boy after the gardener, the donkey galloping all the way to Yarmouth after the gardener's boy.' The letter in question was destined for Ceylon, where Charles Cameron had gone in the vain hope of getting himself appointed Governor of the island:

Dearest Charles,
    On a day so glorious as the present day all Nature seems to say everything, and to bring to silence one's own powers and make

vain one's own attempts. There is *such* a glory over earth and air and sea and sky and shore, and down, and mead and meadow.

This island might equal your own island [Ceylon] now for a richness of effects. The downs are covered with golden gorse and beneath them the blue hyacinth is so thickly spread that the valleys look as if 'the sky were upbreaking thro' the earth'.[1] The sea on one side is cool and tranquil like a child asleep that *may* awake to cry but sleeps that *all over* sleep which is granted only to the child, and to the sea in a calm. The hedges are green and thick, but alas! the truant boys intrude cruel hands to disturb the young life rejoicing there. The trees too are luxuriant here—far more flourishing than they usually are by the sea—and Alfred Tennyson's wood may satisfy any forester. His place is in perfect beauty, but it does not satisfy him. His prairies are really enamelled with the purple orchis and golden cowslip—the orchis being of that royal rich violet which is the robe of Kings, and the golden cowslip and burnished buttercup bordering this purple with a golden band.

He *sees* the beauty but he *feels* it not. His spirits are low, and his countenance serious and solemn. Every trifle of life disturbs him. The buildings *getting* up are a night mare to him, the work-men *not* getting on are a day vexation to him. His furniture has not come. The sculptures for his hall have miscarried or been de-layed. The tradesmen cheat him. The visitors look at him. Tour-ists seek him. Americans visit him. Ladies pester and pursue him. Enthusiasts dun him for a bit of stone off his gate. These things make life a burden, and his great soul suffers from these [illegible] stings.

What *is* the cure? I believe there is no cure. I believe it is a matter of temperament—of blood and of bile.

A little thing pleases him for a little while. The Prince Consort writes him a very friendly letter, sends the Queen's or his own copy of the Idylls, asks for an autograph! and Alfred meditates seriously and pleasantly on it all, declares he does not know what form of answer to write, and then fashions and frames a *perfect* answer . . . All that he has is so great and grand—if he would only live in his own *divine* powers and not suffer the merest

[1] 'That seem'd the heavens upbreaking thro' the earth.' *Idylls of the King*, Guinevere.

terrestrial trifles to magnify themselves into misfortunes heaped on him . . .

He won't give welcome to the Regts here, or know either their men or their officers. He will be so far kind as to lend his stable to the Major, yet 'can never forgive me' because I introduced him to that same Major who sought an opportunity of thanking him and seeing him.

The *looking* at him would be the most capital offence of all if he were Ruler of the Universe. And yet he is so worth looking at: so grand in form and character, and even in his shrinking there is a sad and serious helplessness—and *no offensiveness*. None is meant, none is conveyed. And just now we have the Brother Poet H[enry] T[aylor], glad to see every one and every one glad to see him—so genial and gentle and generous and good. He delights in his fellow creatures whilst A fears them all. He, Alfred, begs me to conduct him to his gate 'for there is some one coming—!' 'Oh a poor old woman hobbling along,' I tell him. 'Oh is it? I thought it was some fashionably dressed lady', is his answer . . .

His health is much better . . . But still the least variableness of weather produces some oppression on his chest—and nothing but constant smoking keeps it down . . .

Tennyson had a horror of having his privacy disturbed by idly inquisitive tourists, and being very shortsighted once fled before the approach of a flock of sheep (which are, after all, of the same genus). It was, however, one of Mrs Cameron's self-appointed tasks to try to make the great man behave graciously towards those who came in a spirit of genuine hero-worship. Hearing that three American admirers on a pious pilgrimage had found the gates of Farringford bolted and barred against them, she went in search of them, marched them back to the house, forced an entry, and leading them to the very sanctum of the Laureate cried, 'Alfred! These gentlemen have come from afar to see the British *Lion*, and behold a *Bear*!' And no doubt it was she who saw to it that when they came to leave each received a signed copy of the *Idylls*. It was Mrs Cameron, too, who during a smallpox scare forced the reluctant poet to be vaccinated. Tennyson saw her approaching with the doctor and the lymph and took refuge in the tower, from whose foot she continued to cry, 'You are a coward, Alfred, a coward!' until finally he was shamed into descending and submitting.[1] As Watts once told Mrs Tennyson, Mrs Cameron 'delights in a passage of arms'.

Tennyson loved Nature in all her moods and, as his poems show, had an excellent working knowledge of botany, ornithology, geology and astronomy. On stormy nights he would come to Dimbola to collect Mrs Cameron and take her down to the shore, and on a night bright with stars he would climb to the roof of his house, where a special platform had been constructed, to get an uninterrupted view of the sky. He enjoyed walking, and Laura, like poor Nell Watts, was often his companion as he strode vigorously over the downs, his long cloak flapping in the wind, the broad hat on his head, a stick in his hand and his boisterous dogs at his side.

And of course Laura and Blanche were also much in Watts's studio—that haven of peace in a house where crises were endemic:

> Here we were perfectly free and at liberty to do and say what we liked. There were no rules, no regulations, and though 'Signor' . . . had a hot temper, it was not the kind that children dread . . . Signor's wrath was only a passing irritability, harmless as summer lightning. We took all sorts of liberties with him, and looked upon him as a playfellow. Granny occasionally told us he was a great man, and a celebrity, but that conveyed nothing to us, and as he had none of the airs of either, the fact of his genius, if we thought of it at all, seemed like something belonging specially to us. Occasionally, thinking him too modest, we gave him a little encouragement. 'Signor, you paint very well,' said Blanche condescendingly one day, as she watched him put some touches to a now famous picture; and he thanked her with a faint, twinkling smile, for the kind words.
>
> Another day Granny, who could not find us a drawing-master, actually suggested Signor should supply the vacant post; whereat we, who thought we were being in some way defrauded, called out in unison: 'But Granny, Signor can't draw, he can only paint.' However, she persisted, and the drawing lesson took place. As we sat round the table with our drawing-blocks, india-rubbers and sharpened pencils, expectant of being instructed to do trees and cottages and elegant landscapes, Signor merely put a wooden

[1] Tennyson was soon afterwards laid up with a bad leg which he attributed to 'faulty vaccination'.

brick on the table, and said: 'Draw that.' We protested angrily that that was too easy, too simple: 'Any one can draw a silly old brick.' But the odd part was, we none of us could do it.

Blanche, who was now thirteen, and the eight-year-old Laura certainly took liberties with Watts, but he obviously encouraged them. When his friend Rickards, hearing that Blanche was learning the violin, wrote to warn him that a girl of his acquaintance had ruined her health in this way, Watts replied (on 1 August 1875) in a characteristic letter which also throws some light on his Freshwater frolicking:

> I quite agree with you that nothing of the kind should be persisted in if prejudicial to health; but I do not believe that playing the fiddle is so. Joachim and Neruda are splendid specimens of vigour, and I am acquainted with several ladies, some quite young, who learn the fiddle without suffering in consequence. In the case you mention, most likely the child is constitutionally defective; if not, let her wear *no stays*, run, jump, play at cricket with her brothers (if she have any), and otherwise exercise her limbs and lungs. I will answer for the violin being innocent of harm to her.
>
> I encourage Blanche in being (at proper times) a regular tomboy. When I am at Freshwater I am looked upon as the property of the children, and often have to yield, when not much inclined thereto, to earnest petitions to 'come and have a romp' (from Blanche and two other little girls), which means much running up and down stairs, and vigorous exercise of all their swiftness and agility, to avoid sharp cuts from switches, or stings from a bunch of nettles, or good sound thumps not seldom resulting in good honest bruises and considerable contusions which they are most proud of and without the risk of which they don't care to use their best efforts, limbs and lungs and ingenuity exerted. The consequence is that they are straight and strong and may laugh at the dangers of moderate study of any kind . . .

Blanche, it may be mentioned in passing, died in her early thirties, though not of over-indulgence in her fiddle.

A few years later, Watts, in whose bonnet bees steadily swarmed and multiplied as he grew older, wrote an article[1] entitled 'On Taste

[1] Printed in *Annals*, iii, pp. 202–26. It is well worth reading.

in Dress' in which he savagely attacked (amongst other female frailties) the wearing of corsets. This led to his receiving the following delightful letter:

Dear Sir,

A party of girls here in Norwood are trying to get up a society calling itself the Anti-Tight Lacing Society, we have had some meetings etc, but much wish to have a president who will fully sympathise with our object—namely that of showing girls and others round us how wicked and ugly the fashion of tight lacing is . . .

I do not know if you know Norwood—the Crystal Palace etc, but this horrible fashion is most prevalent here. We won't have any old women or 'strong minded' (so-called) females in our committees, for we want those who join to be really good advertisements of *anti* tight-lacing—I am secretary of the society . . .

Please do not refuse your name, as President. Everyone either sneers or laughs at us, but we mean to *try* to do some good, and I hope to get some names to *sign* our petition.

Yours faithfully
Gertie Tippla

So Watts became its President.

But to return to Laura. She was still a child when she found herself one day in Watts's London studio while he was painting Gladstone's portrait. The sitting at an end, the artist asked her what she thought of the picture and received a perhaps unexpectedly frank criticism: 'I think his ear is awful, like a piece of raw beef-steak.' Though he patiently explained to her that this was merely the underpainting and that he would 'make it look real afterwards', she continued to protest so vigorously that with a muttered 'Out of the mouths of babes and sucklings . . .' he altered it far more than he had originally intended.

He would also explain his allegories to the eager child, telling her how Death was 'the gentle bosom where we must all lay our heads at last' and how Hope played on when only a single string remained (and did not thereby damage her health):

Darling Signor! no one had ever talked to me as he did, taking all the big facts of life and dressing them up in rainbow words like

the magical colours on his palette. He taught us values, the beauty
of beauty, the joy of joy, the marvel of heroic deeds. No wonder
we loved him. Even to write of him brings a piercing sweetness.
Yet with all his gentleness, he was impersonal; no one could
boast of being his favourite, though it was understood he loved
Blanche best; but what he loved was the youth in all of us . . .

I can see him now, standing in the quiet studio, a slight figure
in grey, with shirt of silk and pleated frill, and a tie of red ribbon,
thin face and neatly trimmed pointed beard, and his quiet voice
articulating very clearly.

He lived entirely by rule to preserve his delicate health, prac-
tising a strict diet that anticipated many of the *régimes* of the
present day. Revalenta Arabica was, I think, the name of one of
the dishes concocted for him. He got up at three o'clock in
summer, and when the light began in winter, and painted all day
until the light failed. After that novels were read to him, and he
loved to be read or played to; but, except for some writing, he
kept his eyesight solely for his work.

Whereas Freshwater long retained memories of the mighty Laureate
and of the invincible Mrs Cameron, the self-effacing painter was
soon forgotten. There were some who recalled seeing him ride his
favourite thoroughbred to picnic at Swainston, while Tennyson led
the way in his big carriage; some who remembered hearing his vain
attempts to play the piano and the violin; but that is all. After Mrs
Prinsep's death in 1887 the Briary passed to Blanche, by then the
wife of Major Herbert Somers-Cocks, and in May 1890 Watts and
his wife made use of the house in their absence when he went to
Freshwater to paint two further portraits of Tennyson. Of a treasured memory of this visit Mary Watts wrote:

Signor had been at work at Farringford, while Miss Liddell and
I had spent the morning together under a big elm on the Briary
lawn, and when one o'clock came we went to meet the party, as
Lord Tennyson and his son had arranged to walk back with
Signor. We had just climbed the little rise that led to a broad
green glade when the three came in sight, and we both exclaimed! For down the great aisle of elms they came, a white

Russian deer-hound flashing like silver through the sun or shade, and the central figure the poet, a note of black in the midst of the vivid green, grand in the folds of his ample cloak and his face looming grandly from the shadow of the giant hat. 'Monumental' Signor would have called him. The slight stoop and the heavier step of age made the youthful figure of his son look all the more what he was, his father's vigorous staff and prop.

And then our eyes fell upon the delicate grey figure of our beloved painter on the other side, the grey hat crowning silver hair, a grey cloak taking pleasant folds while he stepped like a boy, light and neat in every movement. Lord Tennyson was playful, gave us a smiling greeting, and put out the crook of his walking-stick for us to shake hands with.

It was the last time that the old friends were to meet, for within two years Tennyson was dead.

The fate of the third establishment at Freshwater, that of the Camerons at Dimbola, remains to be told—and like everything associated with Mrs Cameron it was dramatic and improbable. Yet it would seem that it was not she but her husband—the invalid and housebound (or at all events garden-bound) octogenarian—who in the autumn of 1875 suddenly took the wild decision to return to Ceylon to join several of his sons who were looking after the family's coffee plantations there. But Mrs Cameron readily acquiesced: 'Where your heart is,' she told Laura, 'there is your treasure also.'

Mary Fraser-Tytler, a visitor to Freshwater that autumn, has described the events that followed:

> The striking of the tents of the Cameron household was full of characteristic unusualness—Mrs Cameron providing for every contingency possible, to the point of unconscious humour. The house was soon in a state of turmoil, their rooms piled up with packing-cases, while telegrams poured in and out, and friends came in crowds to say their farewell. All Freshwater was wailing! rich and poor . . .

Among the contingencies provided for was death, Mrs Cameron including in her baggage two coffins (filled temporarily with china and glass) to ensure decent burial should she and her husband never return; and possibly the 'unconscious humour' was also supplied by

the cow that led the procession up the gangway when they embarked. Mary was not at Southampton to see them sail; but she was
told that almost the whole of Freshwater was, and that since Mrs
Cameron had by then run out of ready money she was to be seen
showering the porters with large mounted photographs of Carlyle
and Mary Madonna in lieu of tips, saying as she did so, 'Take this
instead as a remembrance!'[1]

The voyage was without incident. From some port of call Mrs
Cameron wrote to Lady Tennyson: 'I need not tell you that amidst
all this bustling world of 380 people, my husband sits in majesty like
a being from another sphere, his white hair shining like the foam of
the sea and his white hands holding on each side his golden chain. A
real gem of the ocean; everything glittered like a fairy world, the
sapphire sea, the pearl-white houses, the emerald and ruby boats,
the shining steps, a hundred and thirty-two in number, from the
Quai to the town—all was delicious'. To mark her gratitude for
their safe arrival at Colombo she collected enough money from the
passengers to purchase a harmonium for the ship's captain. Of course
she had brought her camera with her, and in the *Recollections of a
Happy Life* by Marianne North—a woman in many ways almost as
remarkable as herself, who was at that time painting the flora of
Ceylon—we are able to catch a last and characteristic glimpse of
Mrs Cameron at work. 'She dressed me up in flowing draperies of
cashmere wool,' Miss North wrote, 'let down my hair, and made me
stand with spiky coconut branches running into my head, the
noonday sun's rays dodging my eyes between the leaves as the slight
breeze moved them, and told me to look perfectly natural (with the
thermometer standing at 96°)!'

The coffins had not been brought in vain. Mrs Cameron died in
1879, the splendour of the Ceylon hillsides spread before her eyes,
and the word 'Beautiful!' the last to pass her lips. A year later her
husband followed her to the grave, and that other Dimbola at
Freshwater, once a place of so much wonder, is now in part a sort of
motel.[2]

*   *   *

[1] Can any of these still be hidden away in Hampshire attics? Today they are
worth their weight in gold.
[2] One wing is a private house named 'Cameron'. The Briary was burned down in
1934 but has been rebuilt as a private residence, and Farringford is a hotel

There is today a new tourist attraction at Blackgang in the Isle of Wight: a collection of 'Monster models in woodland surroundings' of dinosaurs and other giants of the remote past. Might not 'Tennyson Down' above Freshwater, where a Celtic cross has been erected, be similarly provided (perhaps by Henry Moore) with bronze figures of Tennyson, Watts, Sir Henry Taylor, Mrs Cameron (with camera and tripod), the Prinseps, and those other giants of yesteryear?

---

where an extra pound a night is added to the bills of those who occupy one of the 'Spacious Tennyson Bedrooms'. *Sic transit!*

12

PATRONAGE, PUBLICITY AND PORNOGRAPHY

THE IONIDES family had been Watts's first patrons, but the greatest single collector of his works was to be a Manchester business man, Charles Rickards. It was Tom Taylor who, in 1865, brought Rickards into Watts's orbit and who aroused the artist's missionary zeal by urging him to 'impregnate' the great barbaric North with good art. Any doubts that Rickards may at first have had as to the artistic respectability of his future *protégé* must have been dispelled when, two years later, Watts was made an A.R.A. and an R.A. in swift succession.

Rickards proved from the first the perfect patron. He had money to burn; he desired the betterment of mankind; he had the rare humility to know that he knew nothing about art, and a commendable desire to learn. First he sat for his portrait, then he allowed himself to be painlessly talked into buying, year by year, not only further portraits but also a fair number of those allegories which had hitherto shown a regrettable tendency to return unsold from the walls of the Royal Academy to the artist's studio. He allowed Watts to dictate the positioning and the lighting of his purchases in rooms Watts had never seen—they were to be hung 'with the light on the spectator's left and not too near the window'—and even acceded to the artist's 'rather bold request' to repaper his walls 'any dark colour, red or green, and no matter how rich'; for pictures, he was informed, 'are expensive luxuries, and a man ought to get all the satisfaction he can out of them'. Indeed, term after term the pupil got such excellent marks for conduct and diligence (and, incidentally, the prompt payment of fees) that by 1871 he was pronounced 'now far enough advanced as an art student to be initiated

142

into the mysteries' of the National Gallery by a personally conducted tour.

It cannot, however, be denied there was an occasion when the
pupil refused to eat out of the Master's hand. Watts had appealed to
him to help raise money for one of his unpractical, idealistic schemes:

> I am sometimes tempted [Watts wrote] to try if I cannot get sub-
> scriptions to carry out a project I have long had, which is to erect
> a great statue to Unknown Worth!—in the words of the eloquent
> author of Felix Holt, 'a monument to the faithful who are not
> famous'. I think this would be a worthy thing to do, and if I had
> not unfortunately neglected opportunities of making money I
> would certainly do it at my own expense. I wonder whether it
> would be possible to get any subscriptions with this object . . .

It was not. But nearly forty years later Watts was to pay a much
more humble tribute (including the bill) to 'the unsung heroes of
everyday life',[1] and one can easily imagine how warmly he would
have approved of the Tomb of the Unknown Soldier in Westminster
Abbey.

In 1877 Watts had been given a room to himself at an exhibition
at the Grosvenor Gallery, and of course his pictures had been seen
almost every year at the summer exhibitions of the Royal Academy;
but so far, although he had always advocated the 'full-scale one-man
show' for the proper appreciation of the work of a living artist, he
had perhaps lacked the opportunity, as he admitted to having lacked
the courage, to expose himself thus to the possible mass hostility of
the critics and the public. In 1880, however, Rickards, who had by
then accumulated nearly sixty of the Master's works which he had
always generously made accessible to the interested, decided to
exhibit his whole collection publicly at the Manchester Institution.

Watts was more alarmed than flattered when he heard of
Rickards's resolve, but he raised no positive objection. He did, however, beg his friend to have the light of the exhibition room lowered
as much as possible—indeed 'the more the better. It requires a
hundred years to bring a picture that aims at grave effects to its
proper tone; until after that lapse of time it should not be exposed
to strong light.'

But the artist need not have been apprehensive about the recep-

---

[1] See p. 218.

tion of his paintings. 'From all quarters,' wrote Rickards after the close of the exhibition, 'I continue to receive account of the educational work they have succeeded in accomplishing.' Watts was, of course, delighted, for it was by his allegories—those works by which he set such store but which nobody except Rickards had shown any eagerness to acquire—that he had apparently touched the allegedly stony hearts of the materialistic Mancunians. The most important result of the exhibition, however, was that it persuaded Sir Coutts Lindsay, owner of the Grosvenor Gallery, to consider the possibility, in the not too remote future, of a London exhibition devoted entirely to the work of Watts.[1]

Watts liked to pretend that at this time he could have counted on the fingers of one hand the pictures, other than portraits, that he had sold. This was, as we have seen, far from true, for Rickards already possessed a very fair holding of the allegories. But the fact remained that over the years there had accumulated, in stacks in this studio where no one could see them, a host of unsold pictures charged with uplifting messages for mankind. In the spring of 1881, therefore, he built a Gallery at Little Holland House where they could be hung and where the public could come on Saturday and Sunday afternoons to see them. This led to the loan that autumn of works by himself and Leighton to St Jude's, Whitechapel, whose Rector, the famous social reformer Canon Samuel Barnett—a man who had inherited considerable wealth from the paternal invention of iron bedsteads—was attempting to elevate the unsatisfactory moral tone of his 'largely criminal' parishioners. It was Barnett's aim 'to decrease not suffering but sin', and some of his flock, as they wrestled under his guidance with the obscurer allegories of Watts, may well have felt that when asking for bread they had been given a stone.

Return visits to Little Holland House followed, where one would like to have been a fly on the wall to see Watts and Leighton 'eagerly joining in and making part of the circle of joined hands' with their guests for the singing of 'Auld Lang Syne'. Later, Mary Watts started pottery classes at St Jude's for shoeblacks, and a copy

[1] In 1887, after Rickards's death, his collection of 57 pictures by Watts realised £16,000 at Christie's, small versions of 'Love and Life' and 'Love and Death' fetching £1,207 10s. and £1,155 respectively. No other picture reached four figures, but 'Eve of Peace' made £997 10s.

in mosaic of Watts's 'Time, Death, and Judgment' was placed on the façade of the church.[1] At its unveiling in 1884, Matthew Arnold gave an address in which he referred to the attitude of those who urged the poor to be 'sober, patient, charitable, kind', so that 'after this life they would wake up in a world as little like Whitechapel as possible . . . a form of belief which has been a stay to millions', but 'as thus presented, appears neither entirely solid nor verifiable.'[2] The selfless labours of Canon Barnett and of his wife, (Dame) Henrietta, led to the foundation in that same year of Toynbee Hall, and in 1897 he appealed for £20,000 to build a picture gallery 'as a Diamond Jubilee to the East End'. On 24 April the following lines appeared in *Punch*:

Oh! East is East, and West is West,
   as Rudyard Kipling says.
When the poor East enjoys the Art
   for which the rich West pays,
See East and West linked in their best!
   With the Art-wants of Whitechapel
Good Canon Barnett is just the man
   who best knows how to grapple.
So charge this Canon, load to muzzle,
   all ye great Jubilee guns.
Pictures as good as sermons? Aye,
   much better than some poor ones.
Where Whitechapel's darkness the weary eyes
   of the dreary workers dims,
It may be found that Watts' pictures
   do better than Watts' hymns.

The Whitechapel Art Gallery was opened in 1901, and it has flourished ever since. Very appropriately it was chosen as the setting, in the spring of 1974, for a retrospective exhibition of Watts's paintings and drawings.

[1] When St Jude's Church was demolished, the mosaic was transferred to the façade of St Giles-in-the-Fields Church Schools, Holborn. These too were demolished in 1970, and the mosaic is at present in store.
[2] Arnold's listeners must have been as puzzled by much of his address as was the weary East End social worker, previously unknown to him, by his improbable opening remark to her, 'Ill and overworked, how fare you in this scene?'

In the winter of 1881–82 Sir Coutts Lindsay made a 'bold, not to
say audacious experiment' by staging at the Grosvenor Gallery an
exhibition that nobody could accuse of being 'greenery-yallery': a
representative one-man show of Watts's paintings. More than two
hundred works, covering a period of some forty years, were assembled, and in general the reception was very favourable, though, as
has already been mentioned,[1] some of the allegories came in for
sharp criticism. Every reputable newspaper reviewed the exhibition
fully, *The Times* devoting three long articles to it. In the first, the
critic wrote:

> The exhibition of oil paintings, which was opened to the public
> on Saturday last [31 December 1881], is in several respects of
> unique interest. It is exclusively confined to the work of one
> master; that is the oldest and, broadly speaking, the greatest of
> our Royal Academicians, and the exhibition has been made in his
> lifetime and rendered as complete as possible by his assistance.
> For once, owing to private enterprise, the life-work of a great
> artist has been brought together before the light has faded from
> his eyes and the speech from his lips, and writers and picture-
> lovers have an opportunity of paying that homage to the living
> which is but too generally reserved for the dead. An English
> artist, who has painted our worthiest 'in arms, in art, in song', in
> statesmanship, science, or literature; who has given form to the
> dreams of our poets, the events of our history, and the traditions
> of our faith, pours the chief results of 40 years' labour into one
> great gallery, and says to us practically, 'I have asked nothing
> from you but leave to work. I have worked, and this is the result.
> Throughout my life I have neither sought your praise nor feared
> your censure . . .'

In speaking of the exhibition as covering the life-work of the
artist, the critic no doubt assumed that a man in his middle sixties—
a man who at the age of fifty-two had already proclaimed, 'the best
part of my life is gone'—had virtually reached the end of the road.
Yet in the event, more than twenty years of almost unbroken artistic
productivity lay ahead, and roughly half of the two hundred and
forty-eight pictures that were to be exhibited at the Memorial Exhibition at the Royal Academy in 1905 had not yet been painted.

[1] Page 64.

Moreover, though it must be admitted that most of the finest portraits lay behind him and that many of his feeblest didactic works
were yet to come, even in the last decade of his life there were to be
masterpieces such as 'For he had Great Possessions', 'Destiny' and
'Mother and Child'. On his eighty-sixth birthday he worked for the
last time on his majestic but never completed 'Court of Death',[1] and
in the field of sculpture there was the astonishing 'Tennyson', begun
when he was eighty-one. In fact, the exhibition at the Grosvenor
Gallery should have been considered rather as a belated half-term
than as an end-of-term report.

The sixty or so portraits at the Grosvenor included a number of
those destined for what came to be known as Watts's 'House of
Fame' or 'Gallery of Worthies'. Many others of the series—for
example, Meredith, Lord Roberts, Cardinal Manning and Lord
Salisbury—still lay ahead, and by the end of the century hardly a
great figure of the Victorian age had eluded his brush. In the portraits now exhibited we find literature and the arts represented by
Tennyson (two versions), Browning, Swinburne, Carlyle, Burne-
Jones, Leighton, William Morris, Sir Henry Taylor, Matthew Arnold, Philip Calderon, Leslie Stephen, Stuart Mill, Panizzi, Joachim
and Lecky. The Law was there with Lord Lyndhurst and Sir
Alexander Cockburn, the Army with Lord Lawrence. Among the
politicians were Gladstone, Lord Sherbrooke, the Duke of Argyll
and Sir Charles Dilke; among churchmen Dean Stanley, Canon
Liddell, the Rev. Stopford Brooke and Dr Martineau. There were
foreigners too: M. Thiers, M. Guizot, Garibaldi, Prince Jerome
Bonaparte and Professor Donders of Utrecht. Nor was beauty
absent: Lady Holland, Lillie Langtry (thinly disguised as 'The
Dean's Daughter'), Lady Somers, poor Lady Henry Somerset (rejected by society for claiming in the courts the custody of her
children after having left her homosexual husband), Lady Tavis-
tock, Lady Rosebery, Princess Lieven and Mrs Percy Wyndham.
Only the realm of Science was as yet unrepresented, and Watts
deeply regretted that he was never able to paint either Darwin or
Herschel, although a drawing of the latter was once begun but left
unfinished.

The general opinion of the critics was, as would be expected, that
Watts had succeeded best in portraiture. 'Many of the portraits

[1] Tate Gallery version, 14' × 9'.

here,' said the *Daily News*, 'might be exhibited among the works of Rembrandt, Bordone and Vandyck in Burlington House, and not seem unworthy of their company. It is in his allegorical and poetical pieces rather than in his portraits . . . that Mr Watts's occasional inequality is most manifest . . . In his allegorical works he lives in a strange air, which can hardly be breathed by healthy human art . . .'

The Times felt that to almost every one of his portraits Watts had given 'the look of a man more or less perplexed, if not saddened, by the enigmas of life'. The *Spectator* contrasted them with those of Frank Holl, 'the most powerful portrait painter of the Academy', and found them more penetrating and more sympathetic. 'We have seen portraits (and fine portraits too) by [Holl] of most estimable people—deans and masters of colleges, &c.—who never had a wrong thought in their lives, but to whom Mr Holl has given such a don't-meet-me-on-a-dark-night-kind of look, that we have almost thought he must have in the course of his painting discovered some dreadful secret in those apparently blameless breasts, such "damnable faces" have his sitters shown.'

Inevitably there was some divergence of opinion on individual pictures. The *Globe* greatly admired the full-length portrait of Mrs Percy Wyndham, and *The Times* found it 'the finest of all. . . . There is no modern portrait with which we are acquainted which is at once so beautiful and so dignified as this work; it has a power of conception which might almost be called "majesty", and the colour, though unobtrusive, is especially fine.' But another critic proclaimed it a failure, regretting that Mrs Wyndham stood 'in an attitude such as might be recommended by a second-rate photographer, who imagines his work is going to be artistic when he tells his sitter to be "easy, please, and a little more cheerful if you can".'

But it was the critic of *The Times* who regretted the attitudes of Mrs Prinsep and Lady Dalrymple in 'The Sisters'—a picture in which he did, however, find 'meritorious qualities no less remarkable': 'The arrangement by which the painter has placed the sisters bolt upright, side by side, with a little space between them, as if they were two posts to prevent cows from leaving a field, is wilfully strange and naturally unnatural.[1] The arrangement, too, of the

[1] It would have been kinder, and at the same time more fair, to have compared it to a pair of saints in a Russian icon.

tesselated pavement and the horizontal lines of wall and parapet cutting up the double vertical ones is simply ugly, and the whole effect of the picture is that of a cross composed partly of flesh and blood, partly of architecture. Little more can be said in dispraise, except that the colour is at first sight calculated to give the beholder a shock of surprise.'

The Times's critic was kind about the allegories and 'poetical' pictures in general, 'Paolo and Francesca' very properly receiving particular praise.[1] 'Surely,' he wrote, 'there may be supposed to be some relation between grandeur of thought and the expression of that thought, and to talk as if Watts had done something wrong because he has spoken to us in louder language than ordinary when he had something very important to say seems to us a curiously ignorant criticism.' But 'Fabian' of the *People* voiced a more widely held opinion: 'Sincerely as I admire Mr Watts's work, I do, on the whole, sincerely dislike allegory of the particular kind he affects in art, and I do so, not because it is poetic, but because it is not poetic enough. A personification like "Time", "Oblivion" &c. is to me infinitely less interesting than the prosiest of after-dinner bores. Indeed why the prosy one is such a bore, is that he, too, is a personification rather than a man.'

Worse still, 'Fabian' levelled against Watts the charge that he was 'deficient in the quality of humour . . . Whether his mood be classic, romantic, allegoric, or natural, it is always serenely undisturbed by a perception of the ridiculous.' The painter, who eagerly read every review, was cut to the quick, for like all humourless men he believed himself to be exceptionally well endowed in this respect. So to disprove the accusation he immediately set about the painting of a large and regrettable picture entitled ' "B.C.", or Tasting the first Oyster', in which 'the primitive woman watches with anxious curiosity the effect of the first courageous gulp of the primitive man'. Of it in her manuscript catalogue of her husband's works Mary Watts wrote: 'It must be understood that this picture was purposely intended to raise a smile. The artist had been accused of an excess of gravity in his subjects. It was first exhibited at Liverpool in 1884, when an endeavour was made to find in it some

---

[1] Chris Mullen points out that the composition is 'strongly influenced by Ary Scheffer's painting of the identical scene'. Loshak identifies Francesca as Virginia Somers. Watts had painted several earlier versions of the subject.

serious purpose. In answer to enquiries Mr Watts wrote that there was none—to which his correspondent ironically replied that doubtless "B.C." was to be interpreted as "before clothing".'

However, in general the Grosvenor Gallery exhibition enormously enhanced Watts's reputation. A number of pictures were sold (one landscape fetching a thousand guineas), and through the good offices of Leighton the 'Psyche' was purchased for the Chantrey Bequest. Sir Coutts decided to give a dinner in Watts's honour, and, before consulting the painter, sounded some of the one hundred suggested guests to find out what the response would be; thus it happened that Watts first heard what was afoot when he received a letter from a fellow Royal Academician saying how much he regretted being unable to attend.

Watts was, of course, horrified, and immediately demanded that dinner be cancelled. One or two of those who had been invited— Burne-Jones among them—felt that this excessive modesty was rather tiresome; but Lord Lytton, who had already written praising the pictures in almost extravagant terms, now wrote a further letter which must have comforted Watts. 'Eating and drinking,' he said, 'appear to me grotesquely inappropriate modes (not improved, but the reverse, by the commonly accompanying postprandial oratory) of expressing admiration for a man's genius or gratitude for his work.'

*   *   *

A rich young American with influence in the art world, Miss Mary Gertrude Mead (later to become the wife of the artist Edwin Abbey), had seen when in Paris nine paintings which Watts had sent to an International Exhibition there in 1883. These had so deeply impressed her that she came to London that autumn to visit the Little Holland House Gallery, where she 'accidentally' made the acquaintance of the artist. It is impossible to believe that this meeting was not deliberately contrived, for Miss Mead had instantly decided that Watts must be persuaded to lend a representative collection of his paintings for a one-man exhibition at the Metropolitan Museum, New York. 'I want your pictures to come to America,' she wrote, 'for the sake of the people here, and not for your sake. I want them to come that the people may hear the voice of a great teacher, and believe me, please do believe me, many will listen, for there are many people here who . . . are hungering for a sight of pictures such as yours.'

Watts was at first touched and flattered, then fearful of a hostile reception, and finally 'terrified' that the cream of his life's work, those masterpieces destined for the nation, would sink in mid Atlantic. He therefore proposed an alternative: that he should send instead a series of photographs, worked on by himself in monochrome to correct those false tones that were inevitable in pre-panchromatic days. This suggestion was immediately, and very properly, rejected, and Watts was eventually persuaded by Miss Mead and her ally, Mrs Russell Barrington,[1] to send more than fifty of his best pictures, about half of them portraits, to America. The selection was made by Watts with the help of Mrs Barrington, who also compiled the catalogue together with a long introduction, and the work shipped to New York in September 1884 in the *Canada.*

The pictures arrived safely, but soon there were troubles of every kind. Edmund Gosse, who had expressed the desire to write about the exhibition in the *Pall Mall Gazette,* had been summoned by Watts to be briefed on his intentions. This led to the painter being accused of attempting to 'puff his own works' and 'cram his ideas about them down the public throat'—an imputation, Watts said, which touched him as little as would one of habitual drunkenness; but it hurt all the same. Then came the problem of avoiding the payment of import duty, which was finally solved by putting the whole of the Museum 'into bond' for the duration of the exhibition.

Watts of course wrote ceaselessly, incoherently, and—though he had 'covenanted not to write long letters'—at enormous length to Miss Mead explaining his aims and admitting his limitations: 'I have no more wish to be praised for my work than a bricklayer who builds a wall expects praise for his bricklaying. If the wall answers a good purpose, that is enough.' He instructs her about hanging and about lighting, and begs her to become 'the prophet of Art in America'. Indeed, only his usual crop of miscellaneous illnesses, aggravated by his deep anxiety over the fate of General Gordon in Khartoum, stemmed for a time the flood of his admonitions.

Or was there another reason? He had latterly begun to write almost amorously to his dear Mary, assuring her that the admittedly great difference in their ages was as nothing 'on the shore of the

[1] For Mrs Barrington see chapter 13.

great Sea of Time. One's spiritual existence has no age . . . It is that spiritual existence which you perceived in me that awakened the kinship with your own, so you will come to see as I see—that we are but two children playing on that shore, not unmindful of its mysteries.' It would appear that Miss Mead, reading between the lines, saw danger ahead and was not prepared to play children's games with Watts on the shore of the great Sea of Time—or indeed on any other shore. There were now long silences on her side, and Watts, who had previously addressed her by her Christian name, reverted to 'My dear Miss Mead' and begged to be told if, and how, he had offended. In fact one can hardly doubt that there, but for the grace of God and a chill wind from Mary Mead, went the second Mrs Watts.

In spite of all Watts's fears, the exhibition proved an outstanding success with both the critics and the public. Over half a million people visited it between October 1884 and the following March, and he found it impossible to refuse permission for it to be extended until the autumn. On their return the pictures were shown at Birmingham and at Nottingham, and a selection of them afterwards at Rugby School, with the result that it was not until July 1888 that the Gallery at Little Holland House was properly restocked.

During the summer of 1885, while the exhibition was creating a sensation in New York, Watts received from Gladstone, on behalf of the Queen, the offer of a baronetcy; it was the first time that a painter had been so honoured. Watts had previously been sounded on the matter by Lord Carlisle, but, possibly because he was now rather deaf, he had understood that he was being approached about a C.B. For several days he wavered; then when letters of congratulation, addressed to 'Sir George Watts', began to pour in, he panicked —and declined the honour. 'So you will not let them make you Sir George?' cried Thornycroft. 'Well, never mind, you will be St. George anyway.' To Miss Mead, whose mother was 'dreadfully disappointed', Watts wrote later that he feared that such an honour would expose him to appeals for financial aid which he would be in no position to satisfy:

This was the best reason; some others will not so well bear the light.[1] Would you believe that among them was that I did not

[1] It has been suggested that among these was his fear that, since Ellen had been

think the name would sound well! My love of beauty and harmony is in such excess that it has always been a matter of deep
regret to me that I was not tall and handsome and strong, and
that the sound of my name was unsatisfactory. If I had despotic
power I would . . . oblige change of ugly names.

A jotting in one of his notebooks takes the story a stage further:

Mr G[ladstone] has shown sympathy with effort, the profession
has been honoured, I have been flattered, and the Order has not
been degraded by importing into it an ugly name and mean living.
The honour I should like would be that the Queen would invest
me with a name pleasant to my ears and that would be a constant
incentive, such as Tryamain or Fainhope; does this seem to be
very silly?

Politeness prohibits an answer.

The offer was repeated in 1894 and again declined. 'I must own,'
he said, 'that if thought worthy I should like to be the first of a new
Order.' In 1896 Watts was told that Lord Salisbury was anxious
for him to be awarded the title of 'Right Honourable'. If this were
offered him, he would, he said, accept—'not because it would be
anything to me personally, but I should like to inaugurate this
honour as suitable for literary and artistic labours'. But a fortnight
later Mary Watts noted in her diary, 'Right Hon.; Queen has
refused'. When, however, in 1902 the Order of Merit was instituted,
Watts was among the first batch of twelve civilians to receive it.

*   *   *

'I cannot imagine', Watts once said, 'that any sanely minded individual would find it necessary to refocus his thought, after looking at
the Theseus or the Milo Venus, before entering a drawing-room, or
even a church.'

An artist's attitude to the female nude is as a rule immediately
apparent in his treatment of it.[1] Some soon become so accustomed to
working from it that, whatever may be their feelings when away
from their easels, they will observe and paint a breast with the same

---

his legal wife until 1877, her son by Godwin (b. 1872) might claim to succeed to
the title.

[1] Yet Etty? (see p. xix).

detachment that they would observe and paint a rather large apple in a still-life. Others—Rubens or Boucher, for example—must have been perpetually titillated as they worked; and Renoir, when asked what kind of a brush he used for his nudes, is said to have replied, 'I paint with my penis'. But for Watts, who must surely have suffered from some form of sexual repression, it would appear that the nude remained a perpetual embarrassment; and though he constantly *drew* from it, in his paintings he worked from drawings. Only in some of his earlier pictures—and in particular in his 'Story from Boccaccio'—do we sense any involvement. The nudes in his allegories are almost epicene.

When a certain Mr Richard Johnson wanted to acquire one of his outsize 'Eves' and asked Rickards to arrange the purchase, Watts replied that in the first place Johnson could not possibly have room for it, and 'secondly, it is a perfectly naked figure, and though I hope my endeavour to render it perfectly unobjectionable on that score has not been wholly unsuccessful, still such subjects are more fit for a gallery than a dwelling-house, and one could not expect a household that has not been brought up in familiarity with this class of work to escape being shocked.' He might, in fact, have spared Richards this little homily on nudity, for he ended his letter by saying that he had in any case no intention of parting with the pictures.

It was the erroneous opinion of Mrs Emily D. Martin, National Superintendent of Purity in Literature and Art for the Women's Christian Temperance Union of the United States, that Watts had followed Renoir's example when painting the picture of 'Love and Life' which he presented in 1893 to the American nation.

This, the first of a number of versions of the subject, had been executed by Watts between 1882 and 1884 as a companion piece to his big 'Love and Death' begun some years earlier. It was included among the pictures sent to New York, when a critic wrote of it: 'A yellow figure, with variegated rainbow wings, leads a slender, naked girl, frailty symbolising life, up yellowish red rocks, with an immensity of blue depths behind. Infinitely pathetic is the slender figure: graceful the poetic conception.'

It was generally agreed to be less successful than 'Love and Death'; but, thanks perhaps to Mrs Barrington's long note in the catalogue in which she explained that 'Love' was to be interpreted 'in its most universal sense' as 'charity, sympathy and unselfishness', it does not appear to have shocked the American public. Watts, grateful for the friendly reception his works had been accorded in the States, decided that he would give a picture to the American nation, and 'Love and Life' offered in his opinion what he called 'the widest scope of signification'. It was not, however, until 1893 that the gift was actually made, and the picture, after being shown at the World's Fair at Chicago, was handed over to President Cleveland, who proposed hanging it in the White House.

Then Mrs Martin struck. 'I urged the 300,000 members of the 12,000 organisations of the temperance union,' she told the Press, 'to write letters to President Cleveland . . . protesting against the hanging of the picture in the Presidential mansion. But before the storm had half begun, an order was issued that the Watts work should be sent to the Corcoran Art Gallery [in Washington].'

Watts was, of course, horrified when he heard that he had been denounced as a purveyor of pornography. In acknowledging with gratitude the rescue operation of the director of the Corcoran Gallery, he wrote: 'I confess I was greatly shocked to learn that there was a refusal to hang it in any place on the score that it was immoral. It was the first time, after more than sixty years of work, that anything of mine had been so considered,[1] and I was tempted to write and beg that the picture should be destroyed, and nothing remembered excepting my object (with all humility) in presenting it.'

The powers of darkness had won the first battle; but the war was not yet over. In 1902, President Theodore Roosevelt had the picture brought from the Corcoran Gallery and hung in the dining-room of the White House. Mrs Martin, nearly ten years older now but not a day wiser, rose at once in her wrath:

My first plan [she informed readers of a Philadelphia newspaper] will be to write a letter to President Roosevelt asking for an explanation. I feel sure that he will return me a full and frank answer, and my future action will be entirely governed by the stand the President takes.

It may be that he has ordered the picture to be hung in the

[1] 'The large cartoon of "Hope" was once rejected by a chapel for seamen on grounds of impropriety.' (R. Alston, 'Watts the Painter', in the catalogue of the Arts Council Exhibition.)

White House without inquiring into its history and without knowing that its presence in the home of the Chief Executive of the nation is extremely objectionable to the women of the country. It cannot be that he has resurrected the work from its ten years' obscurity in an art gallery to flaunt any talk of 'art for art's sake' in our faces. My opinion of his sterling character makes it impossible for me to suppose such a thing. The President has always been on the side of purity and morality. Among the women of the National Temperance Union he is looked upon as a knight and a hero . . .

It will be very disillusionizing for the women who have admired him to learn that he has given a place on the walls of the White House to this vulgar nude painting of Watts . . . 'Love' and 'Life' are represented by two naked figures in atrocious postures . . . The women who aided me ten years ago will aid me now, however. Their opinions in such matters remain unchanged. We have no objection to placing such paintings in art galleries, where people must deliberately go to see them, but we do protest against having them in public places or in the official home of the President, where freedom in nude decorations may seem to have the stamp of Government approval.

Mrs Martin this time found little support, and in particular a number of distinguished artists attacked her interference in letters to the Press. 'Those who can find anything sensual in the Watts picture,' wrote one, 'must be anxious to indulge themselves in over-ripe thoughts. The picture . . . is a highly etherialized, hazy study of the nude, in which all sense of nakedness is lost and merely form and soul remain. The President should pay no attention to his thick-skinned critics.' 'Many famous pictures in the nude,' wrote another, 'are, to my mind, as pure as snow', and a third (a woman) suggested that Mrs Martin and her sister smut-hounds should be compelled to describe and illustrate 'what kind of drapery' they would have wished 'Life' to wear.[1]

[1] The White House informs me that over the years 'Love and Life' has made 'many trips back and forth between the White House and the Corcoran Gallery'. Mrs Wilson, wife of the President, sent for it and hung it over the mantelpiece in the President's study. It is now included in the 'National Collection of Fine Arts in Washington, a part of the complex of museums under the Smithsonian Institution.'

In 1893 another version of 'Love and Life' also went abroad to carry Watts's message to a wider public. Monsieur Léon Bénédite, the Director of the Luxembourg Museum in Paris, came to England to choose two modern English paintings for his Gallery and returned to France with Whistler's famous portrait of his mother and Watts's 'Love and Life' (for which the artist firmly refused any payment). It need hardly be added that no Madame Martin rose up to condemn 'Love and Life', and 'Life'—'une figure exquise, à peine femme, tant elle est peu formée; femme à l'extrême, tant elle est souple, gracieuse et faible . . .'—was found to be very far removed from the erotic nudes of the Paris *Salon*.

13

ENTER MRS RUSSELL BARRINGTON

IN ANOTHER of her discursive volumes of reminiscences,[1] Mrs Stirling wrote:

Sir Luke [Fildes] told me that both G. F. Watts and Leighton were much bothered by a lady who was seeking to extract copy from them for a book. They both consulted him in despair as to how they were to get rid of her. Leighton observed plaintively, 'I scarcely dare to go to bed.' 'I said to them,' said Sir Luke, 'there is only one way out—you must both marry!' And, he added, 'Watts married—but Leighton died!'

Though no name is mentioned, this talented but formidable woman was undoubtedly Mrs Russell Barrington, author of invaluable biographies of both Leighton and Watts.[2]

Mrs Barrington is sometimes vague and sometimes inaccurate where dates are concerned, but it must have been about the middle of February 1866,[3] when she was a very young woman and still unmarried, that she paid a visit to Rossetti's studio that was to have important consequences. She wrote that soon after her arrival there

the door opened, and a party consisting of one man and a few large ladies, came in to see the newly-finished picture.[4] I remember the ladies were large because the man looked small in their midst, otherwise I have no recollection of their appearance. The

[1] *Life's Mosaic*, Unicorn Press, 1934.
[2] See the Bibliography.
[3] I am grateful to Mrs Virginia Surtees for establishing this date from internal evidence.
[4] 'The Beloved'—painted in 1865/6 but retouched in 1873.

one figure absorbed all my attention. Habited in a long sealskin coat it was small but in no wise insignificant—on the contrary, it was distinguished in appearance. The face was handsome, with a serious countenance suggesting a latent weariness and melancholy hidden under a crust of reserve. His words were few, but he gazed intently at the new picture. From something Rossetti had said when the party entered the room I had realised that this quiet self-contained personality belonged to Watts—Watts the painter and friend of my friend Mrs Nassau Senior of the rippling golden hair . . .

In 1868 Miss Emily Williams (as she then was) married Russell Barrington, a grandson of the fifth Viscount Barrington. She chose well (we may be sure that it was she who did the choosing), for if Mr Barrington was a nonentity he was rich, amiable, and always as clay in her hands. She herself was cultured, intelligent, well-read, and no mean artist; but above all she was an indefatigable pursuer of artistic big game. The prize trophies of her safari were to be Leighton and Watts.

Though she paid a visit to (old) Little Holland House—on which occasion Russell Barrington, who 'never knew what to say to artists about their own work', embarrassed her by refusing to get out of the carriage—and though she had also contrived to find herself at Freshwater when Watts was there, it was not until the artist was firmly established in Melbury Road that the pursuit began in earnest. She saw at once that his life there, without Mrs Prinsep and her tribe in perpetual attendance, was intolerably lonely; she therefore paid him innumerable visits, listened by the hour to his theories about Art and Life and, most eagerly of all, to his repeatedly expressed regret 'at not having anyone to help him achieve his aims'. So, after talking it over with her husband (a mere formality), she wrote saying that she would be 'proud' to be of assistance to him in any way that he would welcome. On 7 April 1876, Watts replied:

A thousand thanks for your offer. I don't know but what you might help me with some advantage to yourself, because anyone who does help me must go profoundly into the matter, and if real study has any charms for you, why, perhaps, you might be willing to undergo some stiff and stern application; but, I can tell you, help to me in the works I have proposed to myself, and indeed

have plunged into, would be no child's play. If you will come and
see me any day between 2.30 and 5 we may talk over possibilities.
Thornycroft the sculptor has commenced to build two semi-
detached houses next door to me. He intends to live in one and
let or sell the other. It strikes me this house might suit you.

Of course Mr Barrington agreed to buy the house adjoining Watts's,
and a year later the huntress found herself established within pounc-
ing distance of her quarry.

Though Mrs Barrington was no doubt on occasions domineering,
Watts had grown accustomed to having his life run for him by
strong-minded women. Indeed, he needed one within call, and from
the very first he was far from considering his new neighbour a
nuisance. When he was ill or depressed—as often happened—her
little attentions, which included occasional gifts of champagne and
claret (to be taken medicinally, of course) soothed him. Since petty
annoyance sometimes made him lose his temper—'I have a good
nature, but I am irritable,' he confessed—she did her best to keep
his life 'unruffled'. When he was in trouble over a painting he found
her criticism valuable. In fact, in spite of what Fildes is alleged to
have said, it was not until Mary Fraser-Tytler began to make her
successful 'take-over bid' for Watts that any trouble arose. Then
war was inevitable, and it was to be fought to the death.

Mrs Barrington tells her story so well that it seems best to give
much of it in her own words. Until her own studio had been built
she worked in the 'iron house'—a storeroom in Watts's garden—and
it was *he* who suggested that a gate be made in the paling that
separated the two properties. This they also used when Watts
visited the Barringtons, the peasant smocks in which he liked to
work—one of blue linen embroidered in white cotton which Mrs
Barrington had brought back from Brittany—being considered unsuitable for even the briefest appearance in even the rural roads of
Kensington.

A regular routine was established, suited to Watts's carefully
apportioned hours of work and leisure:

Evening after evening the same thing happened. I would go in
first, Mr Barrington generally joining us a little later. In the

winter months Watts was in his sitting-room, always in the same claret-coloured velvet armchair reading. (He never painted by artificial light.[1]) The servant having opened the door and announced me, the book was thrown aside, the spectacles taken off, he would rub his eyes with his fingers and almost invariably begin with, 'Well, what's the news' . . . The most deeply interesting news was naturally how the work got on, how certain experiments with colours had answered, or what pictures had been seen. Watts had what we called 'field days' with certain pigments. One day it would be the effect of burnt sienna rubbed over a ground of light red; another the effect of ultramarine over raw umber . . . How deeply interesting were all these experiments . . .

Discussions over the particular discoveries of the day always ended by his saying, when the servant came to lay the cloth for his evening meal, 'I hope I have improved "Love and Death"' (or mentioning whichever picture he had been chiefly working on). 'I may have spoilt it—I don't know! Come and see!' . . . Then he would take the flat candle-stick that was invariably placed for him on the end of the book-shelf near the door, a paper spill lying in it. Lighting it from the fire, he put the unburnt half on to the moulding above the fireplace. Night after night for all those years this process was gone through in precisely the same manner. I would often warn him that he might burn down his house some day through the little economy, and he would generally answer in the same words, 'I am very careful; I don't like waste—even of half a spill!'

Then, candle in hand, I following, he would go into the passage up the five steps to the double doors of the studio, through the enclosed passage between them, where, from a mysterious little window, we would look down into the sculpture studio[2] on to the giant horse and its rider—'Hugh Lupus' first, and later, 'Physical Energy'—huge ghost-like apparitions as seen by the faint light of the solitary candle; then through the second door into the large painting studio . . . Holding his hand in front of the candle, Watts would throw the light on each part

[1] Except his portrait of Joachim.
[2] Watts's sculptures are discussed in chapter 16.

of the canvas in the different pictures on which he had been working that day. He was always eager for criticism. 'Do you think I have improved it? I work on till I can't see what I have done,' he would often say. The contrast was striking between the impressive strength and size of the paintings and the sensitive frailness of the small hand held up so as to shade the light from everything but the mighty work it had achieved. What a wonderful power had the spirit and mind of this fragile, ageing figure to create and ring out grand anthems in colour and design! . . .

On those winter evenings, when entering the vast, dark, silent studio, where the earnest fever of the painter spent itself in arduous labour from sunrise to sunset, day after day, from one year's end to another, it felt as if rising into another order of life than that we are all living in these modern days, into an atmosphere that inspired aspiration and growth, while at the same time it was resting and calming the nerves. The self-centred individuality of the great artist reigned in it consistently and alone . . .

When the procession returned to the sitting-room, Watts ate his very frugal supper, we talking, or I reading to him. The meal was always the same—the cold remains of the dull little pudding made without sugar which had been hot for his dinner in the middle of the day, and a tumbler of milk mixed with barley-water: summer and winter, never any change. Even out of this very simple fare, Watts, if he was tired, would evolve a tragic self-reproach. To have as much as that distressed him; and when he thought of all the people who were starving he could hardly eat it! I often tried to impress upon him that if he refrained and gave the pudding to a beggar, the beggar would throw it away. It was not amusing enough as food for any beggars I had ever come across. He would easily be laughed out of his tragic moods . . .

After his supper Watts would often settle down to nonsense. He was like a child in his power of enjoying nonsense. Especially when Mr Barrington was also in high spirits the fun would become rampant. Watts had accumulated many ridiculous stories. One upon another he would hurry them out. Terrible puns were made, every kind of off-shoot of high spirits which he was capable of rising to, and when we left him we felt the happy satisfaction that we had helped him to secure a good night. On other winter

evenings, his vitality reawakened, we would plunge into serious
and interesting literature. Burton's 'Anatomy of Melancholy' was
a favourite book, particularly the part describing herbals and the
cures they effected. Bacon's Essays, Ruskin and, at times, the
Old Testament. Any current literature that had reference to
subjects especially interesting, such as criticisms on the art then
being exhibited, we read.

Some strange works Watts would get hold of. I remember two
American books that greatly fascinated him, dealing with somewhat scientific, but distinctly fantastic, new ideas. When I mentioned these ideas to Lord Avebury, then Sir John Lubbock, he
said they were quite unsound as science. Any book that started
the working of Watts's own imagination naturally interested him,
for he greatly enjoyed living in his own imagination. As a rule, in
those days we talked much more than we read. The reading was
the text; the sermon was all our own. The playgrounds we found
for our minds were inspiringly comprehensive. Whether our
knowledge was sound or unsound on all the subjects we scam-
pered over was immaterial; there was enough keen interest,
enough keen vitality aroused by our ideas clashing together to
strike some original matter out of most subjects . . .

Music was another taste that Watts and Mrs Barrington had in
common. He had a piano in his studio—probably the little one
which he mentions elsewhere as having received some years earlier
in exchange for a large and very indifferent painting, 'The Saxon
Sentinels'[1]—and she sometimes played to him of an evening. 'He
liked simple tunes, especially airs by Beethoven and Handel.' And
then he might say, 'Let us have a song. It is good for the health. It
expands the chest.' His favourites were Dibdin's 'Tom Bowling',
'The Banks of Allan Water', 'The Vicar of Bray', 'Sally in our Alley',
'Tell me, my Heart', and others by Bishop. 'The elaborate caden-
zas in these last he achieved with astonishing ease and precision
considering his age and the fact that he had not practised for years.'

He even went so far as to say that he thought he ought to have
been a musician rather than a painter, because 'melodies and har-
monies' came spontaneously into his head whereas ideas for his
pictures had to be laboriously worked out. When Blanche, who came

[1] Now in the York City Art Gallery.

from time to time to stay with him, took lessons from a Polish vio-
linist, Watts insisted on taking lessons too, in order to encourage her.
A photograph exists (see Plate 16), taken by Mrs Cameron, of Watts,
holding a violin and seated between two of his girl pets; but this
was made before Blanche came into his life.

Mrs Barrington also throws interesting light on Watts's method of
painting at that time:

> Before beginning a picture he would often paint over his canvases
> with some colour which would be opposed to the tone he in-
> tended the picture to have . . . Watts dried the oil out of his
> colours by putting them on blotting-paper, reducing them to a
> texture like putty by keeping them under water. His colours,
> when he used them, were nearly as dry as pastel, but without, of
> course, the crumbling quality.
>
> Quite new brushes were, he said, almost useless to him. He
> would wear the outside bristles down on a background, or by
> merely rubbing them on a hard surface till they became a stiff
> little pyramid the shape of a stump used for chalk drawings, and
> then they became great treasures. He said he believed the worst
> thing to paint with was a paint-brush—'except the wrong end!'
> He would use a paper or leather stump or the handle of an old
> tooth-brush filed down to a point, but the best of all, he thought,
> was the finger.
>
> When the putty-like pigment which he put on the canvas in
> distinct touches was nearly dry, he would sometimes take a paper-
> knife, and, using the flat part, would rub it over the touches,
> smearing them together. He would not touch the painting again
> till the smeared surface was quite dry. Then he would work parti-
> ally over it. In this way he contrived to get a bloom of atmosphere
> into his painting, a quality which he invariably aimed at . . .

It is principally from a number of passing references to her
almost daily exchange of ideas with Watts that we learn most about
the character of her hero. There were times when ill-health reduced
him to abject confessions of having failed, to pathetic outbursts such
as

> I am nothing. Oh! you will find out I am nothing! I have no
> genius—no facility; any one could do better work if they sacri-

ficed everything to do it as I do! One thing alone I possess, and I never remember the time I was without it—an aim towards the highest, the best, and a burning desire to reach it. If I were asked to choose whether I would like to do something good, as the world judges popular art, and receive personally great credit for it, or, as an alternative, to produce something which should rank with the very best, taking a place with the art of Pheidias or Titian, with the highest poetry and the most elevating music, and remain unknown as the perpetrator of the work, I should choose the latter.

One despairing letter to Mrs Barrington ends, 'I should like to go into a monastery.'

There was certainly much of the monk in Watts, yet he would hardly have found in a Christian monastery the peace that he sought. His religion was a vague theism—'a church with many doors, illuminated by the great light shining through many windows'; and of his allegories he wrote, 'I lead people to the church door, and they can then go in and see God in their own way'. 'I identify myself and my work with no especial dogma,' he said, and quoted the words of a mystic, 'All beauty is the face of God'. Again and again he returned to the thirteenth chapter of the First Epistle to the Corinthians: 'And now abideth faith, hope, charity, these three; but the greatest of these is charity.' He was always enormously philanthropic.

He was not, he said, *against* the Church, though personally he would not be bound by her decrees. 'Let the Agnostics find something better than the Church before they attempt to demolish her. The indefinite teaching of the Agnostics will never keep the morals of the masses in order. They require a positive creed.' He particularly deplored the attempts of Rome to stifle progress. 'If only,' he would say, 'it had accepted the onward movement of thought and scientific investigation as lawful and right, while still maintaining the spiritual guidance of men, the Church would have kept everything in its hands, and retained, indeed increased its power.'

Above all, he deplored the doctrine of Hell:

The idea that any human organisations such as Churches should create terror in the simple and semi-educated by scares of such retribution . . . and thus create mental suffering which was one of the worst to bear, seemed an abomination to Watts. Through his art he tried in every possible way to inspire feelings which should counteract the terror of inevitable Punishment and Death . . . He dwelt often on the great desire he had of leading those who dreaded Death to regard it merely as an inevitable passing stage in the journey home.

Today the Christian Church has opened its doors so wide that even Watts might have found himself able to enter.

'Watts often confided to me, either in conversation or in letters, his anxieties regarding money and his consequent desire to sell pictures,' wrote Mrs Barrington. Though Mary Watts has scribbled against this in the margin of her copy of Mrs Barrington's book, 'quite untrue', the fact remains that Watts was frequently fussed about financial troubles, real or imaginary, and it cannot be doubted that he discussed with his friend his lifelong horror of falling into debt. The world has, however, benefited from his fear of future poverty because, time and again, it drove him back to portraiture.

Though one cannot agree with the judgment of 'one of the greatest Pre-Raphaelites', who told Mrs Barrington that Watts was 'no good at anything else' than portraiture, it is undoubtedly in this field that he is best remembered today. Yet he always found painting a portrait 'very like torture', and if the sitter was unsympathetic (the future Edward VII) or uncooperative (Carlyle, who made no effort to conceal his boredom), failure might result. The worst moment was when friends and relations came to see the picture. 'You stand first on one foot, then on the other, with nothing to say—waiting for the verdict. When it comes it is generally the one thing that is least bad in the painting which is most criticised.'

A natural shyness (so Watts alleged) made him hate all money transactions where his pictures were concerned, and it was here that Mr Barrington came to his rescue by agreeing, at his wife's suggestion, to act as go-between for artist and prospective purchaser. This prevented what Watts called his 'delicate sensibilities' from being wounded. Burne-Jones helped Barrington to fix the prices and added the sound advice, 'You must never let Watts alter his price. Whatever price he asks for a picture, that he must stick to.'

But this matter of filthy lucre and delicate susceptibilities is nothing like so simple as it may sound. Though Watts was enormously generous to the nation, to deserving public institutions both in England and abroad, and to charities of every kind, he was, in fact, very far from being the guileless innocent that he pretended. True, he hated financial wrangling (and who does not?); yet he was a past master in extracting the last penny from a client. 'Were you the Duke of Portland', Watts would tell him, 'I would charge a much larger sum'; and he would flatteringly add that for a man who bought for love of art and not for re-sale at a profit ('though I venture to add that this picture will be worth much more in the future') he would make a concession: 'Guineas is what I usually work for, but if inconvenient to you we will say pounds'. But the catch was yet to come: 'If not, guineas if you please, as I want to help an old friend who has lost his savings by the failure of a bank . . .' Who but a cad could now write pounds!

A wavering purchaser might sometimes be hooked by the hint that another collector (preferably titled) was nibbling and ready to pay more; and almost casually he would add that this particular picture was perhaps the best thing he had ever done. Another little artifice was the proposal of a 'surcharge' for improvements not allowed for in the original contract. A letter written by Watts on 25 May 1876 to Charles Rickards, on the subject of a self-portrait in armour known as 'The Eve of Peace', is very revealing:

I have been working on the picture of the Knight (my own portrait), have repainted the hand and in other respects improved it. It strikes me, or rather it has been suggested to me, that the introduction of the other hand holding the helmet would greatly add to and improve the picture. This I cannot afford to do, as it would cost me something besides the time and labour; but as it would add perhaps a couple of hundred pounds to the value of the picture, perhaps you would feel inclined to give me an extra fifty guineas for what I should do. You see I am looking at this as a mere matter of business, and I do not at all do more than place the matter before you. I wish I could afford to give my time for this gratis, but I can't.

Yours in haste
G. F. Watts

You will understand that I only write this fearing if you should afterwards hear me say I could greatly have improved the picture you would be vexed.

And what happened? It is hard to say, for Rickards's answer is missing; but to it Watts replied, 'I will do as you wish about the Knight.' In the picture the knight is seen holding the helmet, but the hand is virtually invisible. If Rickards paid the surcharge he certainly did not get his money's-worth.

14

THE PRESERVATION OF A NATIONAL MONUMENT

ON 20 NOVEMBER 1886 George Frederic Watts, widower[1] aged sixty-nine, married Mary Fraser-Tytler, spinster aged thirty-six, of Aldourie, Inverness. The bridegroom was exactly the same age as the bride's deceased father would have been,[2] and her half-brother Edward ('Ted') is said to have handed her over to Watts with the words, 'I give you to the Nation.'

A week before his marriage, in what must appear to be one of the most insensitive letters ever penned at such a moment, the bridegroom-to-be informed an old friend what had persuaded him to take this calculated but improbable step. To Mary Mead in New York—the fish who got away—he wrote:

> For the last two or three years I have been running down, being knocked over by the slightest change of temperature and weather . . . This has necessitated a serious consideration, the result being that a lady whose mind and character command the respect and affection of all who know her is to become my nurse and companion. As I have known her for more than sixteen years she is of course not very young (thirty-six). All my most intimate friends—those who know and realise how necessary it is for me to have constant care—rejoice in the step. Of course, without the reasons I have, at my time of life it might require some stretch of friendship to regard this matter favourably; but my most intimate friends are convinced that I have small chance of being able to

[1] The word is used loosely: Ellen Terry was of course still alive.
[2] Watts had also been exactly the age of Ellen Terry's father.

169

carry out my designs unless I have the watchfulness which is only possible under these conditions . . .

The lady—for she is essentially a lady—has so fine a mind and temper that I can trust myself to her without feeling it will be necessary to give up any old interests and affections . . .

Miss Mead may well have read the letter with a sigh of relief.

One's first reaction is that a suitable body could equally well have been secured by advertisement in the columns of the *Matrimonial Gazette* (if it then existed):

Widower in his seventieth year, sufferer from genuine poor health aggravated by hypochondria, seeks cultured lady of gentle birth willing to act as full-time nurse-companion and thus preserve him to complete his life's work for the nation. Good wages offered, or matrimony if preferred.

And how might the companion advertisement have run?

Cultured spinster, no longer quite young (but essentially a lady), seeks a god to worship. Total dedication and unswerving loyalty guaranteed; money no object.

Happily the marriage, which might on the face of it seem to have been arranged by a very capricious computer, was never to be regretted by either party. But then, Mrs Watts was a very remarkable woman.

Watts first met his future wife in 1870, when she came with one of her sisters to visit his studio in (old) Little Holland House. Mary, then twenty, was the youngest of the three daughters by his first marriage of Charles Fraser-Tytler, a Scotch laird and former Indian Civil Servant. He no doubt knew old Thoby Prinsep professionally, and the rest of the family had met Watts several years before this; indeed, Mary's two sisters had already been subjected to the mild torture of photography at the hands of Mrs Cameron at Freshwater. The girls had subsequently been carried off to absorb culture in Germany and Italy: total absorption it would seem, for Mary, the artist of the party, records that in Dresden she visited the Picture Gallery 'nearly every day for nine months'. Now they were back in England, where Mary was to study at the Slade, and now it was her turn to meet the man with whose work she was already familiar at exhibitions and who had become for her 'the painter of painters' among living artists.

She describes in her *Annals* how she and one of her sisters arrived for the first time at Little Holland House,

> went under its thatched porch, and waited in the room of the blue ceiling till summoned to the studio, to pass with a beating heart through a red baize-covered door. There we read with some feeling of awe a large label—'I must beg not to be disturbed till after two o'clock'—before it was pushed back, to swing again heavily behind us . . .

And there stood her hero—a rather slight figure, brush in hand, dwarfed by enormous canvases.

> In 1870 the beard was only slightly touched with grey, his hair quite brown, very fine in quality, and brushed back from the forehead. I do not recollect that I saw the picture of the knight with bowed head now called the 'Eve of Peace'. I remember the painter much more clearly than his work; but he nevertheless so distinctly suggested to me the days of chivalry that I believe I should not have been surprised if, on another visit, I had found him all clad in shining armour.

Mary alleges that 'from this time forward' she received 'the greatest kindness and help from him'. For reasons which will become apparent, she subsequently wished it to be believed that she established a fairly intimate relationship with him from the very first. If she did not, it was certainly not for want of trying; for it would seem that she set her cap at him from the moment of their meeting in 1870. It can hardly have been mere coincidence that she found herself at Bournemouth in 1873 just when Watts was recuperating there from one of his innumerable bouts of illness; and may she not have been in part instrumental in persuading her father to spend August and September of 1875 at Freshwater? Here she must have made good progress, for before the year was out she had actually returned to the Briary as a guest. Soon we read of her sending Watts what he describes as a 'very beautiful present', probably some specimen of her own handiwork, and receiving in return an open invitation to visit him at 6 Melbury Road whenever she felt inclined; that meant, of course, at those hours when his studio was thrown open to worshippers, most of them female, and many of them young. She soon became an *habituée*, bringing her work to show him and receiving his *ex cathedra* pronouncements on them in awed silence.

Naturally Mary spent long ecstatic hours at the Grosvenor Gallery winter exhibition of 1881–82; but she was not lucky enough to be shown round it by the Master in person, for he was mostly dodging the London fogs at Brighton. She wrote, however, from Scotland in March to congratulate him on his 'triumph', cunningly slipping in a sentence which she must have known would go straight to his heart: 'I have long perceived that whilst before some great masters' pictures I feel wonder, before yours I always feel *better* . . .' Watts replied by return:

> My dear Miss Tytler,
> I think I am old friend enough and certainly am old enough in person to say My dear Miss Mary, or indeed, My dear Mary without the Miss! . . .

There followed purring satisfaction at intentions so accurately understood, modest disavowal of more than minimal success in past achievement, and in conclusion the usual bulletin of ill health— 'sadly knocked up', and so on.

Several years passed, during which Mary continued to be a constant visitor to Melbury Road when Watts was in London, and a regular correspondent when fogs or sickness drove him to Brighton. She played her cards skilfully, and the intimacy between them deepened. She could not decide, she confessed, whether 'being at Church or with you was the best'; 'I *grow*,' she wrote, 'when I am with you.' When, one day, she ventured to say, 'Signor, I think I have been looking for you all my life,' he may well have felt that the engagement—the engagement, that is, of a nurse-companion— could be contracted by him at any moment and on any terms that suited him.

To a letter from her, written in January 1885 and telling him that she intended to become 'the old Maid Aunt', he replied that no doubt one day young Mr Right would come along; he may have thought it unlikely at her age, but it is possible that he began to think it desirable. She was certainly setting the pace, and a pretty

9a. *Sara Prinsep*, 1864
She said of Watts, 'He came to stay three days; he stayed thirty years'

9b. *Time and Oblivion*, 1848
Study for Watts's first allegory. The painting, which is more than ten
feet broad, is now at Eastnor Castle (see p. 62)

10. *Virginia Pattle*, 1849
The most beautiful of the seven famous Pattle sisters, with whom Watts
was in love. She became Lady Somers (see p. 69)

11. *Paolo and Francesca*, 1872-75
In this version Virginia Somers was the model for Francesca (see p. 149)

12a. *Arthur Prinsep*, 1855/56
Thoby and Sara Prinsep's youngest son. This drawing, made in Paris, was used later by Watts for his *Sir Galahad* (see p. 89)

12b. Study for *Hope*
The best-known version of this famous picture is in the Tate Gallery (see p. 212)

12c. 30 fils stamp, Jordan, 1974
The Arab states seem to have taken Watts's *Hope* to their hearts (see p. 212)

13a. Old Little Holland House
The dower house of Holland House, where Watts lived with the Prinseps
from 1851 to 1874. Under Sara Prinsep it became the seat of a
famous intellectual-Bohemian salon (see p. 76)

13b. *Thoby Prinsep*, 1871
A portrait painted for Charles Rickards
(see p. 72)

13c. *Sir Henry Taylor* (detail), *c.* 1870
Author of *Philip Van Artevelde* and friend
of Watts and of the Camerons (see p. 127)

14. *Mrs Nassau Senior*, 1857/58
Sister of Thomas Hughes, author of *Tom Brown's School Days*, and a
valued friend of Watts. The picture, which is one of a handful of full-length
life-sized female portraits, was exhibited at the Royal Academy in 1858 under
an assumed name, F. W. George, but no one was deceived (see p. 102)

15. *Julia Cameron*
A photograph taken by Lord Somers. Julia, the famous
photographer, was the most brilliant, the most eccentric, and the 'ugly-duckling'
of the seven Pattle sisters

16. *The Whisper of the Muse*
Photograph of Watts by Julia Cameron, taken at about the time
of his marriage to Ellen Terry

brisk one at that. Was she hinting that she wanted to marry him? He felt uneasy, unsure of himself. After the disaster of his first marriage, would he not be crazy to contemplate a second where once again the difference in age was so enormous? He knew well enough that he needed nursing and cosseting, yet could he with propriety admit her into his house on any other footing than that of his wife? She was, after all, a lady, not a trained nurse to be paid by the week. His letter was cool, and in it he called her 'a silly child'. She understood, and perhaps she wept.

In April she suggested coming to see him, but received no encouragement; disillusioned and miserable, she returned for consolation to her painting. She had already studied at the South Kensington School of Art as well as at the Slade, and she now began to take lessons in modelling from the French sculptor, Jules Dalou; at the same time she threw herself energetically into the movement that was soon to become the Home Arts and Industries. Meanwhile spring turned to summer, summer to autumn, and with each day that passed Watts grew increasingly aware that he was missing her company more than he cared to admit. He consoled himself by visits to the Westminster Aquarium to see 'Zazel' nightly shot from a cannon's mouth—an act of courage that so impressed him that he persuaded her to sit for her portrait. But Zazel was no substitute for Mary, and in December he broke the silence and wrote to ask how she was. This led to the resumption of her visits, but she saw that she was making no real headway.

One day in the following July she arrived at Little Holland House with a portrait she had just painted, bringing with her the man who had sat for it. There seemed nothing sinister in this; to criticise the picture it was obviously advantageous to have the sitter to hand. But a few days later she wrote to tell him that she and her model were thinking of getting married. The news, so sudden, so utterly unexpected, felled him to the ground and brought on a sharp attack of lumbago. He implored her to do nothing rash. He begged for half an hour alone with her. She came; but we do not know what was said—only that he was assured that as yet nothing was finally settled.

It may sound uncharitable to suggest it, but is it not just conceivable that all this was simply a ruse: that Mary calculatedly dangled this man in front of Watts in order to make him clarify the situation, to force him to a decision? She was now a spinster of thirty-six. Attractive, highly talented and of a good family, she must surely have had other offers of marriage a dozen or more years ago and have rejected them; could it be mere coincidence that at this precise moment an apparently eligible and potentially acceptable suitor should suddenly appear? Once she had almost landed her divine painter; then he had got off the hook. Now was her last chance. *He* might not be certain that he needed her; but *she* was. Of course Ronald Chapman, as the son of the Wattses' adopted daughter[1] and writing while his mother was still alive, makes no such outrageous suggestion in his biography of Watts. But the fact remains that, as time was to show, Mary had a will of iron. If it was a game that she was playing, she played it to the end and with consummate skill.

On 12 July Watts, unable to bear the suspense any longer, wrote to Mary, 'I want you to tell me very distinctly when you are engaged, or consider *That* to be within distance of a decided *probability*. I do not think that it should depend upon the question of money! That is not nice. When you have made up your mind as to that future, or even *That it may be*, I consider that, all things taken into account, we should become strangers. But you know that I shall always be— yours affectionately, Signor.'

Then he realised that he was playing his hand badly, that he had not produced his one big trump. No doubt he was many years older than his rival (we do not know the young man's age, or even his name), but at least he was better off financially. So, three days later, he wrote again—this time to warn her of the misery that struggling to make both ends meet would entail, of the unhappiness it would cause her 'to watch the deepening lines of anxiety on another face, to be pinched by small necessities—especially with a family.' Still hitting below the belt (if we may mix the metaphor), he added casually that his own income was between £1,000 and £1,500 a year.[2] But he could not close his letter on so sordid a note:

I want you to know that I have come to feel for you the most pro-found and tender respect and the most absolute trust in the

1 Not Blanche, but Lilian Mackintosh (Mrs Michael Chapman)—adopted about 1889.

2 Surely a gross underestimate. Perhaps he did not wish to frighten her by appearing indecently rich.

qualities of your nature. I do grieve to lose the much that might have been thought, and done, and seen together. But all this is selfish; and knowing this, I do not allow any personal feeling to influence me in the advice I give you to be prudent and very resolute in your prudence . . .

For Watts there now followed anxious days and contradictory reports. Everything was settled: she was to marry her man in October. Nothing was settled: she might not be marrying him after all. On 17 July Watts took advantage of a moment of alleged disengagement to propose, and Mary, playing her game to the last, asked for time to consider her answer. Eight days later she went to him 'to tell him that my *life* was his. There are no words for an hour like this— only tears of joy. The noblest heart all mine, all mine.'

Watts should now have been the happiest man in the world; in fact he was besieged by doubts and perhaps also troubled by a slightly guilty conscience. How would Mary's family receive the news? Would he prove a 'jarring element' and create discord? What would they feel about his first marriage—a subject, he had told Mary, 'which I must for ever decline to discuss even with you!' but one, she had already hinted, that might arouse the disapproval of her half-brother and head of her family, Edward? Was she sure, he asked, that she was making the right decision? Mary was very sure; but she asked, was *he*? He replied, 'Don't be a Goose!'

For the moment the engagement was to be kept secret; so secret, indeed, that even three months later he could write to Miss Mead saying that his continued ill health *may* end in his taking a step which will surprise his friends. In September, however, Mary went to Aldourie to break the news to her family. Ted, she wrote, was 'glad about my great happiness and proud of my prince of painters', but felt that 'a little offering of game—"various"—black cocks— grouse and partridges'—would give better expression of his pleasure than would a letter. We do not know whether Watts, who elsewhere spoke of shooting as 'a disgraceful and unmanly amusement', ate them—for his Mary's sake, or how he thanked the sender. But poor Ted had other and sadder things to occupy him, for meanwhile his three-year-old son and heir had fallen from his pony, receiving injuries from which he died soon afterwards.

Naturally the letters that passed between Mary and Watts were loaded with bulletins, anxiety and expressions of sympathy, but not to the total exclusion of declarations of carefully weighed affection. Mary wrote:

I want when you take me to be just a sort of pillow that helps you to rest, and perhaps something more, too, but *not an anxiety*. And I think I can promise you to do without any luxuries, even comforts if it is necessary, for getting into debt is worse than having too little to eat! It will be best to begin as if we were much poorer than we are. It is so easy to increase expenses . . .

Watts replied:

I shall be disappointed if you do not bloom out like a flower that is transplanted into favourable soil. I want you to feel, if I do not profess the passionate feeling which would not be becoming to my age, I can love you very much with the love that joins itself closely round goodness and had its roots deep down in perfect trust, and that the door of your cage shall be wide open and there shall be no wires but silver films instead! . . .

Mary was more than satisfied:

Thank you my beloved Signor for all you say. What you give me—I mean the kind of love—is like everything else I have got from you, just what I want. I do want to be perfectly trusted. I do better when I am—if I am held cheap I become so. I hope and believe you will find me though *very* imperfect, very ignorant, and very different from the clever women you have had for your friends, at least as big hearted, and as true as any . . . I am a good deal dependent on the atmosphere I live in, and years seem only to make me more aware of its effects for good or for evil. I think it has been one reason to prevent my accepting a sort of medium happiness in married life, for I knew I should be deeply impressed by the intimate life, and have had fears of taking an impress from a lower type than my ideals. I have no fears now . . .

Mary returned from Scotland and the date of the wedding was fixed. It took place, very quietly, on 20 November, from the house that her stepmother had bought at Epsom, various Fraser-Tytlers having arrived from Aldourie on the previous day. After the ceremony the bride and bridegroom went by train to London—'to *my* home with *my* beloved', as Mary wrote in her diary.

We do not know what wedding present Watts gave Mary, but she was giving him one of incalculable value: eighteen more years of creative activity and eighteen years of married happiness.

15

'A POISONOUS SNAKE'

ANY MAN who has found himself simultaneously pursued by two or more adoring women (and what unfettered male has not?) will know the extreme difficulty of keeping them from meeting. Watts showed great skill as a painter and as a sculptor, but it was surely little short of genius that enabled him so to arrange matters that Mary (if she is to be believed) first met Mrs Barrington only 'very shortly' before her marriage. When one remembers that the Barringtons lived next door to Watts, and that this 'coxing-and-boxing' had been going on for nearly a decade, one must really begin to think in terms of the miraculous.

The two women felt very differently towards their hero. Mrs Barrington was married (and for all we know, happily married). She was not emotionally involved, which made her position much easier than Mary's. She was an artistic lion-hunter with literary ambitions, and her biographies of Watts and Leighton had been gestating for a great many years when they finally appeared in 1905 and 1906 respectively; Mary was therefore being very unjust in describing Mrs Barrington's *Reminiscences of G. F. Watts* as 'an unreliable book brought out hastily within three months less than a year after his death,'[1] and surely rather petty in refusing for many years to read it. When she eventually did read it (in a second-hand copy; she was not going to promote sales by buying a new one), she scribbled offensive comments in the margin, and in one of her notebooks she substituted 'a poisonous snake' for the name of the author. In her *Annals* she dismissed the viper in three or four withering lines. 'I never saw her after September 1890. She and I never really knew each other. I have this winter (1911–1912) for the first

[1] Manuscript notebook.

178

time seen and read her published recollections of my husband, and have thus been made aware that she did not really know him.' Yet this is the book that even Ronald Chapman, who might be expected to support his 'grandmother', describes as 'the best work for the light it throws on Watts's character'.

A letter written by Mary to a friend in July 1905, shortly after the publication of Mrs Barrington's *Reminiscences*, speaks for itself:

> I only know that book of Reminiscences by advertisements 'of the unique opportunities and most intimate friendship', the bad taste of which appears not to strike the mind of Reviewers— save perhaps that of *The Times*. The writer always assumed a proprietorship in my husband—distasteful to him and much more so to me. She seldom saw him during these last *18* years of her '29 years of *intimate* friendship'. She never saw this house [Limnerslease]! and by our going late to London (often only in August and September) she had practically ceased to be a neighbour. I have not seen the book—but if she describes him as irritable she is a foolish woman, as everyone will know that *she* must have rubbed him up very often! as she did *me always*.
>
> Her book, and reports that others were offering to write for publishers, forced me into making the announcement in the papers,[1] which I *hated* doing, but I felt it was due to the public. I should like first to have told all friends and privately asked for letters, but this was impossible . . .

Three days later, she wrote further:

> When I see you again some day I will perhaps let you know a little more about the lady who wrote the Reminiscences. I do not want to read them until it is necessary for me to do so. They will make me very angry I know, and I am advised that neither I nor any friend of mine should take any notice of what is said in the book at present.
>
> I shall hope my book will be so compiled as to give an account that is quite beyond question . . .

Mrs Barrington was, as one would expect, much more charitable. 'It was during this year [1886],' she wrote, 'that he talked to me of

[1] Of her forthcoming biography, and inviting any who had letters from Watts to get into touch with her.

the idea he had of marrying, but wrote in the summer that he wished it to be kept a great secret, a very great secret!' (Against this passage Mrs Watts has scribbled '*Lie*. He wrote to no one till he had told the Prinseps through Julia Stephen'). 'He said he was certain that we [she and Mary] should become "great friends", as we had "the same interests and tastes." "You will perhaps find her a little shy and reserved, but I don't think you will have any difficulty. We are both to have perfect confidence and freedom, and none of my habits are to be changed." ' She saw the Wattses several times after the wedding and before they sailed for their honeymoon in Egypt, and according to Ronald Chapman (who does not give his source) she told Watts, in Mary's presence, that he was 'mad to entrust himself to such untried hands' and that he would die during the voyage (which in fact he nearly did). 'A furious quarrel had ensued. But Mary saw that once and for all she would have to be resolute . . .'

Watts wrote to Mrs Barrington a number of times, and at some length, during his honeymoon. He was, of course, already ill by the time the ship reached Malta, and so obliged to interrupt his journey for a fortnight. But by Christmas they had reached Cairo, where he found the Sphinx enormously impressive but the Pyramids, for being in competition with the Libyan mountains, disappointingly puny. Six leisurely weeks were spent in a hired *dahabiah*, the 'Vittoria', in which they sailed up the Nile as far as the first cataract, Mary earnestly studying Egyptology and Watts the 'grand pectoral muscles' of the *fellaheen*. Then on medical advice Watts, still troubled by a cough, took the baths for several weeks at Helouan before they continued their journey to Athens and Constantinople. During these 'six months of delight' Watts painted a number of small landscapes and several portraits; but the memory of all he saw was to bear more fruit later.

Some of his experiences were recorded in his letters to Mrs Barrington, and quoted in her *Reminiscences*; but, needless to say, the original letters are not to be found in the archives at the Watts Gallery. He told her (she says) 'how admirable a companion' he had found in Mary—and in the circumstances it was generous of her to quote this in her book. But no sooner were the Wattses back in London than the two women were at one another's throats. In a letter written by Watts to Mrs Barrington on 2 October 1890, the writer looks back on the three of four years of bitter warfare that had ensued, and blames her for creating a situation that was intolerable to his wife. The actual letter is missing but two drafts survive, one of which reads:

My dear Mrs Barrington,
   You are to see me before you go on a visit. When I see you I must have some serious talk with you which, as I am still very deaf, would be difficult—so it must be deferred. I acknowledge and am grateful for much and unvarying past kindness and more; but this could not justify your unwise persistent determination in the beginning to make Melbury House and Little Holland House joint concerns. My wife distinctly showed you that this was not agreeable to her, and you must remember she was a stranger to you! You obliged a duel which distressed her, for her nature is most kind; but she felt that either she or you must be master of the situation. However unreasonable she might have been (and few wives will think she was), you were wrong!
   It should have occurred to you that a jealous temper (and you could not know whether she had one or not!) might have been made very suspicious by assumption of right to be absolutely at home, or even of such very unusual intimacy, and this might have sown the seeds of great bitterness and most lasting unhappiness. You were wrong! You will say most likely that you never showed any disposition to assume the position, but I will illustrate the matter. When Mr V. Prinsep married, though he [and I] had been brought up in the same home since he was fourteen years old, I shut the garden gate leading to this house and sent him the key. When I married and we first came home, I put a wedge in the latch (not fastening up the gate but hinting that we wished to be alone at least some part of the day). What did you do? Took our wedge out and threw it away! This was the key-note. You were wrong! You may say, Why was I not told this honestly? No telling could be more distinct than my wife's manner . . .

Watts had told everyone that his marriage would make no difference whatever to old friendships. To Mrs Barrington this no doubt sanctioned her continued use at all hours of the garden gate, but a woman with greater tact would have understood from the wedge that it did not. The trouble largely stemmed from Mrs Barrington's complete misjudgment of Mary's character. Mary looked so deceptively gentle: a harmless little nurse-companion who had indeed succeeded in marrying her patient but who would never attempt to interfere with the established pattern of his life. She could hardly have been more wrong; behind that demure exterior was a will of iron, and Watts had no choice but to stand by his wife in the war that was now inevitable. Though his marriage brought him in most ways deep happiness, there may well have been moments when he wished he had engaged a paid nurse.

He breathed a sigh of relief when, early in November 1887, he and Mary sailed for Malta to spend the winter at Sliema. But things turned out badly. First came the news, just before Christmas, of Sara Prinsep's death. This greatly upset him, and he cried, 'How sad the dismemberment of that sisterhood!—like the pages of some beautiful book torn out one by one.' He had—quite unreasonably, one may think,—a slight feeling of guilt that he had deserted Sara, and someone had once acidly remarked of him to Augusta Holland, 'No one has received more kindness than he has and no one has lost, always by his own neglect, so many friends'. Shortly before his second marriage he had written to Mary:

> I could almost wish you could find it in your heart to write to Mrs Prinsep and say in your own way you wish she could look upon you as a sort of daughter. Poor thing, she is in a bad state of health and things have gone very ill with her for many years past . . . I fear being ill and ill at ease she may feel that somehow I am deserting the family with which I have been identified for some seven and thirty years.

It must seem highly improbable that any such letter to Sara ever came to be written.

Then, a day or two later, Watts was taken seriously ill, and it was not until the middle of February that he was considered sufficiently recovered to exchange, on medical advice, Malta for Naples. In March they reached the French Riviera, where Watts was well enough to make studies from which he later painted 'The Alps behind Mentone' and 'Sunset over the Alps'. At the same moment, and not so very far away, a neurotic young Dutchman with flaming red hair who had just arrived at Arles, was also painting what to

Watts would have seemed the wildest daubs, yet which were pictures one day to be eagerly contested in the sale-rooms in which his own were derided or forgotten.

By May Mentone had become too hot, and the Wattses moved on by way of San Remo and Turin to Aix-les-Bains, where Watts was again taken ill. A week in the more bracing air of the Haute-Savoie revived him, and in June he found himself home again and once more in the forefront of the battle.

From Aix, Watts had written to Miss Mead in America, whose long silence had been troubling him. She was coming to London soon, and he felt it wise to warn her of the tension that existed. Though the letter contains much that he had said a dozen times already, it is quoted almost in full because it shows how endlessly repetitive he always was and how necessary he thought it to justify yet again the improbable step that he had taken in marrying:

My dear Mary Mead,

I was very sorry to think during the long interval of silence after I wrote to you, that perhaps disapproval of the step I took in marrying might be the reason. No doubt at my age, for I had reached my seventieth year, such a thing might seem to want explanation. During the last few years I had been getting into a very bad state of health, worse and worse, requiring constant care indeed, and attention no one could bestow who could not be with me at all times as this state of things was putting an end to all the work I hoped to do, I felt justified in asking one who for the last sixteen years had made no secret of her profound interest in my objects and attachment to myself. It looks rather like a selfish calculation, but I knew she would be happy. I could return affection to a nature of the finest fibre, capable of developing all that is good in me and aiding in all my best projects.

I look forward to your making her acquaintance and I want you very much to come to see me as soon as you can. . . . I shall be at home, I hope, in ten days. *Write to L.H.H.* and *say when you will come*—but please come alone. Our good friend Mrs Barrington (you will find her at home and working hard and admirably!) makes a mistake sometimes in a little want of judgment bringing mutual friends, as if her introduction as the mistress of the ceremonies was necessary. This is of course *entre nous*. My wife particularly wishes to make the acquaintance of my friends through me . . .

Miss Mead came and went, but of her visit we know nothing. On 27 September 1888 he wrote to her again—and we may assume that it was his wife who ordained that he should now call her by her second name, Gertrude; henceforth there was to be only one Mary in his life:

My dear Gertrude,
  What has happened? Not only have you not written to tell me that you enjoyed your visit, which from the friendship that seemed to have grown up one might have expected, but you have not answered my letter. This is so unlike the Gertrude Mary [sic] I used to know, that I am seriously anxious . . .

He is trying, he says, to view the matter quite impartially, but 'cannot find anything we have done to weaken your interest or destroy your friendship'. So he is forced to the conclusion that Mrs Barrington has been making mischief, through a mutual friend:

[Mrs Barrington] and Mary do not sympathise, but her grievance if fairly stated comes to this *only*: that Mary could not consent to have an intimacy which could only and should only be won by mutual respect and sympathy, forced on her by actual violence. This hardly calls for resentment on the part of mutual friends. There must be more . . .

People, he continues, have been saying that Mary is 'extravagantly jealous', which is quite untrue. 'Mary is delighted that my friends should have the affection for me which she (foolishly) thinks they ought to have.

I am far from wishing to influence you against my neighbour. She has a thousand good qualities. I am in debt for unvarying kindness and could count upon any aid; but this does not give unlimited right! I write this to you because I am greatly grieved and because my time runs short. When you go back to America it is hardly likely that I shall see you again, and there is no one I had and shall have a greater affection for. I wish also to place you at your ease if you have exchanged your friendship or feel that you cannot have both; then my great desire will be, I will say *our* great desire will be, that you should do what will make your visit to England most pleasant.

My neighbour with, as I said, excellent qualities, has the misfortune of creating difficulties between friends; this is the third time she has placed me in a serious position with old friends, and the twentieth time it might have happened had I listened to insinuations and accusations, and I really feel that this must not happen again. And at the risk of seeming ungrateful, which I certainly am not, I shall consider whether I should not take the step of honestly declining to continue intimacy. I have written this without Mary's knowledge because I know she would be against your being vexed, and you must not consider you have to reply unless you can say that representations of ill treatment have not caused the change of feeling which is patent, and for which I am sure you think you have sufficient reason . . .

Two days later he wrote again, saying that he much regretted his former letter, which had been prompted by his learning that Miss Mead intended to stay with the Barringtons. 'I must own I was greatly provoked and really distressed by an act of such want of judgment, to say the least, as may still lead to serious consequences.' He then repeated most of the contents of his allegedly regretted previous letter.

Miss Mead sensibly declined to let herself be bullied. She must have written to say that she would first visit the Barringtons in London, then join the Wattses when they went to Brighton to escape the London winter. On 19 October both Watts and Mary replied, now adopting a new line in which jam cloaks the pill. Mary wrote:

We are so glad you can come to us at Brighton; it would have been more 'bitter' if you had gone away without a goodbye . . . I am glad you are going to stay with Mrs Barrington—so much nicer than going into lodgings. I always take people as I find them, and expect others to do the same. I should never have said anything to you about her, but that with some reason I have a wholesome dread of her hearing much about our little life here—so very precious to me!—that I cannot bear to think of garbled versions of it going about. That is all I want you to think about—by no means to feel I grudge her your friendship or mind a bit her coming in every day with you! a pleasant excuse! . . .

Watts wrote:

Mary I know has written to you. I only scribble a line to say do not let any sort of difficulty exist about your going to Mrs Barrington. *There is no war between us,* and why on earth should you not come in to see us with or without your hostess? Better without, I own. I think you will greatly enjoy your visit. She knows a great number of the best people of all kinds, and has a thousand merits. You must not understand more than I mean if I say, Take care. I do not say she will repeat confidences, but she has a craze *to show how very much she knows about everybody,* and is sometimes injudicious to the extent of creating real trouble. Also she has a curious tendency to think people cracked. I am sure that you will not believe that I wish to interfere with the friendship which exists between you, and she herself told me you were the most intimate friend she had . . .

'There is no war between us'! Here Mary might well have written 'Lie' in the margin.

For two years there is no news from the battle front, though we can rest assured that bitter fighting continued whenever the Wattses were in London. Presumably Miss Mead paid her promised visit to Brighton, where Watts worked during the winter on his big 'Court of Death', one of his many 'Eve's, 'The Habit does not make the Monk', and other paintings. Then he caught bronchitis, which led to pneumonia and complications which kept him in bed from February until April. Brighton having failed him, he made the experiment of spending the following winter at Monkshatch, near Guildford, the home of his old friends Andrew and May Hichens. May, before her marriage had been a Prinsep—the daughter of Thoby's elder brother, Charles, who had died in 1864; she was yet another of those homeless children whom Thoby and Sara had taken under their wing. In 1918, after her husband's death, she became the second wife of the second Lord Tennyson, the Laureate's son.

This, as Mary tells, was an eventful visit:

The winter months as they passed found [Watts] so well that the idea of a winter home in the neighbourhood—a cottage, perhaps to which a studio could be added—was constantly in our minds. One lovely sunny morning Andrew came in from a walk, enthusiastic about a site for a house he had found, and a quarter of an hour later we were standing on a little sandy knoll, well wooded and possessed of some very fine trees, and as it then seemed, building our cottage in Spain. 'Too delightful for accomplishment,' Signor thought; but Andrew saw no difficulty, if the land could be secured.

It was, and Hichens insisted upon buying it himself and renting it to 'the beloved little man' (as he and May called Watts). Building began in April 1890, with (Sir) Ernest George as architect—who surely was rather careless in forgetting to make a staircase from the first floor to the second. In May, Watts was at Freshwater painting the portrait of Tennyson already mentioned, and then in October there occurred that unspecified crisis with Mrs Barrington which provoked the long letter given earlier in this chapter. Surely we may see the hand of Mary in this decision to build a house far removed from Mrs Barrington and yet within easy reach of London, and to acquire sufficient land around it to prevent the latter from moving in next door? Watts was, of course, obliged to keep on his Melbury Road house; but as the years went by he spent increasingly less of his time there, and though he himself saw Mrs Barrington now and then, she and Mary never met again.

The new house—a big and ponderous red-brick building at Compton, two or three miles from Guildford below the Hog's Back —was ready in 1891. The Wattses named it 'Limnerslease'—' "Limner," ' wrote Mary, 'to keep the remembrance that it was built for an artist, and the word "lease", as having a double meaning, for we played a little with the old English word "to leasen", which meant to glean, our hope being that there were *golden years* to be gleaned in this new home.' Wilfrid Scawen Blunt, when sitting for his portrait there in 1899, described it as 'an ornamental, not too ornamented cottage[1] of the usual Victorian kind, which he had christened

[1] It was large enough to have been converted later into three quite substantial houses.

"Limnerslease", much to his friends' amusement . . . Burne-Jones used to call it "Dauber's Den", "Painter's Palette", and other nicknames.' Here, watched over by his guardian angel, the Grand Old Man of English painting was to spend most of the last thirteen years of his long life.

16

'ENGLAND'S MICHELANGELO'

'WHY DON'T you stick to painting?' Rodin is said to have asked Renoir when he heard that the painter had turned in his old age to sculpture. 'I am too old to paint,' replied Renoir; 'I must do something easier.' Perhaps this was simply intended as a snub; if not, then it must sound to the layman rather like taking up ice hockey on discovering that one is too decrepit to play bowls.

It may well seem strange that Watts, who as a boy had worked in Behnes's studio, should have waited until he was in his fiftieth year before seriously turning to sculpture. Though it was Leighton who called him 'England's Michelangelo' (for Watts would never have overtly made so extravagant a claim for himself), Watts must surely have 'owned the soft impeachment', and his project for a 'House of Life' had clearly been envisaged as a challenge to the Sistine Chapel. But Michelangelo was also (among other things) a sculptor, and Watts, who had dared to call himself 'a poor relation of Pheidias', was now to compete with the great Florentine in this field too. Indeed, had Watts carried out his 'House of Life', redesigned St Paul's Cathedral, and addressed a handful of immortal sonnets to Ellen Terry and Arthur Prinsep, he might well have laid claim to being 'a poor relation of Michelangelo'. He once said—though it is hard to know what he meant by it—'I would like to have done for modern thought what Michael Angelo did for theological thought.'

When in Italy in the forties Watts had sometimes amused himself by modelling in clay or wax, and small figures so made were later occasionally used as studies for paintings. He is also said by Mary Watts to have carved at this time, in Nelson's studio in Rome, the alabaster 'Medusa'[1] now in the Watts Gallery, of which another version in stained marble was made for Rickards in 1870–1871. The fact that handling wet clay gave Watts rheumatism may have contributed to his reluctance to continue with sculpture, for even carving is usually preceded by modelling in clay. This obstacle was, however, to be overcome when an Italian named Fabrucci, who became his sculptural assistant in the seventies, introduced him to a method of working with pieces of tow soaked in a mixture of size and plaster powder (*gesso grosso*) which hardened into a substance that he could 'cut, indeed almost chisel, into the forms he wanted'.

But what made Watts suddenly turn, or return, to sculpture in 1866 was an appeal, difficult to refuse, from his old friend Reginald Cholmondeley to carry out for Condover Church in Shropshire a memorial to his elder brother, Thomas Owen,[2] who had tragically died within a few weeks of his marriage. The kneeling figure that Watts completed in 1867 is undistinguished; its importance lies in the fact that it set his feet again on a path that he was to continue to tread until the very end of his life.

Lack of space makes it impossible to discuss in any detail more than four of Watts's sculptures: 'Clytie', 'Hugh Lupus', 'Physical Energy' and 'Tennyson'. Besides these there were, principally, the following:

> LORD HOLLAND, 1869–70. Bronze seated life-sized figure of the third Lord Holland, made with some assistance from Sir Edgar Boehm (Holland Park).
> DR LONSDALE, Bishop of Lichfield, 1869–71. Life-sized recumbent figure in alabaster, Lichfield Cathedral. There is a plaster version at Compton.
> AURORA, *c.* 1870–80. A failure, cast and then abandoned (Compton). Several models, including a housemaid, a Life Guardsman and a professional male Italian model (Colorossi) all posed for it. It was intended to be carried out in gold and ivory,

---

[1] Gutch rejects an early date for this on the grounds that the head has a Pre-Raphaelite look, and places it around 1873–1874. I see no reason for doubting Mrs Watts's dating, and suggest that the influence is in fact Hellenistic (cf. the head of Alexander in the Uffizi) or renaissance.

[2] Thomas Cholmondeley had changed his surname to Owen, that of the family from whom he had inherited the Condover estates through the female line.

like the famous chryselephantine 'Athena' of Pheidias. Mary Watts refers to it as 'Venus'.

LORD LOTHIAN, 1871–74. Life-sized recumbent marble figure with supporting angels in Blickling Church, Norfolk. Replica in Jedburgh Abbey.

DAPHNE, 1879–82. Marble head and shoulders, intended as a companion piece to the Clytie, but left unfinished (Tate Gallery).

By general consent, Watts's 'Clytie' is the most successful of his smaller sculptures. The well-known legend that inspired it may be read in Ovid's *Metamorphoses*. Clytie, a sea-nymph, loved Apollo, whose principal duty it was to drive the chariot of the sun; but though she each day watched amorously his progress across the sky, she never succeeded in winning his favour. So the gods, in pity, turned her into a sunflower.

Various versions of the 'Clytie' exist: one in marble (now in the Guildhall), two in bronze (Tate Gallery and Watts Gallery), and a number in plaster or cement, one of which was acquired by George Eliot. Probably two other marble versions were also made. The Guildhall 'Clytie' was exhibited in an unfinished state at the Royal Academy in 1868 and completed ten years later. As with the 'Aurora', various models were pressed into service. 'Long Mary' (the co-operative housemaid at Little Holland House whom Watts and Mrs Prinsep had persuaded to pose in the nude in the cause of art) was, as on occasions in his paintings of the period, the chief inspiration; she it was who, in the words of a journalist quoting Browning, enabled Watts 'to display his old admiration for the "superb abundance where a man might base his head".' But Colorossi once again provided the muscles, and 'a beautiful little child, not yet three years old—Margaret Burne-Jones—was laid under contribution, and was studied in her mother's arms' (Mary Watts). According to Mrs Barrington, memories of Ellen Terry also 'gave value to the conception and inspired the working of the marble', which was largely carried out by Watts himself.

One could hardly have expected that such a gallimaufry could have resulted in a work conspicuous for its homogeneity. But it did, and Swinburne, in his *Notes on the Royal Academy Exhibition, 1868*, loudly and properly sang its praises:

Not imitative, not even assimilative of Michael Angelo's manner, it yet by some vague and ineffable quality brings to mind his work rather than any Greek sculptor's. There is the same intense and fiery sentiment, the same grandeur of device, the same mystery of tragedy. The colour and passion of this work are the workman's own. Never was a divine legend translated into diviner likeness . . .

So England's Michelangelo had produced a 'Michelangelo'!

In 1870, Hugh Lupus Grosvenor, 3rd Marquis of Westminster,[1] decided to commission for Eaton Hall, his house near Chester, a 'heroic' equestrian statue of Hugh Lupus ('Le Gros Veneur'—'The Fat Huntsman')—the Norman Earl of Chester after whom he was named. He first approached Landseer; but Sir Edwin replied that he was too busy, and at sixty-eight too old, to undertake such a major work. So Lord Westminster turned to Watts, who accepted in a pompous letter: 'Something worthy even of the Nation', and so on. He longed, of course, 'in an affair of such importance to work for the dignity of art alone . . .', but alas! the bills kept on coming in . . .

Meanwhile Westminster, who had been studying his Ormerod's *History of Cheshire*, began to have doubts about the moral character of his hero, a man who 'dissipated his goods, was much given to his belly, had many bastard children and so on'. Might not some local saint—there was, for instance, St Oswald, 'a capital man, and he fought his battles too'—be more suitable? Rather surprisingly, Watts still preferred to immortalise the obese old lecher, and Westminster agreed to abide by his original choice.

A small sketch of an equestrian figure—one that is in fact closer to the later 'Physical Energy' than to 'Hugh Lupus', but which served for both—was modelled and cast; but Watts was enormously occupied at that time with other work, and his ejection from old Little Holland House further delayed his start on the big sculpture. Meanwhile he and Westminster corresponded intermittently about armour and stirrups and falcons; about Hugh Lupus's sword in the British Museum; about what breed of horse should be portrayed, and then about the precise position of the animal's limbs. At last, in 1877, Watts was able to use a studio in Melbury Road, where the base for the group was mounted on a trolley so that it could be run out on rails into the garden (which became his regular practice with

[1] Created first Duke of Westminster in 1874.

big works). Mrs Barrington tells us that Watts also made 'a frame-work of wood—a section of a horse—over which he nailed large sheets of brown paper, and cutting these to the shape of the horse, he drew lines in charcoal which indicated the action he meant to express.'

Summer after summer for the next six years Watts laboured away, working out of doors when the sun shone, and in conse-quence getting sunstroke. For critic there was Mrs Barrington ready to come through the fence at any moment, for model a Percheron mare brought by the Duke from Normandy; and Mrs Barrington tells how, one sunny day in May, she watched the arrival at Little Holland House of a groom leading 'a gorgeous white steed . . . as white as the horse in Watts' "Sir Galahad"—with rippling, shining mane and tail, and partly covered with beautiful purple silk trap-pings'. When off duty the horse was stabled at Cliveden, which Westminster had bought in 1870.

By 1879 the work was far enough advanced for the Duke to pro-nounce it 'magnificent'; then, two years later, Watts discovered 'a radical defect', cut it to pieces and virtually began all over again. But at last, in 1883, it was finished to his satisfaction and 'drawn down Melbury Road under an enormous sheet on its way to Mr Moore's foundry at Thames Ditton' for casting—a process that took nine months. In September of the following year it was delivered—all seven-and-a-half tons of it—at Eaton Hall; and there it still stands, beside what survives of the ducal mansion.

Though a carping critic with a tape-measure has demonstrated that the horse's hind thighbones are of unequal length, Marion Spielmann declares—and we cannot but agree with him—that 'we need not be disturbed in our conviction that the monument is an extraordinarily fine and noble performance'. It is, however, less original, and of course far less well known, than its successor, 'Physical Energy'.

While working on 'Hugh Lupus', Watts had constantly at the back of his mind the thought of a second 'heroic' equestrian figure in which he would be 'untramelled by costume or period'.[1] His aim, he

---

[1] I have not seen 'Hugh Lupus'; but I presume that it and 'Physical Energy' are roughly the same size, for the Duke of Westminster has kindly informed me that the former weighs 7 tons and the horse's tail $1\frac{1}{2}$ tons.

said, would be 'to create a figure that should suggest man as he ought to be—a part of creation, of cosmos in fact, his great limbs to be akin to the rocks and the roots, and his head to be as the sun.' A friend who visited his studio while the sculpture was in progress spoke of it as 'impressionist'. Watts replied:

> All art is impressionist; the men who use the term do not carry out their own ideal. The aim of their impression is to make evident their own dexterity; the aim should be to give the impression of some great truth of nature, something so far too great for expression that finally it must remain indefinite. The infinite looming large behind the finite. That is the impression which great art alone can convey. I do not wish my man to be like any model you could find anywhere, and I do not wish my horse to be like a natural horse. I want them both merely to represent the characteristics of the human and of the animal.

'Physical Energy' was thus envisaged as something very different from the representational and historically accurate 'Hugh Lupus'.

It would appear that 'Physical Energy' was begun as soon as 'Hugh Lupus' was off Watts's hands, and Mrs Barrington gives an interesting account of an ingenious method the sculptor now devised to enable him not only to keep the limbs of horse and rider of the desired length, but also to make changes in their position:

> Iron bars had been made of the right length for the limbs of the man and horse—the length of these of course never changing as they represented the bones, and at the end of each was a hook or an eye. Before the muscles had been added to these bars the hooks were fastened into the eyes, and turned into the direction Watts meant the limb to take. If he wanted to alter any direction of the line of any limb after the modelling of the flesh had been added, he had but to saw through the tow and plaster, adapt the hook and eye to a different angle, and fill in the gap with fresh tow and plaster.

In one respect the method had a disadvantage. Since Watts, who was never satisfied with what he had done, could make these alterations at any stage, man and beast were constantly being temporarily deprived of one or more of their limbs. Again and again the work appeared to his friends to be finished, yet when they next visited the studio they would find that the perfectionist had once more dismembered it. In 1886 Millais declared that it wanted 'not a touch more' and begged Watts to have it cast at once, adding, 'I'll subscribe to the casting'; but Watts refused. Four years later came fresh demands from other admirers, and in 1898 an offer from the Government to have it cast at the nation's expense; but still Watts was unwilling. 'I never come to it,' he said, 'but I see something fresh to be done to make it better.'

Mrs Stirling describes, in *Life's Little Day*, a visit that she paid to Watts's studio while he was at work on 'Physical Energy':

> The scene which met my eyes stamped itself unforgettable upon my imagination. Against the light was the great statue of Physical Energy, which, reared aloft in the enclosed space, looked colossal. A scaffolding was raised around it, and on this, with the great white beast towering above him, Watts stood, infinitesimal of aspect beside that gigantic emanation of his mind—a frail old man creating with indomitable will that splendid image of Eternal Youth.

In 1899 Rhodes, who was sitting to Watts for the never-completed portrait now in the National Portrait Gallery, was shown 'Physical Energy'. 'He was visibly impressed,' wrote Mary Watts, 'and said: "That's what I should like to have to commemorate the completion of the Cape to Cairo railway. I would write on the base the names of the first subscribers."' It had been Watts's intention to write a 'roll of great names on the pedestal: Genghis Khan, Timon [sic!] the Tartar, Attila and Mahomet'; did he realise, one may ask, that three at least of these four men were among the greatest butchers of all time, Timur (Tamerlane) alone being held responsible for the deaths of thirteen million men, women and children? The names of the subscribers might have been less exotic; they would at all events have been more appropriate.

Watts deeply admired Rhodes as 'the last great Englishman of his type'. When, therefore, on Rhodes's death in 1902 Lord Grey asked whether the sculptor would allow a bronze cast to be made and set up by his grave in the Matoppo hills, the latter willingly gave his consent on condition that the gesso should afterwards be returned to him so that he could continue to work on it. The cast was duly made, but because of the difficulty of transporting it up country it was sent instead to Groote Schuur, Rhodes's house on the slopes of Table Mountain, and later most effectively incorporated in the Rhodes Memorial there.

In the spring of 1904, before its despatch to South Africa, 'Physical Energy' had been exhibited in the courtyard of Burlington House. By that time Watts had made certain alterations to the gesso, including the uptilting of the rider's head, and in 1906, after the sculptor's death, a further cast was made and placed in Kensington Gardens. A graphic account of this casting appeared in the *Daily News* on 22 November 1906, but those who wish to get some idea of the drama of this fascinating but always hazardous operation may turn more easily to the celebrated description of the casting of the 'Perseus' in Cellini's *Autobiography*. In 1960 came a third cast for the British South Africa Company, which was set up at Lusaka (Zambia) on an exaggeratedly high pedestal and unveiled by H.M. Queen Elizabeth the Queen Mother. Later it was moved to Salisbury, Rhodesia, where one must hope it will be allowed to rest in peace.

'Physical Energy' was universally acclaimed as a noble achievement, undoubtedly the masterpiece of Watts's large sculptures. One thinks inevitably of Rodin, who visited the '*vénéré maître peintre et sculpteur de l'Angleterre*' at Limnerslease in 1903 and afterwards wrote a gushing letter of thanks to 'Mistress M. S. Watts'. But Watts, who had even attacked Michelangelo's 'David' (though he spoke warmly of his *tondo* at Burlington House), also had considerable reservations about Rodin, whose 'Penseur' he saw in London a few months before his death. He said of it to his wife that had he been told that it represented prehistoric man he would have replied, 'Yes; possibly it belongs to the order of the lumpy Hippopotamus and such other creatures. It is unintellectual, and that surprises me.' To his friend Christopher Turnor, the architect of the Watts Gallery, he explained that

to treat the muscular development of the body as Rodin had done was unpardonable. All the muscles of the body were represented as at tension and quivering, which they would not naturally be in that attitude; in all statuary everything should be seized and expressed at a moment of rest—even when representing energetic action—and this especially is the case of a man supposed to be deep in thought.

As Gutch has pointed out, Watts's thinking was often confused: 'His "Physical Energy" has just that inner strength of Rodin's works. By all his own criteria, it must be accounted a failure; the rider's back has a lumpy muscular formation, his body and legs twist at a high point of tension and the exaggerated proportions of the rider's back can hardly be described as beautiful. Yet it is his only [sculptural] work where we feel a genuinely original form has been created as a result of an idea. In this sense, it has ideal form.' 'Physical Energy' is in many respects much closer to the work of Rodin's pupil and one-time collaborator Emile Bourdelle—for example his 'Herakles', which it anticipates.[1]

'Physical Energy' still rides in triumph through the leafy glades of Kensington Gardens, admired by many who neither know nor care who created it; on the foothills of Table Mountain the rider still gazes with the eyes of the visionary across the endless plain. Over the years it has received a good deal of publicity, not all of it fortunate. A wit[2] once described it as 'a eunuch riding a gelding', and certainly neither horse nor rider appears to be very highly sexed. Then an unhappy rumour began to circulate among the native population in South Africa that the group at Groote Schuur symbolised the White man riding the Black, followed by the suggestion, happily never acted upon, that indignation might be silenced by painting the horse white. In 1956 permission was given by the Trustees of the Watts Gallery for 'Physical Energy' to be used as the trade-mark of Energen Foods, and in 1964 as a cap-badge for the pupils of Lusaka Boys' School. So Watts's masterpiece is still not altogether forgotten.

In 1970, when there was some discussion in the Press as to whether a memorial to Sir Winston Churchill should take the form of an equestrian figure, Mr Christopher Sykes wrote in the *Listener*:

. . . We live in a dismounted age, whereas when Verrocchio made his statue of Colleoni, horses were a necessity . . . Once railways had made horses less needful . . . practical knowledge

---

[1] Bourdelle kept a work of Rodin's in his studio to remind him (he modestly informed the author when he visited the sculptor's studio more than fifty years ago) how much further he had come than his master.

[2] Some say Oscar Wilde, who might of course have seen the unfinished statue in Watts's studio. There is a letter from Wilde to Watts in the Gallery archives.

of horses became much rarer, and as it did so an instinctive feeling for horsemanship was not often found among artists. Only thus can I account for the hideous oddity of two of the best-known equestrian statues in London: one by G. F. Watts described as *Physical Energy* situated in Kensington Gardens; the other in Whitehall and supposed to be a portrait of Lord Haig.

Both are manifestly influenced by the Colleoni statue: both show the horses extended, resting on three hooves with one forefoot proudly raised, as in Verrocchio's masterpiece, but with a major difference. Both these later statues show the hind legs extended to the full and closed together, and thus depict an equine position which may appear powerful to an ignorant eye, but is in fact one of the uttermost weakness. A strong man on foot can overthrow a horse in this position, but in nature it is one that a horse only adopts when it wants to urinate[1] . . . Both [statues] are designed to excite feelings of conventional respect and awe. Both fail because the artists did not know one end of a horse from the other . . .

Watts was all his life a keen horseman. He admitted that he did not want his horse to be 'like a natural horse'. Whatever may have been his reason for choosing this particular posture, it was surely not that he 'did not know one end of a horse from the other'! As (Sir) Desmond MacCarthy wrote at the time of the first Post-Impressionist exhibition in 1910, 'A good rocking-horse has often more of the true horse about it than an instantaneous photograph of a Derby winner.'

It is the fate of those who live to a great age to watch the friends of a lifetime vanish one by one. Tennyson was in fact eight years older than Watts, but the poet's death in 1892 shocked him deeply and, to his great sorrow, left him for a time so ill that he could not act as pall-bearer at the funeral in Westminster Abbey. When, six years later, Lord Brownlow, Lord-Lieutenant of Lincolnshire, proposed that a statue be erected at Lincoln to the county's most illustrious son, Watts, who had painted no less than seven portraits of Tenny-

---

[1] 'I know two things about the horse,
And one of them is rather coarse.'
(Lord Alfred Douglas)

son, offered to do the work for nothing but the cost of the casting. A wax model was submitted to a committee set up by Lord Brownlow, and Watts, now in his eighty-second year, began a task which might well have daunted a man of half his age.

The 'Tennyson'—a heroic statue which shows the poet with his great wolfhound, Karenina, at his side and a 'flower in the crannied wall' in his hand—was carried out in a barn close to Limnerslease which Watts now acquired for this purpose. Progress was slow until 1902, when 'Physical Energy' had been taken from Melbury Road to be cast; then, day after day and even in mid-winter, Watts would be at work on the 'Tennyson' from dawn until the light failed. A too shallow base created many technical difficulties, and at one point a fresh start had to be made. 'I think what it ought to have been,' said Watts sadly when, in 1903, the gesso was torn from him to be cast in Frome.

The bronze was erected, a year after Watts's death, near the Cathedral Chapter House on the site—and this would have pleased the sculptor—of a demolished public house, the Dolphins. On the occasion of the unveiling, Canon Rawnsley wrote a poem which concluded with the lines:

Colossal on the green the poet stands
Lost in high thought; the hound is at his side,
Looks up for guidance to his master's face
While he looks down for guidance to the grace
Of some wild flower that in his reverent hands
Proclaims how Life by Love is unified.

In 1959, to celebrate the one hundred and fiftieth anniversary of Tennyson's birth, the statue (known locally as 'the disappointed cabby') was cleansed of bird-droppings by air-and-water jet. This led to the discovery that the bronze was beginning to deteriorate as the result of some kind of metal fatigue or bronze disease for which there was once no known cure, and in an article in the *Lincolnshire Echo* (23 August 1967) entitled 'Tennyson is facing a second "death"' the hope was expressed that if the worst came to the worst a new bronze could be cast from the gesso now at the Watts Gallery. It has, however, recently been treated, and (to judge from photographs) with complete success.

Some have described Watts's last great sculpture as an anti-climax; others see in it a miraculous achievement of a frail and ailing old man in his eighties. It was surely both. Certainly the work is not free from fault: in particular, the head seems uncomfortably small. But the overall effect is monumental, and Watts, could he have seen his 'Tennyson' where it stands today, backed and flanked by the great walls and towers of the Cathedral, would surely have felt that he had not laboured in vain.

17

INDIAN SUMMER

IN THE summer of 1891, Watts, his health temporarily improved by a rigid adherence to the 'Salisbury Diet' (which consisted of living almost entirely on pounded raw beef[1]), took possession of Limnerslease. It was primarily conceived of as a fog-free winter residence; but with each year that passed Watts found his summers in London increasingly curtailed, no doubt as a part of Mary's campaign to keep him from the clutches of Mrs Barrington.

But London sometimes called, and the French painter Jacques-Emile Blanche, who visited Melbury Road about 1900, describes the peace that prevailed there—presumably at a moment when Mrs Barrington was not in circulation:

> As soon as inside one felt soothed, in the serenity of pure art. There were drawing rooms full of precious objects, where two ladies like shadows came and went, arranging flowers in bowls and vases; from the garden slid the golden light of the end of a fine day, and through the little diamond-shaped leaded window panes, the heroic horseman, Physical Energy, was visible . . . At last, a sort of monk came in, wearing a choirboy's scarlet cap . . .'

Limnerslease, however, was soon the Watts's true home, and Julia Cartwright (Mrs Henry Ady), who visited them there in the mid-nineties, wrote in glowing terms of the beauty of its setting: its grassy lanes; its bluebells, primroses and nightingales in spring, its heather in autumn; its deep silence at all times. 'The house itself stands on the crest of a knoll planted with tall Scotch firs, which lift

[1] His cook was so ingenious in disguising its beastliness that Watts informed her that she too was 'aiding in the production of his pictures'.

their ruddy stems and dark-green boughs against the hillside. It is a picturesque building, with deep mullioned windows, quaint angles, and slanting roofs, overgrown with virginia creeper and clematis'; she does not mention its bogus half-timbering:

> Within all is rich and warm in hue. The red gleam of copper, the glitter of Algerian and Indian brass-work brightens each dark corner. Persian rugs and Oriental hangings relieve the blackness of old oak chests and cabinets, and the latest specimens of home arts and crafts stand side by side with Damascus pottery or Arab fretwork. The walls are hung with the works of great masters, living or dead. On one side we see drawings of Rossetti's 'Blessed Damozel', and Burne-Jones's 'Sponsa di Libano', on the other, autotypes of Michael Angelo's Sibyls and Raphael's Madonnas. Many, too, are the paintings by Mr Watts's own hand, views of the Tuscan Apennines near Careggi, and glimpses of Mediterranean waters, or early versions of well-known pictures, the 'Genius of Greek Poetry', and 'Olympus on Ida'.
>
> But another hand besides the master's own has helped to decorate that home, and at every turn we find signs not only of Mrs Watts's taste but of her inventive faculties and artistic skill. The gesso reliefs, representing the symbols of ancient religions, which adorn the white-panelled ceilings, are her work. . . . The same gesso work appears in the arched recess above the master's favourite seat, by the corner of the hearth. Here the richest golds and greens and blues are delicately blended together, and angels and powers bearing appropriate symbols represent the different aspects and meanings of life . . .[1]

Watts, when he came to Limnerslease, was in his seventy-fifth year—in those days an age at which most men, even such as enjoyed the best of health, would have been content to sit back and let the world go by. And Watts's health was always precarious. Excessive heat, cold, wind, rain or fog always made him ill. He still had migraines. If there was an influenza germ within ten miles of Limnerslease or Melbury Road it infallibly tracked him down. He suffered, simultaneously or in turn, from rheumatism, arthritis, boils, gout, eczema and insomnia. His eyes gave him a lot of trouble,

---

[1] *The Life and Work of G. F. Watts,* the Art Journal Office, 1896.

and he was very deaf. He sprained his foot; he ruptured himself when trying to ride a bicycle;[1] and there were other less attractive ailments all duly noted in her diaries by his devoted wife. Yet during the last thirteen years of his life he produced a corpus of paintings that many a robust artist might have been proud to claim as his total *œuvre*.

Indeed, having decided when in his fifties that life was over for him, at eighty-five he boldly declared that he was 'beginning to know how to paint' and that his best work was yet to come. One is reminded of Hokusai, who in his ninetieth year, as he lay dying, cried to heaven for 'ten years more', then 'just *five* years—and I could become a *real* painter'. But one cannot, however, imagine Watts on his deathbed writing (as did Hokusai) to an old friend, 'I am going to take a room at the corner of Hell Street and shall be happy to see you whenever you happen to be passing'.

Admittedly, some of Watts's very last pictures were failures: one thinks, for example, of 'Evolution', with its dreadful maggoty infants; but among them was a handful of admirable works, and those critics who like to maintain that his reputation as an artist would have been enhanced had he laid down his brush and been content to cultivate his garden—had he, as was suggested, named his house 'Limnersease' rather than 'Limnerslease'—are surely mistaken. If, however, he had laid down his *pen*, the world would have been little the poorer.

Incidentally he *did* cultivate his garden—or rather, he helped to create one, himself pruning back the tangles of bramble with a reaping-hook for fear that an unknown hand might destroy 'too much of the beauty of wild nature', and keeping a careful watch that axe was never laid to any tree however moribund. He rode, too, with Mary up Sandy Lane, according to tradition the track trodden by generations of pilgrims on their way to the shrine of St Thomas at Canterbury. He even became a member—though not an active one —of the Compton Cricket Club, and only a few weeks before his

---

[1] J. St Loe Strachey, in some notes he made of a conversation with Watts on 1 June 1895, wrote, 'He approves of bicycles and decried Ruskin for abusing so good a means of getting the town into the green fields. . . . He touched the handle of my machine and said, "All this might be made decorative . . . What a splendid thing our Saxon or Norse ancestors would have made of a railway loco-motive—a great fiery dragon!"'

death his tired eyes were seen to light up at the sound[1] of ball on bat in some nearby field.

Several of Watts's more important late works were explained by the artist to Augustus Hare, the illustrious author of so many books on Italy, when he visited Limnerslease one December day in 1893:

This afternoon Victoria[2] took me to see Mr Watts. A drive through wooded lanes and water-meadows; then the carriage stopped at the foot of a wooded knoll, and we walked up little winding paths through the bracken and Scotch firs to the house— a rustic hermitage. You enter directly upon the principal dwelling apartment—two low rooms, with old carved furniture and deep windows, and much colour and many pictures. The ceiling is in panels, decorated in stucco by Mrs Watts. At least she has finished one room, and is going to do the other with an epitome of the religion of all the nations of the earth—'A work,' she said, 'which gives me much study.'

Soon Mr Watts came in, like a pilgrim, like a medieval hermit-saint, in a brown blouse and slippers, with a skull-cap above his white hair and beard, and his sharp eager features, in which there is also boundless tenderness and refinement. He sat by me on the window-sill, and began at once to talk of Lady Waterford[3] . . .

Mr Watts took us into his studio, an immense and beautiful room added to the cottage. Here were many of his pictures, the work of years, on which, from time to time, he added a few touches. He likes to have many of his works around him, and to add to them thus. At the end of the room hangs his vast 'Court of Death', which can be lowered by pulleys whenever he wishes to add to it . . . 'Death' is throned in the upper part of the picture. 'I have given her wings,' said Mr Watts, 'that she may not seem like a Madonna. In her arms nestles a child—a child unborn, perhaps, who has taken refuge there. By her side the angels of silence guard the portals of the unseen. Beneath is the altar of Death, to which many worshippers are hastening: the old mendicant comes to beg; the noble offers his coronet; the warrior does not offer— but surrenders—his sword; the sick girl clings for refuge to the

[1] He had eventually found a hearing-aid of great help.
[2] His cousin, Victoria Rowe.
[3] See p. 99.

17. *Sir Charles Dilke,* 1873
This sensitive portrait makes those that hang near it in the
National Portrait Gallery seem crude by comparison

18a. *Love and Life*, before 1885
The Tate Gallery version of a
composition which aroused the wrath
of the Purity Superintendent of the
Women's Christian Temperance
Union of America (see p. 154)

18b. (*below left*) Plaster casts of figures
modelled by Watts when working on
Love and Life

18c. (*below right*) Study for *Satan and Sin*,
c. 1850?
A design that might fairly be described
as erotic (see p. 56)

19a. Watts's Studio in Melbury Road, 1904
This was 'New' Little Holland House, built for Watts in 1876 by
Frederick Cockerell. Watts stipulated that there should be no
spare bedrooms – 'to avoid complications' (see p. 122)

19b. *Physical Energy*
Watts's famous sculpture in Kensington Gardens. There are also casts
at Cape Town and at Salisbury (Rhodesia) (see p. 194)

20. *Mary Watts*, 1887
Formerly Mary Fraser-Tytler, the artist's second wife. The picture was
'painted straight off in four colours on a single-prime canvas'
at Pera (Constantinople) during their honeymoon (see p. 180)

21a. *Mrs Russell Barrington*, 1881
A bust by Mary Thornycroft of Mary
Watts's bitterest enemy. This 'poisonous
snake' (as Mary Watts called her) was
of great help to Watts when he first
came to live in Melbury Road

21b. *Clytie, c.* 1868
The most 'Michelangelesque'
of Watts's sculptures.
Swinburne wrote of it,
'Never was a divine legend
translated into diviner
likeness . . .' (see p. 191)

22. Watts in Old Age
Photograph taken at Limnerslease, Compton

23a. Mary Watts and her helpers painting panels for the
Mortuary Chapel at Compton (see p. 224)

23b. The Niche at Limnerslease
Mary Watts reading to her husband (see p. 202)

24a. The Watts Gallery, 1961

The Gallery was built in 1903/04 with Christopher Turnor as architect.
Turnor, though for a time associated with Sir Edwin Lutyens, was not a
professional architect. He owned large estates, and is chiefly remembered
as an agriculturist, educationist, and authority on emigration (see p. 226)

24b. Limnerslease, c. 1895

The house was built for Watts in 1890/91 by (Sir) Ernest George, who forgot
to include a staircase from the first floor to the second (see p. 187)

feet of Death. I have wished to paint Death entirely without terrors.

'You wonder what that is, that other picture of a figure of a rich man in Eastern dress whose face is half-hidden, buried away in the folds of his garment. I meant that for the man who was "very sorry, for he had great possessions". He cannot give them up. He has tried, but he *cannot*. He is going out into the world again, and yet—and yet he is very sorry.'

He said, 'I am within two years of eighty, and I have worked all my life, but I do not feel old or feeble. I do not even use a maul-stick, and I intend to do my best work yet.' He said he had no wish to go into the world again. Living was outliving. Holland House, the second home of many years, was swept away from him, and all its intimates were passing away, and its memories perishing. Nothing else in London could attract him.

He had wished to make large pictures of Hope, Charity and Faith. With the two first he had no difficulty, but he lingered long over the third. He showed us the picture he had done—of a woman seated, looking upwards, an Amazonian woman, sheathing her sword, and bathing her blood-stained feet in a brook of clear water. 'She has found out that all that was no use—no use at all.' His words, his thoughts, his works, all seemed imbued with the truest spirit of religion. 'With theology,' he said, 'I have nothing to do.'[1]

Hare has little to say about Mary Watts, who was no doubt duly self-effacing. Her whole life, her every moment, her every thought, was wrapped around her god. She rose with him at dawn. She read to him in the evenings as he lay in the little gesso'd niche which has since been so wantonly defaced. She noted his tritest *obiter dicta*. She pasted into some twenty notebooks the backs of envelopes on which he had scribbled his endlessly repetitive and barely legible little thoughts (those conceived and written when in his bath present-ing especial difficulties), and later employed a secretary to attempt their decipherment. She kept a diary in which she entered each even-ing's harvest of reminiscences of his early life elicited by a tactful but remorseless catechism, and after his death had an invaluable

[1] *The Story of My Life*, vol. 6. George Allen, 1896–1900.

manuscript catalogue of all his traceable paintings painfully written in Carolingian minuscules.

For all this probing and gleaning, which provided her with much of the material for her *Annals*, we are deeply in her debt; we would have been still more so had she not been blinded by her hero-worship to the very existence of any human weakness in her husband. As an American reviewer wrote when the *Annals* was published: 'The virtue of a saint really lies in the fact that at bottom he is human like the rest of us, and after a hundred odd pages of rigorous sublimity one longs violently to have Watts, just for an instant, swear at someone or kick the studio cat; but such lapses the chronicler never permits.'

The Grand Old Man was of course greatly and deservedly revered, and his most trifling commands had to be punctiliously executed. For example, his coachman, ordered one day to bring the carriage round to the front door at three o'clock, arrived two minutes early and was told to drive away and return at the proper time. 'His servants', wrote Mary, 'were often reminded that he required to have things done very precisely, sometimes adding this little counsel of perfection: "Remember the daisies!"—pointing out that one of the smallest and commonest works of nature was thus exquisitely finished; therefore the smallest things in life should neither be ignored nor slurred over.' A servant today (did the genus exist) would no doubt react to a botanical parable of this kind by giving instant notice. But in those far-off happy times the master was always right, and Watts's employees seem to have worshipped him almost as much as did Mary:

> I told Thompson[1] [wrote Mary] that a visitor to the New Gallery had said he [Watts] was 'the greatest man in the world'. I thought that would be praise enough even for Thompson; but he swallowed it whole, merely remarking, 'That's nothing at all, Madam. I've heard that said a score of times—and a great deal more besides.'

As for Mary, her idolatry knew no bounds. She took every little politeness of friends and visitors, every scrap of flattery or syco-

[1] Watts's faithful assistant. He died several months before Watts—probably (thought Mary) 'to be there to meet his master'.

phancy, at its face value and lovingly recorded it. After visiting Watts, Gertrude Jekyll felt that she had been 'in paradise' and another woman that she had been 'in church', while Lady Pembroke considered his whole life a prayer. A girl and a child were seen to kiss their hands to the Gallery in Melbury Road as they passed it. We learn that 'little Blanche' slept with Signor's photograph on her heart, and that a working man had said, 'We look upon Mr Watts as a National Trust'. 'Marguerite' confessed that Signor was the first person who made her want to try to be good. A visitor to the gallery was overheard by Miss Meyrick to say how gladly she would give two years of her life to add to his span, whereupon Miss Meyrick could not resist crying out, 'Many of us would!'

'Unsolicited testimonials' were, of course, the sweetest:

> I was standing [at the New Gallery] near, not before, Signor's portrait . . . when a little old lady, a stranger, moved towards me, and pointing to that portrait, said, 'Isn't that a beautiful face for a painter?' to which I answered, 'Yes, I do think so, and I must tell you that you have said this to his wife,' whereupon she covered her face with both hands. 'Oh,' she said, with a sort of sob in her voice, 'then a blessing be upon you.'

This was the beginning of a beautiful friendship, and soon the old lady was proudly hanging a reproduction of the portrait, the gift of Mary, between those of Beethoven and Mozart.

Many of Mary's 'precious moments' with Signor were, she confessed, too precious for commitment to paper—and we can only be grateful; but often she is explicit: 'A quickening influence flows out upon me from him.' ' "How happy we are!" he said tonight as he turned upon his pillow.' 'Even if he tells me what one knows, he says it in a way that makes it sound more true than it ever was before.' ' "Well", he answered directly, in that dear voice that rings so true in every simple word he says.' 'His eyes shut, an unutterable calm in his expression . . . A sleeping angel wrought in silver, he seemed.' 'My little love! How we enjoy our books together, he following every word, I the voice—oh happy time!' 'I wonder sometimes if anyone ever lived so beautifully in all the smallest details.'

The Song of Solomon might almost have inspired the following:

> My dear one is to me like moonlight—something calm, silvery,

mysterious—a light that makes the expanse of heaven look larger and dims out earth's details for a little while. I see the outline of things better for his light.

And when painting a miniature of him, she wrote:

Trying to paint him again full face. How exquisite that little head upon the white pillow! The spirit slung like a lamp through those beautiful brown eyes. The silver hair like wings about his head. The temple of as high a nature as flesh was ever made to cover— save perhaps the One.

One of these miniatures, a profile, is now at Compton; it is a thing of rare beauty—almost like a little Vuillard. Mrs Stirling was not exaggerating when she wrote that Mary Watts 'subordinated her own very remarkable genius to the task of keeping prominent that of her husband'.

In the third volume of Mary's *Annals* are to be found ninety-nine of her husband's 'Thoughts on Art' and eighty-five of his 'Thoughts on Life', together with the evidence he gave before the Commission which in 1863 investigated the position of the Royal Academy in relation to the fine arts. It also contains articles on various topics that interested him: 'On Taste in Dress', 'On Plain Handicrafts', 'Our Race as Pioneers', and so on.

Watts freely confessed that he had been 'denied by nature the gift of words', and even the loyal Ronald Chapman felt obliged to admit that many of the 'Thoughts of Chairman Watts' recorded here and in the notebooks were 'flat', where 'flat' could be short for 'flatulent'. Some might have come from Christmas crackers or found a place among the more fragrant vapourings of Wilhelmina Stitch— for example, 'Bury your sorrows in the garden and they will come up as flowers'. Others are undeniably true but hardly worth the recording: 'Each line I draw is one nearer the last'; 'Those who stand high, when they slip have the further to fall'; 'If a man goes as far as he possibly can in any one direction, it is but fair to suppose he would go further if he could'. Yet others are obscure—for example:

Man physically a luminous body like the Sun, perhaps the whole humanity a Sun, perhaps the Sun a sentient body. This is but the principle that all is an emanation from the Creator and part of Him. The whole system Him. The whole stellar and planetary system may have its palpitations, fluctuations and aspirations, the circulation in our veins! our very ideas Stars, Planets and Comets.

The brain that invented and the hand that fashioned the drill and used the tool to drill a hole that would only admit a hair, could certainly have made a watch and perhaps have invented the telephone.

In this vast store of wisdom there appears to be only one snippet that sparkles—only one that Chesterton might possibly not have disowned as a paradox: 'The next divine teacher who visits the earth will not say, "Blessed are they that have not seen, and yet have believed"; he will say, "Blessed are they that see and yet believe".' But perhaps some more sympathetic searcher might discover in these acres of verbiage gems that have escaped the eye of a cynic.

Apparently Mary did not consider this particular aphorism worthy of (or perhaps suitable for) inclusion in her *Annals*; and there is another confession which, hardly surprisingly, she also omits: 'The fact is, though I have kept it a secret (not intending to do so), I am a very dull person . . .' She does, however, rashly quote two examples of the 'wit' that never deserted her husband even at the very end of his long life:

Mr Walter Earle was sitting beside his sofa and happened to tell him that in a bookseller's shop he had overheard a customer ask for a reproduction of 'Mr Watts's painting of "Lot's Wife",' and at the same time pointing out a photograph of the picture 'She shall be called Woman'. Laughing heartily, Signor exclaimed, 'Well! I wanted her to have plenty of salt.' And again, though more gravely, he replied with the same readiness, when a friend had described somebody as one 'who gave herself airs',—'Ah!' he answered, 'airs which are never graces!'

If only there had been someone to pull Watts's leg occasionally! But nobody did—or if anyone did, Watts failed to notice it. Vanessa Bell, describing a visit to Limnerslease in 1903 with George Duckworth, wrote to a friend: 'Georgie remarked (can you imagine it!) that he had been ashamed to look at the drawings [of nudes] at the

R.A. prize-giving and had felt in want of a fan all the time.' Watts took him perfectly seriously, and embarked upon a long monologue on the place of the nude in art. Only children teased Watts; but that was different, and even they were ordered by Mary never to let him lose at 'Old Maid'. Among these children was a very pretty girl named Lilian ('Lily'), described by Mary as 'daughter of Henry D. A. Mackintosh, Esq.' Motherless from infancy, she was adopted by the Wattses about 1889 at the age of ten, and in due course sent to Roedean, where Watts, who thought the school uniform ugly, insisted upon her being allowed to wear Pre-Raphaelite dresses. In 1906 married Michael Chapman,[1] who was killed in the First World War. She herself died at Compton in 1972 in her ninety-third year, beautiful and charming to the last.

Watts's religious unorthodoxy, his muzzy theism, was a perpetual source of sorrow to Mary. 'Sometimes I wish my sweet would talk to me of what he believes and holds to,' she wrote. She did not, one imagines, care to hear him say that it was 'left to Christianity to institute the most awful tortures the world had ever seen', or that 'the only Christian people I have ever heard of are the Burmese Buddhists'; but she may have sympathised with him when he declared that it was 'ridiculous' that God, on being asked by Moses to show his face, consented only to reveal his hinder parts.[2] 'Why did I come into the world?' he one day cried. 'I won't again if I can help it . . . I am ashamed of myself for not having done better.' Yet she must have been comforted when he said, 'The older I grow, the more I am aware that the only real existence is the spiritual.' 'His words,' wrote Mary, 'made me realise what the loosening from earth would be to him. "Ah, but my sweet," I said, "you will soon ask for a paint-brush when you get the new life." "That I am sure I shall," he said laughing.'

Like Tolstoi, whom he greatly admired, Watts also held unorthodox views on the subject of inherited wealth. When W. T. Stead, the famous journalist and founder of the *Review of Reviews*, quoted to him the saying, 'God Almighty has plenty of cash, and all the millionaires are but his money-bags', Watts drily remarked, 'Then I wish He would add to His other duties the appointment of an

[1] See p. 230.   [2] *Exodus* xxxiii, 23.

auditor.' 'Who knows,' said Stead, 'the auditing may come hereafter.' 'Maybe,' replied Watts, 'but we know nothing.'[1]

It may be remembered that Watts, after his return from Italy in the forties, had been deeply moved by the misery of the poor. The four 'propaganda' pictures that he had then painted—'Found Drowned', 'The Song of the Shirt', 'The Irish Famine' and 'Under a Dry Arch'—had been exhibited at the Grosvenor Gallery in 1881–82, where they had been either ignored by the critics or dismissed as works 'upon which visitors to the Gallery will not like to linger'. When in 1896–97 a second important one-man exhibition of Watts's paintings was held at the New Gallery, these disturbing pictures were not included.

But with the passing of the years Watts had moved still further to the Left, and two paintings exhibited at the New Gallery—'Mammon (Dedicated to his Worshippers)' and 'For he had Great Possessions'—told clearly enough what he felt about the greed of the rich. Of the former picture, which was to be presented to the Nation, he wrote in the catalogue:

> The god, his face expressive of avarice, cruelty and insolence, and his head flanked with ass's ears, seated towards right, and decked in gorgeous but ill-fitting draperies; his right hand rests heavily on the head of a crouching woman, and his left foot is placed on the prostrate figure of a man; in his lap are money bags.

Another work with the same message—'Industry and Greed'—was in progress at the same time, but not sufficiently advanced to include in the exhibition. It shows a sturdy young labourer toiling away for the enrichment of an old miser (curiously like Watts!) who stands behind him, clutching his money-bags. A smaller version of this picture so impressed an impoverished young locomotive footplate man, Mr Percy Collick, that in 1939 he purchased it out of his hard-earned savings from Mrs Michael Chapman. Fifteen years later, when an exhibition of Watts's work was held at the Tate Gallery in celebration of the fiftieth anniversary of the artist's death, Mr Collick, by this time Labour Member of Parliament for Birkenhead, wrote indignantly to the Editor of *Reynolds News* to refute an attack on Watts made in its pages by Mr Tom Driberg:

[1] *Review of Reviews*, June 1902. An interesting 'character sketch' of Watts, from which lack of space alone prevents more extensive quotation.

I do not think [Tom Driberg] could have made such comment if he had seen Watts' paintings, 'Found Drowned', 'The Seam-stress', 'Under the Arches' [sic] and 'Industry and Greed' . . . Tom Driberg says he will not go to the exhibition at the Tate. On the other hand, I would strongly advise all my generation of Labour stalwarts to go and make up their minds for themselves. Ask to see the pictures I have mentioned, and if they are not there, ask why.[1]

Mr Collick added that he had recently met in Vienna a Jewess who during the terrors of the Nazi War had received 'renewed faith and hope' from a photograph of Watts's 'Hope'. This was not the first time that the picture had served as a pick-me-up. Mary Watts mentions a letter her husband had once received, 'written by a stranger to tell him in the simplest language that in a dark hour of life in a grimy northern town a photograph of his picture "Hope" had arrested attention in a moment of extreme crisis', had been pur-chased with his few remaining shillings and had changed the whole course of his life. Nor was it to be the last. Chris Mullen states that 'reproductions of the painting were given to Egyptian troops after their defeat in the 1967 War', and the current Jordanian 30 fils stamp carries 'THE HOPE' lithographed in shades of beige. How delighted Watts would have been!

Watts often spoke to Mary about social matters and politics. In her diary for 1 August 1895 she noted: 'Signor talking of the wave of conservatism sweeping the country: "All these sensible men to whom I talk seem carried along by it. It makes one doubt one's own judgment, and yet it is clear enough that the unequal balance of wealth and poverty is there, and cannot be permanent. A change must come, in spite of the opposing party whose vested interests have grown up round them until in their security they have for-gotten that the advantages they possess demand duties."'

Yet in that same year, in an interview given to a reporter of *The Young Woman* named Hulda Friederichs, he said:

No, I am not a politician—not because I do not care enough, but

[1] None of these was exhibited. The condition of three of them was at that time very bad, and Mr Collick did not lend his picture. 'Under a Dry Arch' and 'Found Drowned' have since been restored.

because I should care too much. And I have only strength enough for my work, and for nothing else besides . . . The other day a cutting was sent to me from an Italian paper in which it was stated that I had refused to become a '*Baronetto* in the House of Peers' because of my Socialistic tendencies. But I am not a Socialist by any means, although I take what are called broad views of social questions. So far from being a Socialist, my inclinations are all the other way. I love pomp and ceremony; I would like to see a duke wear his ermine, and a king his crown . . .

Also I would like the working class to retain their distinctive dress, which was not only infinitely more picturesque, but also infinitely more dignified than the present straining to imitate the clothes of the wealthy, which, of course, can only be done by buying what is cheap and ugly and machine-made. But I know that the pomp and stateliness of olden times cannot return . . .

It was also in 1895 that Mary had noted in her diary: 'One of Signor's sad days: "The country eaten up by vice. The habit of the upper classes of taking money that is not earned and for which they give nothing, is a sign that vice is sapping the national character. It has travelled downwards, and betting is the common theme of boys in the street."' Mrs Barrington, who saw something of Watts when he was in London in the summer of 1895, wrote that he had always had a tendency 'to allow certain subjects to become focalised as bugbears in his mind, and as his fits of nervous excitement, "not to say irritability" (to use his own words),[1] increased with great age, his indignation at the evils of certain customs knew no bounds. He deprecated gambling and racing in the strongest terms.' He had just read with horror an article in *The Spectator* which Richard Hutton its editor ('who was, he believed, a religious man'), had allowed to be published and in which it was stated that gambling—'a habit [said Watts] which was known to be often the cause of suicide, of forgery, of ruin'—was not in itself immoral.

'The most striking pictorial outcome of these abhorrences,' wrote Mrs Barrington, was the 'Jonah', a 'work of inspiration' which was exhibited at the New Gallery. Painted in 1895 in the white heat of indignation, it was described by Watts in the catalogue as showing the 'full-length, gaunt-like figure of Jonah, standing facing, with

[1] But see p. 179!

outstretched arms; behind him, on a mural tablet, are depicted scenes representing the sins of the people, drunkenness, gambling, racing, &c.' It is a remarkable but repulsive picture, and fascinated Evelyn Waugh when he visited the Watts Gallery shortly before his death. It, too, was presented to the Nation.[1]

When the Boer War broke out, Watts, 'like a seer of old' (wrote Mary), cried, 'I see blood, blood, blood everywhere.' Yet, surprisingly enough, he was convinced that this war was just and necessary—that 'some active and progressive people must replace [the Boers], and at present no people seem better to do it than we are.' These sentiments, published in the *Nineteenth Century Review*, were read with 'inexpressible sadness' by the leader-writer of the *Outlet*, who was at a loss to understand how the painter of 'Mammon' could believe it right 'to "replace", that is, to exterminate, a people that cannot "appreciate" the country that it has won by incredible hardships . . . To do ourselves justice the majority of us, after we had stolen the diamond mines, would have been content to let the Free State alone—all of us perhaps but Mr Rhodes and his gang.'

But Watts was quite unrepentant. It was his opinion that 'the Temple of Mammon, the Turf, and the gin-shop will do more to bring about the downfall of a nation than any amount of fighting'. He advocated two years' compulsory military service even in peacetime, and he now thus encouraged a civilian who had volunteered for South Africa: 'I trust you will come back safe after the splendid experience of the battlefield, compared with which every other experience must be tame. Every man who volunteers is to be envied.' To Lord Grey, whom he had earlier informed that England wanted 'a good squeeze to make her think', he wrote (on 15 December 1899):

I want more blue jackets for the future, and have been advocating the establishing of a number of training schools all round the coast, the more the better, in which all the children of the slums we can get hold of may be taught judiciously and pleasantly (this would want good looking after) to be not only sailors but active

1 A large gift of paintings was accepted for the Tate Gallery in 1897, and the first seventeen (of what now amount to some fifty) portraits by the National Portrait Gallery in 1895.

intelligent citizens capable on any emergency. It is evident that every man among the Boers is capable at short notice of being turned into an efficient soldier; so it was with us in the Middle Ages . . .

Perhaps Lord Grey did not answer, for some weeks later we find Watts writing again, repeating his proposal and pointing out that though the '270,000 yearly sent to prison and the 100,000 tramps'[1] were beyond redemption, his 'absolutely simple plan' could save both England's position in the world, and the next generation from a similar fate. 'I was for some months on board a Man of War,' the old sea-dog continued, 'and know how admirable the training is for making the character prompt, precise and obedient.' No answer survives.

Watts himself rather obscurely celebrated the Boer War with a painting entitled 'Love steering the Boat of Humanity'—the smaller and original version of which is now in Japan, the larger at Compton. 'The Nation's suffering during the war in South Africa,' wrote Mary, 'prompted its conception. Man's condition of conflict in the midst of forces from above and below, the recognition of his own importance to control, yet with the sustaining faith that the hand of Love directs his course.' Watts once said in conversation, 'These ideas are always trotting in my mind, and sometimes I want to mention them.' And then, smiling and pointing at the picture, he made what was very nearly a joke: 'Poor Humanity has caught a terrible crab!'

Among other crusades waged by Watts at this time was one against the wanton destruction of birds for their plumage. (Yet he himself wore a sealskin coat.) His 'A Dedication' (1898–99), which shows an angel weeping over a handful of plucked kingfishers laid on an altar, is inscribed 'To all who love the beautiful and mourn over the senseless and cruel destruction of bird life and beauty'; it would have made a good poster for Conservation Year. Some years earlier, Lillie Langtry, when she came to pose for Watts, had arrived wearing a little poke bonnet crowned with 'an opulent feather', which the artist immediately ripped off. Mrs Langtry had further cause for irritation when Watts, after being accorded forty (one account says a hundred) sittings for a second and full-face portrait,

[1] These figures seem enormous but may well be correct.

erased the head and substituted for it that of a Mrs Robert Crawshay.

Another crusade was directed against alcohol and smoking—the latter dismissed as an evil habit on the grounds that 'anything that is bad for a growing boy cannot be good for a grown man':

Being naturally sickly [he wrote], I had orders to take care of my body. I have never smoked. Greater things were done in the world, immeasurably greater, before tobacco was discovered than have ever been done since. The cigarette is the handmaid of idleness. I do not say that possibly it may not be a sedative to overwrought nerves, but overwrought nerves are things that ought not to be. Of wine I have taken very little. In my earlier days I used to take a little, but for a long time I have never touched any form of alcohol.[1] At meals I never drink anything, not even water. Tea—yes, in moderation . . .

The autograph-hunter (in reality a harmless pest, since he can simply be ignored) also infuriated him. 'I should like to ask the autograph hunters,' he said, 'why, instead of forcing a scrap of writing out of those whom personally they do not know, they do not go and sit on the hillside and get the Creator's autograph, as they can see it in the skies, the clouds, and the flowers . . .' Very probably he was unable to resist replying to one or two of them to this effect, thus providing them with something far more to be valued than the Creator's autograph, which could not be pasted in a book.

Watts was, however, ahead of his time in many ways. In an age when few people cared, he condemned the pollution of our rivers by factories. Before it had become obvious to all, he sadly observed the steady decline of the British character, the growing idleness and apathy, and quoted what a German had once said to him, 'My father used to say to me, "Buy English goods, however dear they are"; now I tell my sons, "Don't buy English goods, however cheap they are".' 'England's position,' he wrote,[2] 'is one of peril, the object of envy and distrust . . . Our insular position is no longer the protection it was formerly.' He predicted 'a gigantic war in Europe into

[1] Watts to James Smith, 17 October 1898: 'How very kind of you to send me the wine!' No doubt it was drunk by his guests.
[2] Most of the jottings bear no date.

which it will be difficult for any European power to avoid being drawn, and which will give the Nihilists the reason they want to strike in and sweep away all existing institutions, upon the plea that they have one and all been tried and found wanting.' It would be a war, he wrote, that would leave Germany 'mistress of Europe'. How very nearly was he right!

Watts's eightieth birthday in 1897 was celebrated by an enormous children's party, and by the presentation of a number of addresses, one of which carried a specially composed but rather commonplace sonnet by Swinburne. A fortnight later Miss Elinor Hallé and Miss Geraldine Liddell gave a musical evening at Little Holland House for Watts and Joachim, at which a small string orchestra 'played to the two masters with Love as the rosin to their bows', and Joachim replied with Bach and Beethoven. Watts, who had beforehand expressed the hope that the evening 'would give as much pleasure to others as it was misery to him', found when it was all over that he had very much enjoyed himself.

In July of the following year Mary achieved a little miracle: she got Watts to Scotland! It was, she said, at his own suggestion, but we may be sure that the clever woman had long been making propaganda for the beauties of her homeland. They arrived at a lodge on her father's estate which they were to occupy during their stay, in what a Scot calls a 'mist'; but since Watts, when he stretched out his arm, could not see his hand, the poor Sassenach probably mistook it for a fog. Next morning, however, Nature relented and there, spread at his feet, lay Loch Ness in all its glory, encircled by blue and purple hills. On the whole he was to be lucky with his weather, and was indeed even persuaded to welcome the occasional rain since it 'varnished the picture'. He trudged across the moors, was rowed on the loch or sailed on it in a friend's yacht; with a ninety-two-year-old crofter and a family party he ascended on horseback 'dear Dynyardil', on whose summit the crofter distributed Gaelic blessings.

Watts had brought with him to the lodge a small portable 'shelter', capable of being set up facing in any desired direction, to serve as a studio. In it he made a number of sketches from which he painted 'Loch Ness' and other pictures after his return to England—a return which was delayed by many weeks as a result of his catching

a cold which turned to pneumonia. He did not see the 'monster', and
he never set foot in Scotland again.

Watts had always enjoyed music. His little old cottage piano had so
far served his needs, but it proved inadequate when he received a
visit from a professional pianist; in 1892, therefore, a group of
friends (among whom was Ruskin) clubbed together to present him
with a Broadwood grand for Limnerslease. This gift delighted him.
It pleased Watts to imagine that he was a composer *manqué*—indeed that, given some knowledge of musical notation, he would have
been able to enrich the world through the wonderful music that
came to him as he slept. 'In his dreams alone,' wrote Mary, 'could he
create music, and this not infrequently; but one such dream I
remember more clearly than any other, his description of a magnificent anthem that he had just awakened from hearing, of which he
told me had it been possible for him to write the score down, it
would have stood for ever as one of the great things of the world.
"Hallelujah, God is great", were the words, he said: "it was quite
superb in its grandeur".'
   Mary Watts was a very remarkable woman. She gave her painter a
new lease of life, She brought to his closing years a happiness that
he had never before known. But she did his reputation nothing but a
disservice by stuffing her already over-long biography with such
nonsense.

In September, 1887, Watts had written a letter to *The Times* and the
Spectator, suggesting that the fiftieth anniversary of the Queen's
accession might appropriately be celebrated by a monument raised
to 'the unsung heroes of everyday life'. At the time nothing came of
his scheme; but twelve years later he carried it out at his own expense in 'Postmen's Park'—a garden near the General Post Office on
the site of the old churchyard of St Botolph's-without-Aldersgate.
   It took the form of a number of tablets of Doulton pottery, rather
'sanitary' in character, on which were briefly recorded deeds such as
might today earn a George Cross. These tablets are protected from
the weather by a penthouse of the kind that sometimes shelters
bicycles, and the whole is as humble as were the heroes it commemo-
rates; it might even be described as 'shoddy'. Thirteen of the
tablets were placed there in Watts's lifetime, thirty-four more by

his widow and another five by public subscription, the last being unveiled by the Postmaster-General in 1930. Space for ninety more remains, but according to *The Times* (5 December 1962) 'no suitable names have been put forward to fill the gap'. Surely the Second World War would have provided more than enough?

Among those commemorated are several children who gave their lives for others even younger than themselves: Solomon, aged eleven, 'died of injuries, 6 September 1901. After saving his little brother from being run over in Commercial Street, said, "Mother I saved him, but I could not save myself."' Younger still was Harry Bristow, aged eight, who at Walthamstow on 8 November 1890 'saved his little sister's life by tearing off her flaming clothes, but caught fire himself, and died of burns and shock'.

Today, in the beautifully kept garden planted with camellias and lilies, typists eat their midday sandwiches under the shadow of the gigantic Barbican development; but few seem to have time to spare a thought for Ernest Benning, a young compositor who, 'upset from a boat one dark night off Pimlico Pier, grasped an oar with one hand, supported a woman with the other, but sank as she was rescued'.

By the closing years of the century it had become apparent to Watts and Mary that what they considered to be an evil artistic influence was beginning to invade England from the Continent. We do not know precisely what they themselves saw: hardly, one would imagine, the Toulouse-Lautrec exhibition at the Goupil Gallery in 1898, of which the art critic of the *Daily Chronicle* had written, 'Monsieur de Toulouse-Lautrec had only one idea in his head— vulgarity'; but in France there were known to be men who called themselves 'Impressionists' and painted decadent rubbish, and there could be little doubt that, all over the world, art was 'going to the dogs'.

A few weeks before Watts's death, Charles Hallé, the proprietor of the New Gallery, had visited him at Limnerslease, and in his *Notes from a Painter's Life* he has left us an interesting account of a long conversation that he had with the artist. The exhibition referred to in it is presumably that of the International Society of Painters, Sculptors and Gravers, who had rented the New Gallery earlier that year:

[Watts] said that from some examples of modern work he had just seen, he felt that painting and sculpture had better cease to be altogether, than that they should be devoted to the cult of ugliness and obscenity. He begged me to close, sell, or burn down the New Gallery sooner than allow it to become a centre for everything he held to be most degrading in art. He did not blame me, because he knew I was in no way responsible for the exhibition which had so excited his wrath; and he also knew that I was exactly of his way of thinking; but his grief and rage that such things could not only be tolerated, but senselessly applauded, in a country where he, Burne-Jones, Leighton, Millais, and others had worked so hard to revive the sense of what was noble and beautiful, was a sad experience . . .

The catalogue of this exhibition reveals that it contained nothing even mildly provocative. The French were represented by such innocuous things as a Camille Pissarro and an early Monet, a Renoir bronze and several Rodins; among English painters we find Pryde, William Nicholson, Ricketts and Charles Shannon, and there were two fine Whistlers—'Symphony in White' and 'Off Valparaiso'.

Watts and Burne-Jones, wrote Hallé,

died with despair in their hearts about the art they loved so much, and the headlong pace at which it was hastening to become a corrupting influence in the world, instead of what men had always hitherto striven to make it, an influence for good. Throughout Europe there was no ray of light on the horizon, nothing but a sea of mud; no thought, no beauty, no workmanship—nothing but sensationalism of a degrading kind, and a method of work out of which no good could possibly come; as, for the first time in the history of Art, it struck at the roots of just those qualities which make fine Art possible . . .

In this same spring of 1904 a twenty-three-year-old Spaniard had returned to Paris from Barcelona bringing with him a remarkable picture he had recently painted of an old beggar playing a guitar. It bore the same message as did Watts's 'Under a Dry Arch' and his 'Irish Famine', and like his 'Hope' it was a 'symphony in blue'; but had it been given a sub-title it could only have been 'Despair'. What would Watts have thought of it? Might he perhaps have been touched by its intention even if he had been repelled by its execution? And what would he have thought could he have known that one day the most casual, the most obscene scribblings of this Picasso were to fetch more in the sale-rooms than almost anything that he himself had ever painted?

18

LOVE AND DEATH

THOUGH MARY was dedicating her life to her 'Signor', the artist in her could not long remain suppressed. In the early years of her marriage it found its principal outlet in the Home Arts and Industries Association, an activity in which her husband also soon became involved.

Founded in the mid-eighties, the Association had had a humble enough beginning. A lady of the manor, seeing a crippled boy sitting outside his cottage door knitting, had decided that more interesting work might be found for him, and so started a small wood-carving class in the village. Her example was followed in other villages, and soon, under the patronage of Lord and Lady Brownlow, the Association was formed. Watts and Mary contributed money with their customary generosity, Watts painting two *ad hoc* portraits to raise a thousand pounds; and no doubt the influence of Ruskin, William Morris and William De Morgan was felt, directly or indirectly, by all who became involved.

Mary's interest was chiefly in the aesthetic side of the work; Watts also stressed its moral value. In an interview given in 1896 to a reporter of the *Westminster Gazette*, he said that the object of the H.A. & I.A. was not to enter into competition with any industry; it was

> simply and solely to give amusement in leisure hours to those who have now nothing to fill up the hours after work, and consequently seek a vent for the activity natural to the human bee when not reduced to animal apathy, in betting and gambling which too often leads to drunkenness and final ruin. Let these youths and men be taught by some cultured, voluntary teacher to

222

take delight in drawing, carving, brasswork or anything else that tends to develop the innate taste for creating something beautiful which lies in all human beings.

'Formerly a carter took the greatest pride in the bells and trappings of his horses,' he continued. 'That taste cannot yet be dead; it wants resuscitating.' He told of a semi-imbecile boy who took to wood-carving like a duck to water. Then there was a 'shy young navvy' who only at his third attempt brought himself to enter the house where wood-carving was being taught, but who soon became 'the best carver in the class. His whole appearance underwent a change for the better; the innate sense of the beautiful had been awakened . . .' Still more affecting, he said, was the way in which these grimy-fingered yokels took pains to avoid soiling the books they were lent to copy from, 'and in one instance a big man was seen with a clean handkerchief wrapped round his finger and thumb, carefully turning over the pages.' Today this same 'big man' would no doubt be earning forty or fifty pounds a week, would have a car and a colour TV and take his family on an annual package-tour holiday to the Costa Brava; his enthusiasm for wood-carving or basket-making would probably be minimal. *Autres temps, autres moeurs*!

Mary naturally wished that Compton might play its part in this revival of village handicrafts, and the discovery of a fine bed of clay in the grounds of Limnerslease seemed a clear indication that pottery was the craft to be introduced. When in 1895 the Compton Parish Council, deciding that there was no space left in the churchyard for further burials, acquired a new plot—a piece of rising ground not far from the house—Mary saw her great opportunity; she would provide it with a mortuary chapel, designed by herself and carried out with terracotta decorations made under her direction by the villagers. In the following year a kiln of a pattern approved by William De Morgan was set up in the grounds of Limnerslease, and evening pottery classes started. 'The Squire, the Rector, and the Lady of the Manor', alleging that they were unable to attend of an evening, 'came during the day each to make their brick with its pattern on it'—and so escaped contamination.

The structure, including all the terracotta work, was finished by 1898, and on 1 July of that year the Bishop of Winchester dedicated the Chapel. 'The ceremony was very touching, and Mr Watts, in the scarlet robe of the Oxford D.C.L., was one of the procession.' The establishment by Mary of the Compton Potters Art Guild (to be discussed in the following chapter) delayed by several years the decoration of the interior of the building, which was carried out, presumably at Limnerslease, on gesso panels afterwards attached to the Chapel walls on a framework of metal lathing galvanised to prevent rust. In April 1904, only three months before his death, Watts painted a small and rather feeble version of his 'The All-pervading' for the altar; but not until 1906 was the last touch put to the decoration of the interior.

Mary's building enterprises and her boundless philanthropy were becoming such a drain on Watts's income that he was soon obliged to sell works which he had intended never to part with. On 27 November 1898 he wrote to James Smith, a keen collector of his paintings:

> You shall have 'Chaos' for 600—it is a favourite of my wife's and we have been unwilling to sell it; but she wants to build a Lodge for a caretaker at the Chapel, and I want to make a beginning in the shape of a memorial to the heroes of everyday life, a desire I have long had . . . All this makes it very necessary, as you may suppose, to sell a picture or two.
>
> I am very glad you were so much impressed by my wife's work. I think highly of it, and believe it and the way it has been carried out may have some influence for good. Already I see a change in some of the people about.

The Watts Mortuary Chapel is a creation of genius, unique in England. Let us look more closely at the fabric—and first at the exterior. Here the colour comes as something of a shock, for though Mary optimistically hoped that it would 'tone down in time', in fact the Chapel, for all those black Irish yews planted to steady it, still strikes as discordant a note of scarlet on that green Surrey hillside as do the superannuated London buses that ply in the jungles of Ceylon. Symbolism pervades everything, from the ground plan, which combines the Circle of Eternity with the Cross of Faith, to every square inch of decorated surface. There are friezes representing the Spirit of Light, of Love, of Truth, and of Hope, and every buttress is a Tree of Life. The pillars of the doorway, 'rising from bases upon which there is a suggestion of a half crushed evil with closed eyes, bear the great name "I AM",'[1] and support a Garment of Praise. These areas of crowded Celtic imagery are cunningly off-set by much larger areas of plainest brickwork.

The exterior, in spite of its terracotta decorations, gives an overall impression of plainness. So, too, do those of the rococo churches of Bavaria or the Byzantine churches of Mistra and the Kremlin, where an external simplicity also in no way prepares the visitor for the astonishing richness that awaits him within. The entire wall surface of the Watts Chapel is smothered with angels and cherubs' heads, with sprawling vines and pert little clusters of wild-flowers, with *art nouveau* strap patterns, texts and medallions all carried out in gesso in low relief and gilded or painted in glowing colours: Mary modestly dismissed it as 'glorified wallpaper'. A brilliantly original effect resulted, perhaps almost accidentally, from the cross-and-circle ground-plan, which produces internally the impression of walls six feet thick.

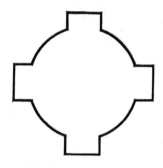

It was Watts who dreamed of creating a House of Life; it was his wife who, in her own highly personal way, realised that dream. One may love the Chapel, or (as many still do) one may hate it; but no one can fail to be amazed that so complex, so *professional* a building could have been produced by a woman with no architectural train-ing, assisted (so far as we know) only by the local builder and black-smith and a handful of enthusiastic but ignorant villagers. If, when

[1] Mary Watts, *The Word in the Pattern*, London, W. H. Ward, n.d. In this little book we are told all about the symbolism but virtually nothing about the building of the Chapel.

reading the *Annals*, one is at times stirred to irritation by its cloying adulation, then a visit to the Chapel is the instant antidote. Here one can forgive Mary everything; indeed, one can pause to wonder whether the world might not have been the richer had she devoted the best years of her life to her art rather than to her aged, ailing hero.

The Chapel was not, as has so often been asserted, in a strict sense, a *memorial* Chapel; Mary built it to the glory, not of her god, but of her God. But her god was to have his memorial too.

It cannot be doubted that it was Mary's idea to build, only a few hundred yards from Limnerslease, a Gallery where a representative collection of her husband's works would be available for all time to the public—a collection which would keep before the Nation the standards of true art for which he had lived and fought and which were now being undermined by Continental corruption. Ernest George was not this time to be employed as architect—perhaps because he had now become too expensive, or perhaps because he had blotted his copybook by forgetting the staircase at Limnerslease. A local man, Mr Christopher Turnor, was invited to draw up plans and to make a model which was carefully vetted by Mary, and on 23 February 1903, the painter's eighty-sixth birthday, Watts laid the 'corner stone'—actually a terracotta plaque inscribed in Lombardic capitals:

GEORGE	BENISON
FREDERIC	ON THE HOUSE.
WATTS	BENISON
PLACED THIS	IN THE HOUSE.
FEBRUARY	BENISON
23rd 1903	FROM THE HOUSE.

Work went ahead at a speed almost unimaginable in these days of strikes and 'go-slows', and on Good Friday (1 April) of the following year the Gallery was opened to the public.

The building had been designed to serve a dual purpose. In the centre came the Picture Gallery, at each end a hostel 'for some of the clay-workers, engaged in what is known as "The Terra Cotta Home Arts", who come from a distance'. It was carried out in rough-cast and roofed with red Surrey tiles; and though the lighting of some of the rooms leaves much to be desired, the exterior has a curious charm to which few visitors to the Gallery today are insensitive. The pictures shown consisted of 'muffins' which had remained unsold, various studies, a few of Watts's favourite small pictures which he had never consented to part with, and a few more which can only be described as failures. Later, when endowing the Gallery, Mary Watts stipulated that if at any time the collection was permanently removed 'to any City or Town or Cities or Towns in disregard of my late Husband's desire that the Country as distinct from the Town should have the advantage of artistic influence', then her Residuary Estate should be distributed among various charities which included 'The Provident Surgical Appliance Society of No 24 Basinghall Street . . . in the City of London' and 'The Home of Rest for Horses of West Croft Farm Cricklewood in the County of Middlesex'.

There can be no doubt that Watts, though Mary makes no specific mention of it, saw the Gallery with some at least of his pictures hanging in it; for even in May he managed to walk as far as the Chapel, and one day went up to London to attend at Queen's Hall a concert given to celebrate the diamond jubilee of his friend Joachim. He returned to London on the 25th of the same month, when he not only saw the bronze of his 'Physical Energy' in the courtyard of Burlington House but, in the light of this experience, began alterations to the gesso in Melbury Road. He was also painting, and the splendid 'Destiny', entirely carried out that spring, shows that his vision was still undimmed, his hand still unfaltering. It was still his proud boast that he never needed to use a mahlstick.

On 4 June his physician, Dr Keightley, looked in at Little Holland House to see how his patient was; he found him hard at work and complaining of nothing more than a slight soreness of the throat. That night Watts went early to bed, never again to leave it. For a month he remained 'as it were unconcernedly in both worlds, the one as present to him as the other'; then, on Friday 1 July, finally and peacefully he crossed the boundary that separated them.

Mary and Lily slipped out of the house by the back door, to avoid the importunity of reporters who had been waiting day and night on the front doorsteps.

* * *

'ARTIST WATTS DEAD—BRONCHITIS CAUSES DEMISE OF BRITISH GENIUS': thus the *Chicago Post* broke the news to the people of America.

Indeed, almost every newspaper in the world reported it. Watts was 'the English Titian', 'England's Michael Angelo', 'the great Painter-prophet', 'the Grand Old Man of English Art', 'an Idealist of the first water', 'the great Symbolist', 'the Painter of Eternal Truths', 'a Preacher in paint', 'the greatest of the moderns', 'a vigorous veteran whose great ideal was nobly realised', and so on. Though the critic of the *St James's Gazette* commented acidly that 'certain morning papers' had not given Watts the space he deserved because 'by the side of a [cricketer] who had made a three-figure score on the previous day, G. F. Watts counted for nothing', the fact remains that he was accorded what by present-day standards seems little to complain of. Over the next few weeks many thousands more words were poured out in eulogies on the departed. A score of poetasters also sought, as was then the fashion, release of pent-up feelings in verse, 'H.I.R.' concluding a sonnet in the *Westminster Gazette* with the couplet:

> For in the Elysian Fields at last are met
> Watts, Titian, Reynolds, Gainsborough, Tintoret.

This brought a reproof from a rival columnist: 'Why Mr Watts should be supposed as especially anxious to meet these gentlemen is, and will probably ever remain, a mystery . . . There must be many other great artists playing on those fields who would be, one imagines, quite as good company, Whistler, Andrea Del Sarto, and Phil May, for instance . . .' No doubt rhyme demanded Tintoret's inclusion.

There were, of course, plenty of long and serious obituary articles and appraisals by well-known writers such as Chesterton and Harold Begbie; they contained, however, little that has not been recorded elsewhere in this book. Meanwhile Mary was endlessly active with scissors and paste, finding solace in filling page upon page of two news-cuttings albums and correcting some of the more glaring inaccuracies. When, for example, the Vicar of Croydon declared that Watts 'whispered as he lay dying, "I believe in the everlasting Light, ever new and ever old, from everlasting to everlasting blessed for evermore",' she noted curtly that this was a mere flight of the good Vicar's fancy. The body was cremated at 'Broadwood' (Brook-wood), the ashes buried at 'Crompton' (Compton), and so on. By a curious irony, the principal officiating clergyman was named Gamble.

The funeral was a simple one, attended principally by relations, close friends, the staff, and the villagers. The ashes were placed in an urn designed by Mary and interred, not within the Chapel but on the highest point of the hillside above it, where Mary was later to erect a rather unimpressive little cloister. And so 'the great artist was left to his long sleep on the sun-kissed hillside'. He had not wished for an Abbey burial; but a memorial service was held in St Paul's Cathedral, where the largest version of his 'Time, Death and Judgment' (his gift) hangs in the nave and mosaics after his design of St Matthew and St John decorate spandrels of the dome.

19

THE WIDOW OF COMPTON

THOUGH THE light had gone out of her life, Mary was not at first alone at Limnerslease; for there was Lilian Mackintosh, the girl that she and Signor had adopted, at hand to comfort her. But Lily (as she was always called) was now twenty-five and strikingly pretty, so it can hardly have come as a surprise to Mary when, less than two years later, she announced her engagement to Michael Chapman, an Old Etonian who had established an engineering business in Toronto. They were married at Compton in September 1906 and left together for Canada shortly before Christmas.

Writing to a friend soon after they had sailed, Mary admitted that in the future she would inevitably be much alone. 'I realise,' she said, 'how much my Lily's sweet companionship was to me, but I am going to write and edit letters and my time will be full, and I shall live in Signor's thought so I do not dread loneliness.' Her time was indeed to be full. She was not yet sixty, still enormously energetic and endlessly busy with enterprises of various kinds. There was the great definitive life of her husband to be written: one that would tell the truth (or so much of it as was suitable) and so put the nose of the regrettable Mrs Barrington permanently out of joint. There was a catalogue of Signor's life work to be compiled, for which, over the past ten years, she had been accumulating material. There was more to be done at the Cemetery, where the cloister was to be built and a well-head carried out to her own design. There was the Gallery to be cherished; and above all there was her love-child, the Compton Potters' Art Guild—as yet in its infancy. It was not for nothing that in 1906 a Berlin newspaper referred to Compton as 'the English Bayreuth', for like that other great widow, Cosima Wagner, Mary, who had dedicated her life to her husband while he lived, was no less determined to fight to keep his memory green.

The Potters' Art Guild—a by-product, as it were, of the Mortuary Chapel—had been started before Signor's death. In December 1900 Mary had written to a Mr James Nicol, asking if he would consider coming to Compton to manage a pottery run on commercial lines. 'I believe [she wrote] that neither man nor woman can do better than try to make a *delightful* village industry—beautiful things beautifully made, by people in beautiful country'. But Nicol, who already had a good job, felt obliged to decline. Nothing daunted, however, Mary wrote a second time and at great length, ostensibly asking him for advice but in reality urging him to think again:

I am much obliged to you for your letter and cannot of course ask you to leave a position in an established business where you have the chance of partnership in the near future; but you are good enough to be interested in our work and may possibly hear of some one who is able to 'come over and help us'. I will try to define better the position I have to offer.

Our work here began four years ago this month—a small class of perfectly untrained hands met here in the evenings to do some decoration—con amore—for the little chapel in the newly made burying ground of this village. Four out of the number soon became permanent hands.

I designed the chapel (which was my husband's gift) and all the decoration, and began the scheme with two objects: to carry out my husband's earnest wish to give our village people interesting work, and to make the field where the dead were to lie, at once a spot of interest to the villagers.

A few people sneered, and I believe it was generally thought that the attempt would fail, and that some big firm would come in for the order. I had many fears myself, but hoped, and went on. Our own little chapel grew up, and had built into it many beautiful thoughts—and is of interest not only to the village but to many who come far to see it.

After its completion, having no idea of trying to sell anything, I parted with our kiln-burner and one other permanent hand, and for six months the evening class alone went on—that being the amateur or play-side. I then saw the difficulty I should have in getting the work burnt, so I asked the burner to come back, and proposed that he should try to make a few pots to repay some part of the expense of having him permanently. He came—but he told me plainly one could never *sell* anything! However he took to the wheel and to modelling and from that time our orders are ever increasing. Since last year's Home Arts and Industries Exhibition there have been far too many for us to carry out. I think and believe that the moment has now come when with a capital from Mr Watts, a good business manager (who if he is the right man would be worth paying a big salary) and with my suggestions and designs, a very good industry may be made not only here, but also on the banks of Loch Ness (my old home) where a class has been started under this one, and is enthusiastically taken up.

At this moment I believe I am justified in having a very great hope that if I can find the practical manager, there is a big opening for our work. In the present fashion for gardening and garden decoration I believe we have a good assurance that we can keep the work from being given chiefly to Italians, and also that *at Compton* we may give better shapes than the modern Italian. I also hope that there is a good opening for interior decoration work for houses, for churches, and for memorial tablets, and *I* do not fear now that the seed we planted four years ago, and which is now a growing plant, will fail, if it is rightly treated. I believe it is a tree of life. I am encouraged to think this, as a similar work begun by a lady I know in Ireland—in furniture making and wood carving—is now so flourishing that she is paying £1400 a year in wages. We have an opportunity of showing at an architectural exhibition in March in London, and also in Glasgow.

Any one coming to us will have a share in a harmonious and happy life. He would see, if that interested him, the work of a great master going on side by side with his own. He would probably have the opportunity of seeing interesting and remarkable people, who like to see Mr Watts work, and are nearly always interested in the clay studios.

Mr Watts wishes to encourage the industry and is prepared to spend all that is necessary for its true development—not that I wish it to be a *charitable* gift from him, but money laid out, not hoping at first for any return, or ever for anything but a small percentage—desiring to see and to have the pleasure of knowing that a beautiful work is being created about him.

If you in any way see your way to finding us such a man I need not say how grateful I will be. You would I think also feel that you were helping on a useful work.

Yours very truly
M. S. Watts

To an altruist, such an appeal was irresistible. Mr Nicol came, he stayed, and the venture flourished.[1]

In an article published in *Country Life* in 1902, the writer, referring to the value of terracotta for garden ornaments and the disappointment so often experienced through breakages in transport from Italy, tells his readers what Compton has to offer:

> In a picturesque tiled[2] 'workshop', nestling on the side of that curious Surrey ridge, the Hog's Back, Mrs G. F. Watts has comfortably housed the work which has only in the last year been growing from the recreative evening class into a village industry, the first object of which is to establish a little colony, in the heart of the country, of intelligent happy workers, who, trained in eye, hand and mind, will take pride in making, as the Guild of Artists did long ago in Italy, their village name known in association with their craft.
>
> The progress already made is astonishing, and the work in terra-cotta turned out here is quite as good as that coming from Italy. Vases and pots of exquisitely graceful outline, plain or ornamented with designs of interlacing serpents or linked hands, richly worked tiles and panels, some meant to be built up into great centre-pots, others intended for decoration, garden seats, sundials ranging from simplicity to elaborateness—these are some of the things to be seen stacked in the showroom or lying about outside. The staff employed is, in so young a work, necessarily small, but is growing steadily, for the industry has great possibilities for a workman with real artistic gifts . . .
>
> As orders come in as fast as they can be executed, there seems to be a bright future for the industry. It is certainly full of

[1] Watts became godfather to Nicol's son, George Frederic Watts Nicol.
[2] The building was in fact mostly thatched with heather, but after being burnt down in 1922 it was rebuilt and tiled.

vigorous life, for, besides making its own way so well, it has thrown off a branch to Scotland . . . The educational value of such artistic work as the Compton industry is very great, for mind as well as hand. The ornament designed by Mrs Watts for the decoration of the pottery is not only beautiful in itself, but full of symbolism, and likely to set the lads working upon it thinking as little else in their lives could.

Certainly the big garden pots were admirable, and the *art nouveau* cherubs that adorn a number of the graves in the Watts cemetery are now, after many years of ridicule, once again found acceptable by the *avant-garde*. Even the more regrettable trivia—the whimsy book-ends and simpering little saints, the porous bowls whose unfired colours crumble at a touch—are eagerly sought after by collectors of Edwardiana. In the days before every village had its 'artist-potter' and every school its kiln, the Compton pottery was a great draw; but the death of Mary Watts in 1938, together with the outrageous wartime purchase-tax on pottery, dealt the Compton venture a crippling blow. Though it struggled on into the mid-fifties, its taste did not move with the times and its doom was sealed; for by then, collectors were beginning to want either genuine *art nouveau* or something 'contemporary'. Mary would have been sad indeed could she have known that the building that once housed her thriving village industry was to degenerate, within less than twenty years of her death, into a store of a combine of grocers.

Another and more immediate, if less direct, concern of Mary's after her husband's death was the Memorial Exhibition of his work, held from January to March 1905 at Burlington House and succeeded in due course by other substantial exhibitions in Dublin, Edinburgh, and elsewhere in the British Isles. In London two hundred and forty-eight of his works were shown, and the critics were as generous with their praise as is their custom when a famous artist has recently died. Sir Charles Holroyd, first Keeper of the Tate Gallery and soon to be appointed Director of the National Gallery, wrote to Mrs Watts that the Burlington House exhibition was 'the noblest thing, and fills me with reverence and gladness that such a man should have been amongst us. He is like a great eagle up above all of us, the rest mere barn-door fowls and sparrows on the housetops only . . . His technique I feel to be as noble as his ideas.'

Nor was music silent, for Sir Charles Stanford composed a 'Watts Symphony' (op. 94).

But for all this adulation, collectors were never prepared to pay for his works the extravagant sums they readily gave for pictures by Leighton and several other popular Royal Academicians. The prices realised at the McCulloch sale at Christie's in 1913 are instructive. The 1865 version of Watts's 'Fata Morgana', a large and important work, was sold for a mere 1,700 guineas,[1] whereas Millais's 'Sir Isumbras at the ford' fetched 7,800 guineas. Other pictures which then sold for more than the Watts (the only one of his works in the sale) were Burne-Jones's 'Love among the ruins' (4,800 guineas), two paintings by E. A. Abbey (5,400 and 4,800 guineas), two by Orchardson (4,400 guineas each), two by Alma Tadema (2,600 and 1,950 guineas), and Cecil Lawson's 'Marshlands' (2,800 guineas).

Then, as each year passed, the prices of all Victorian pictures fell, and it must have been a source of infinite sorrow to Mary to watch, impotent and incredulous, the swift decline of her god and the no less swift ascent of those dreadful Impressionists and Post-impressionists. In 1934 the exquisite portrait of Ellen Terry, 'Choosing', which today would certainly fetch a five-figure sum, realised only £320 at Sotheby's! But Watts's nadir was probably reached at what Graham Robertson referred to as the 'Compton bargain basement'—the sale at Limnerslease in 1939, a year after Mary's death, when charming little drawings went for a few shillings each and others were burnt because there were no bidders, while paintings hardly fetched the price of the paint—'let alone the cost of putting it on'.[2]

In this connection it is perhaps not *too* frivolous to quote a review, said to have appeared in a Tasmanian newspaper, of an unidentifiable painting by Watts on exhibition in Hobart. It seems that the editor, unfamiliar with the world of art, reasoned that a local housepainter would be the man to deal with it. The poor innocent wrote:

Mr. Geo. Watt, the famous artist, is to be congratulated on the

[1] In 1934 it was sold at Sotheby's for £240 and in 1960 was offered to the Watts Gallery by a London dealer for £800, but not purchased.
[2] 'The paint's worth that—let alone the cost of putting it on.' (*Punch* cartoon showing an auctioneer selling a painting). But how can one explain that on 14 September 1939 Hugh Walpole was able to exchange, at the Leicester Galleries, a Watts nude for 'a superb Despiau drawing, a Degas, and a little James Pryde'?

substantial job he has just turned out . . . He has painted a picture of a lady on a horse, and it looks very pretty. The lady's face is picked out in flesh colors, with arms to match, and the delicate rose pink on the cheeks form a nice contrast to the ultra-marine blue eyes. The lady's hair seems to have been laid off rather carelessly and is very streaky, and looks as though it had been done with a new brush. It would have been better if the brush had been broken in on the body of the horse first . . .

The picture seems to have had several coats of the best oil and lead color, and the paint has not been spared on the sky, which is very thick and cloudy . . . [It] is painted on canvas. There is a lot of suction in canvas, and the job could have been done cheaper if zinc had been used instead. There are some figure in the fore-ground, £3 17s 6d, which perhaps refers to the price of the job. If so, the price is a bit stiff (even for day work), and pans out at about £2 9s 2d per yard. Taken altogether, and as the frame is gilded in a first-class manner, the artist deserves the custom of anyone who goes in for that sort of thing.[1]

With the advent of the militant Suffragette movement the rural calm of Compton and its Gallery was, in Mary's opinion, threatened; but 'the vigiliance of Superintendent Jennings of the Godalming Division of the Surrey Police, and of his men enabled us [she wrote] to frustrate what we have every reason to think would have been a serious attempt to do mischief to our Collection.' When Velasquez's 'Venus' at the National Gallery was slashed, it was even considered necessary to defend the honour of Watts's nudes by the employment of a night watchman.

Then came the First World War. Michael Chapman returned from Canada and enlisted, while Lily and their infant daughter, Anthea, joined Mary at Limnerslease. A son, Ronald, was born in 1917, and the following year his father, who had won the Military Cross, was killed in action in France; he had seen the child when on leave a few months before his death. During the War a part of the Gallery buildings was used as a reading and recreation room for soldiers billeted in the neighbourhood. Few people know that at that time

[1] Quoted in the *Argonaut*, 19 September 1904, allegedly from an account in the Tasmanian *Clipper*.

Mary also decorated the interior of a small tin tabernacle at the Cambridge Military Hospital, Aldershot, to serve as a mortuary chapel.

It cannot always have been easy for those two strong-minded widows, Mary and Lily, to live day in and day out in proximity, and jealousy was undoubtedly one of Mary's weaknesses. Possibly, too, she was now beginning to find the boisterousness of her 'grand-children' and their young friends rather wearing. At all events, in the early thirties Lily Chapman moved with her family to Hasle-mere, leaving 'Gaga'—as the younger generation irreverently called their 'grandmother' (who was 'Donna' to her friends)—in the safe hands of faithful servants at Limnerslease.

Mary was anything but gaga—at all events until within two or three years of her death, when Lily returned to look after her. Though now in her later seventies her mind was clear and her energy inexhaustible. Those who remember her at this time speak of her as formidable: 'a bit of a Tartar' was an expression used by two different people. Though not the Lady of the Manor she ruled the villagers, reproving them sharply if their gardens were untidy and their children if they omitted to curtsey to her. (One such child, on being reprimanded, replied, 'Mother told us not to as we're just as good as you'; Mary's answer has not been preserved). Local post-cards were sold at the village shop at a penny each, but the pro-prietor was made by Mary to sign a document obliging him to charge twopence for the one of Watts. Surprisingly enough, Mary does not seem to have played the Lady Bountiful, and no one remembers her distributing wholesome but simple food to the needy or even photo-gravures of 'Hope' to the poor in spirit.

The little woman with the piercing eyes and the trailing black skirt—she never wore anything but black after her husband's death—was often to be seen in the Gallery, now under the care of her friend Rowland Alston who had helped her since 1923 and whom she appointed official Curator eight years later. Re-arrangement of the pictures, which she had hung in serried ranks, was firmly dis-couraged, and it was not until after her death that Alston was able to display them more selectively and rationally. Mary was much loved; but she was also much feared.

It was perhaps fortunate that she did not live to see the outbreak of the Second World War, when Limnerslease was commandeered by the Government and a part of the Gallery used as a store for books from the Warburg Library. She died peacefully on 6 September 1938, the great tasks she had set herself accomplished, the great sacrifice she had made rewarded.

*   *   *

More than thirty-five years have passed since then. The A3, against the construction of which Mary had fought valiantly but unavailingly, has become a noisy battlefield which shatters the calm of Limnerslease—now converted into three separate houses. But the Gallery, shielded from the by-pass by rising ground, is still an oasis of peace. Visitors come—some six thousand of them each year. There are the devotees of Watts who make the pious pilgrimage from afar. There are the locals with week-end guests who have already seen Guildford Cathedral, Loseley and Clandon but who have to be yet further entertained. There are—easily recognisable— the half-starved dieters from Enton Hall and the glutted patrons of Compton's famous hostelry, the Withies. There are the casual passers-by—week-end motorists brought in by idle curiosity, or ramblers by a sudden shower. There are those who put something in the contributions box and those who pass by on the other side. But perhaps most endearing of all were three simple and engaging youths (one announced that his father was 'Tinker Smith'), who goggled as they timidly entered this esoteric and incomprehensible shrine. Then Tinker Smith's son said, ' 'Oo did these?'

'George Frederic Watts—an artist who died in 1904.'

'Well—'oo does 'em now?'

CHRONOLOGY: GEORGE FREDERIC WATTS

1817	Born in London, 23 February
1827	Began to work in the studio of the sculptor William Behnes
1834	Self-portrait aged seventeen
1837	'A Wounded Heron' and two portraits exhibited at the Summer Exhibition of the Royal Academy. Met his first important patron, Constantine Ionides
1843	Awarded a first prize of £300 for his cartoon 'Caractacus' in the first Houses of Parliament competition
1843–47	Visited Paris on his way to Italy. The guest of Lord and Lady Holland in Florence and at Careggi, and travelled to Rome, Naples, etc. Remained at Careggi with Lady Duff Gordon after the Hollands left. Painted 'A Story from Boccaccio'
1847	Returned to England with 'Alfred inciting the Saxons', which won a first prize of £500 at that year's Houses of Parliament competition
1848	'Time and Oblivion'—his first big allegory
1849–50	Studio at 30 Charles Street. Painted 'The Irish Famine' and other pictures dealing with the misery of the poor
1850	Visited Ireland
1851	Became the guest for twenty-four years of Mr and Mrs Thoby Prinsep at Little Holland House
1852	Offer to decorate Euston Station at his own expense rejected
1853	Brief visit to Italy
1856–57	Travelled in the Levant for his health
1859	Completed the fresco 'Justice' (begun in 1853) in the New Hall of Lincoln's Inn

1863	Gave evidence before the Royal Commission appointed to inquire into the position of the Royal Academy
1864	Married Ellen Terry (aged 16)
1865	Separated from Ellen. Met Charles Rickards, soon to become his greatest patron
1866	First meeting with the future Mrs Russell Barrington
1867	Elected A.R.A. and R.A.
1870	Began 'Hugh Lupus' for the Marquis of Westminster. Met Mary Fraser-Tytler, later to become his second wife
1875	Little Holland House demolished. Built the Briary at Freshwater for the Prinseps and joined them there
1876	Built (new) Little Holland House (6 Melbury Road) as a London home but continued to winter at The Briary
1877	Divorced Ellen, who a fortnight later married Charles Wardell
1880	Rickards' collection of Watts's pictures exhibited at Manchester
1881–82	First one-man exhibition in London (Grosvenor Gallery)
1883	'Hugh Lupus' completed, 'Physical Energy' begun now or soon after
1884–85	Exhibition at the Metropolitan Museum, New York
1885	Offered baronetcy by Gladstone but declined it
1886	Married Mary Fraser-Tytler (aged 36)
1886–87	Honeymoon in the Mediterranean and Egypt. Feud between his wife and Mrs Barrington on their return
1887	Death of Sara Prinsep
1887–88	Winter and spring in the Mediterranean and at Aix-les-Bains
1890	Visited Freshwater to paint his last two portraits of Tennyson
1891	Occupied Limnerslease (Compton), built as a winter home away from London fogs and Mrs Barrington
1894	Second offer by Gladstone of a baronetcy, again declined
1896	The building of the Mortuary Chapel at Compton begun by Mary Watts
1898	Visit to the Scottish Highlands. Statue of Tennyson begun (completed 1903)
1902	Accepted the newly instituted Order of Merit
1903	Building of the Watts Gallery at Compton begun

1904   Last revisions of 'Physical Energy'. The Watts Gallery
        opened. Death of the artist in London on 1 July

        ————————————

1905   Memorial Exhibitions at the Royal Academy and else-
        where in Britain. Mrs Barrington's *Reminiscences* of Watts
        published

1912   Mary Watts's *Annals of an Artist's Life* published

1938   Death of Mary Watts

1956   Closure of the Pottery

1972   Death in her ninety-third year of Lily Chapman, adopted
        daughter of the Wattses

BIBLIOGRAPHY

ALSTON, Rowland, *The Mind and Work of G. F. Watts, O.M., R.A.*, Methuen, 1929

ANON, 'the Potter's Wheel, *Country Life*, 15 March 1902

ANON, the Masterpieces of G. F. Watts, 1918

Arts Council Exhibition Catalogue, G. F. Watts, 1954

BARRINGTON, Mrs Russell, *G. F. Watts, Reminiscences*, George Allen, 1905

BARRINGTON, Mrs. Russell, *Life, Letters and Work of Frederic Leighton*, George Allen, 1906

BATEMAN, C. T., *G. F. Watts, R.A.*, Bell, 1901

BAYES, Walter, *The Landscapes of G. F. Watts*, Newnes, n.d.

BELL, M., *Watts*, Bell, 1905

BENSON, E. F., *As We Were*, Longmans, 1930

BESSBOROUGH, the Earl of (ed.), *Lady Charlotte Schreiber, Journal*, John Murray, 1952

BLUNT, Wilfrid, *G. F. Watts* (The Master Series, No. 37), Purnell, 1963

BLUNT, Wilfrid, Letter in *Burlington Magazine*, January 1964

BOASE, T. S. R., 'The Decoration of the New Palace of Westminster', *Journal of the Warburg and Courtauld Institutes*, 1954

CARTWRIGHT, Julia, 'George Frederic Watts, R.A.', Easter Annual of the *Art Journal*, 1896

CHAPMAN, Ronald, *The Laurel and the Thorn: A Study of G. F. Watts*, Faber, 1945

CHESTERTON, G. K., *G. F. Watts*, Duckworth, 1904

CRAIG, E. and St JOHN, C. (eds.), *Ellen Terry's Memoirs*, Gollancz, 1933

DALRYMPLE-CHAMPNEYS, Sir Weldon, Bt., *Le Chevalier de L'Etang and his Descendants*, O.U.P., n.d.

DIBDIN, E. R., *George Frederick Watts*, Cassell, 1923

DRAPER, W. H., 'The Watts Frescoes at Lincoln's Inn', *Burlington Magazine*, 1906

du MAURIER, Daphne (ed.), *The Young George du Maurier; Letters 1860–67*, Peter Davis, 1951

FITZPATRICK, K., *Lady Henry Somerset*, Cape, 1923

FORD, J. E. and LAMONT, T., *Pictures by George Frederick Watts*, New York, Fox, Duffield, 1904

FRY, Roger, 'G. F. Watts', *Burlington Magazine*, 1904

FULLER, H. T., *Three Freshwater Friends: Tennyson, Watts and Mrs Cameron*, The County Press, Newport, 1936

GAUNT, W., *Victorian Olympus*, Cape, 1952; Sphere Books and Cape, 1975

GERNSHEIM, H., *Julia Margaret Cameron*, Fountain Press, 1948

GRIERSON, E., *Storm Bird: the Strange Life of Georgina Weldon*, Chatto & Windus, 1959

GUTCH, R., 'G. F. Watts' Sculpture', *Burlington Magazine*, November 1968

HAMMERSLEY, V. and FULLER, H. T., *Thackeray's Daughter*, Dublin, 1951

HARE, Augustus, *The Story of my Life* (vol. 6), George Allen, 1896–1900

HARE, W. Loftus, *Watts*, Jack, n.d.

HAYDON, Benjamin, *Autobiography*, ed. by Tom Taylor, Longmans, 1853

HEWETT, O. W. (ed.) . . . *and Mr Fortescue*, John Murray, 1958

HILL, Brian, *Julia Margaret Cameron; A Victorian Family Portrait*, Peter Owen, 1973

HUXLEY, Gervas, Victorian Duke: *The Life of Hugh Lupus Grosvenor, First Duke of Westminster*,

ILCHESTER, The Earl of, *The Chronicles of Holland House, 1820–1900*, John Murray, 1937

JESSEN, J., *George Frederick Watts*, Berlin and Leipzig, Schuster & Loeffler, 1901

LOSHAK, D., 'G. F. Watts and Ellen Terry', *Burlington Magazine*, November, 1963

MACMILLAN, Hugh, *The Life-work of George Frederick Watts, R.A.*, Dent, 1903

MANVELL, Roger, *Ellen Terry*, Heinemann, 1968

Masterpieces of G. F. Watts, London and Glasgow, Gowans & Gray, revised edition, 1913

NEVILL, Ralph (ed.), *The Reminiscences of Lady Dorothy Nevill*, Arnold, 1906

ORIGO, Iris, *Images and Shadows*, John Murray, 1970

PASTON, G., *Haydon and his Friends*, James Nisbet, 1905

PHYTHIAN, J. E., *George Frederick Watts*, New York, Stokes, 1906

PIPER, David, 'In Defence of G. F. Watts', *Listener*, 13 January 1955

RAYMOND, E. T., *Portraits of the Nineties*, Unwin, 1921
RICKETTS, C., 'Watts at Burlington House', *Burlington Magazine*, 1905
ROSS, Janet, *The Fourth Generation*, Constable, 1912
RUSKIN, J., *The Winnington Letters*, ed. Von Akin Bond, Allen & Unwin, 1969

SCHLEINITZ, O. von, *George Frederick Watts*, Bielefeld and Leipzig, Velhagen & Klasing, 1904
SCHREIBER, Lady Charlotte, see Bessborough, the Earl of
SHORT, Ernest, *Watts*, Philip Allan, 1924
SHREWSBURY, H. W., *The Visions of an Artist: Studies in G. F. Watts, R.A., O.M.*, Epworth Press, 1918
SKETCHLEY, R. E. D., *Watts*, Methuen, 1904
SPIELMANN, W. H., 'The Works of Mr G. F. Watts, R.A.', *Pall Mall Gazette*, Extra Number, 1886
[STEAD, W. T.], 'Mr G. F. Watts, R.A.', *Review of Reviews*, June 1902
STIRLING, A. M. W., *A Painter of Dreams; the Life of Roddam Spencer Stanhope*, John Lane, 1916
STIRLING, A. M. W., *Life's Little Day*, Thornton Butterworth, 1924
STIRLING, A. M. W., *Life's Mosaic*, Unicorn Press, 1934

TERRY, Ellen, *The Story of My Life*, Hutchinson, 1908 and Gollancz, 1933
TERRY, Ellen, see Craig, E. and St John, C.
TROUBRIDGE, Laura, Lady, *Memories and Reflections*, Heinemann, 1925
TWISTLETON, Hon. Mrs E., *Letters, 1852–1862*, John Murray, 1928

WATERFIELD, L., *Castle in Italy*, John Murray, 1961
WATTS, Mary, *George Frederic Watts, the Annals of an Artist's Life*, Macmillan, 1912
WATTS, Mary, *The Word in the Pattern*, W. H. Ward, n.d.
WEST, W. K. and PANTINI, R., *G. F. Watts*, Newnes, 1904
Whitechapel Art Gallery Exhibition Catalogue, G. F. Watts, 1817–1904, 1974
WOOLF, Virginia and FRY, Roger, *Victorian Photographs of Famous Men and Fair Women*, Hogarth Press, 1926

INDEX

The works of George Frederic Watts are indexed separately below. Plate numbers of the colour illustrations are given in roman, those of black-and-white illustrations in arabic numerals. 'George Frederic Watts' is abbreviated as GFW.

THE WORKS OF G. F. WATTS